# Managing the New Generation

A practical guide for understanding and meeting workplace expectations of Generation Y

## Carolin Rekar Munro

Impackt Publishing
We Mean Business

# Managing the New Generation

First published: October 2014

Production reference: 1241014

Published by Impackt Publishing Ltd.
Livery Place
35 Livery Street
Birmingham B3 2PB, UK.

ISBN 978-1-78300-088-3

www.Impacktpub.com

# Credits

**Author**

Carolin Rekar Munro

**Content Development Editor**

Sweny M. Sukumaran

**Proofreaders**

Maria Gould

Ameesha Green

**Production Coordinator**

Melwyn D'sa

**Reviewers**

Sue Honoré

Itamar Sharon

**Copy Editors**

Tanvi Bhatt

Simran Bhogal

Karuna Narayanan

Faisal Siddiqui

**Cover Work**

Melwyn D'sa

**Acquisition Editor**

Nick Falkowski

**Project Coordinator**

Venitha Cutinho

# About the Author

**Carolin Rekar Munro** is the Associate Professor and Intellectual Lead for Leadership and Human Resources in the MBA and B.Com programs for the Faculty of Management at Royal Roads University in British Columbia. She is also an adjunct professor for Central Michigan University's Global Campus, teaching in the MA in Education. She received her Masters' and Doctoral degrees with a focus on developing human resources and leadership from the University of Toronto. She also has a Certified Human Resources Professional (CHRP) designation from the Human Resources Professionals Association, a Certified Training and Development (CTDP) designation from the Canadian Society for Training and Development, and is certified in values-based leadership from the Barrett Centre, Myers-Briggs Personality Inventory, and Emotional Quotient Inventory.

Carolin manages a successful consulting practice, *Eye of the Tiger Consulting* (www.eyeofthetigerconsulting.ca), in which she collaborates with leaders on change management, employee engagement, organizational renewal, strategic planning, performance management, developing and sustaining high performing teams, succession management, and leadership development (for aspiring leaders, executives, and the youth community). Carolin has worked with clients in Canada, the U.S., South America, the Caribbean, and parts of Europe. She is also a national and international conference speaker.

Since 2008, Carolin's research portfolio has focused on Generation Y. Specifically, she has been investigating the following three key issues: the leadership role and competency profile required by GenY as they move into leadership; the organizational initiatives that need to be in place to identify, develop, and retain GenY talent; and the anticipated changes as leadership roles are filled by GenY, and how these changes can be navigated to ensure a smooth transition in organizational functioning and staff relations. Carolin is currently embarking on a study of how organizations internationally are preparing GenY for leadership roles, the competency profile required of GenY to lead internationally, and the changes GenY plans to make in doing business globally.

Her published work includes: the emerging organizational landscape with Generation Y at the helm; developing and sustaining high performance teams; Return on Investment (ROI) from training and development initiatives; leadership models to transition teams from dependence to interdependence; best practices in teaching and learning; wellness management of HR practitioners; transitioning to e-learning environments; bridging multi-generational differences; and the mentoring needs and expectations of Generation Y human resources practitioners. This is Carolin's second book, the first was *Management of Human Resources*, which is required reading for courses in Human Resources in many Canadian colleges and universities.

In the community, Carolin is involved in a number of national and international initiatives. For Education Beyond Borders, she is Chair of the Advisory Board, member of the Strategic Partnership Committee, and member of the facilitation team, who recently returned from Tanzania as part of a leadership development and community education project. As well as this, Carolin serves on the Human Resources Association's Educational Standards Committee and on the National Steering Committee for the Canadian Society for Training and Development.

I am indebted to a number of people who guided and coached me along the way, inspired me to persevere and give my best, and listened patiently to my many escapades into the world of Gen Y. A resounding and heartfelt thank you to: my mom and dad; my sister, Angela and her family—Steve, Robbie, Ashleigh, and Jessica; my brother, Steve; my dear friends, Wendy and Kieran; my family at Royal Roads University, especially Dr. Stephen Long, Shirley Russell, Cyndy Mason, Dr. Ingrid Kajzer Mitchell, Don Caplan, and Dr. Pedro Marquez; and the team at Impackt Publishing, especially Nick Falkowski and Venitha Cutinho. A special note of gratitude to the many Generation Ys who I met along the way, and a special thank you to those of you who graciously accepted the invitation to be interviewed for this book. All of you inspire me. Thank you for your presence in my life. A special heartfelt "asante sana" to Allen E. Mollel for always being at the other end of a text message when I needed encouragement to go one more mile.

# About the Reviewers

**Sue Honoré** is an independent business researcher, a learning consultant, and a project manager. Over her career, she has held international managerial roles in both, global blue chip organizations and small companies. She is a cross-functional consultant and has worked in Strategy, Learning and Development, Research, IT, and Logistics.

At Ashridge Business School in Hertfordshire, UK, Sue acted as an internal learning consultant for 6 years, but is now an associate focused on research, in particular young people (Generation Y) and their managers at work. A major international Gen Y research project was completed in 2013 and ongoing research is looking into tapping into the experience of Baby Boomers. Other subjects include human interaction in a virtual MBA program, innovation in executive education, and ROI in customer service. Sue has taught for the Chartered Institute of Personnel Development, judged e-learning awards, and spoken at many conferences. She is also on the Executive Committee of the Oxfordshire Family History Society and is editor of its journal, which won a major award in 2013.

Sue's first degree is in biological sciences, with a postgraduate qualification in Business Management and an MSc (Distinction) in Networked Learning from Lancaster University. In her continued aim to be a polymath, she has recently gained an Advanced Diploma in Local History from the University of Oxford.

**Itamar Sharon** is the founder of GeneratY. With GeneratY, he helps organizations with managing Generation Y. He believes that this generation can be of great value for an organization, but only when they are triggered and managed in the right way. By giving advice, workshops and presentations, he creates awareness within an organization and helps them benefit from the great potential their young workers have.

Itamar lives in Amsterdam (the Netherlands) and is 28 years old.

# Contents

| | |
|---|---|
| **Preface** | **1** |

| | |
|---|---|
| **Chapter 1: Generation Y – Who Are They?** | **7** |
| So, what's burning? | 8 |
| Unpacking the attributes of Gen Y | 9 |
| Exploring Gen Y's needs and expectations | 10 |
| Can you live up to Gen Y's expectations? | 10 |
| Can your organization live up to Gen Y's expectations? | 11 |
| Shattering myths about Gen Y | 12 |
| Myth number 1 – Gen Y is entitled | 12 |
| Myth number 2 – Gen Y has no work ethic | 13 |
| Myth number 3 – Gen Y is disrespectful | 14 |
| Myth number 4 – Gen Y is self-centered | 15 |
| Myth number 5 – Gen Y wants to run before they can walk | 15 |
| Shattered myths? So what now? | 16 |
| Meeting the Gen Y community | 17 |
| Reframing challenges as opportunities | 18 |
| Leaning in to change | 19 |
| Google it... | 19 |
| Summary | 21 |

| | |
|---|---|
| **Chapter 2: Attracting Gen Y Talent to Your Company** | **23** |
| So, what's burning? | 25 |
| Turbo-charging our job ads | 26 |
| Converting our ads from mild to sizzling hot! | 27 |
| Putting the lion's roar in your content | 28 |
| Tapping into social media – are you digitally networking? | 30 |
| Tweeting away your time - #tellmeyourstory | 31 |
| Blogging back to the basics | 32 |
| Facebook – do you like me? | 34 |
| The ABCs of heading back to school | 35 |
| Selecting the "perfect" candidate | 36 |

| | |
|---|---|
| Meeting the Gen Y community | 37 |
| Reframing challenges as opportunities | 38 |
| Leaning in to change | 39 |
| Google it… | 39 |
| Summary | 40 |

**Chapter 3: Acclimatizing Gen Y to Your Workplace – Training that is Sticky, Stickier, and Stickiest** — **41**

| | |
|---|---|
| So, what's burning? | 44 |
| Revealing the learner within – the 360 degree request | 45 |
| Gen Y – who shows up for training? | 45 |
| Delivering training – how do YOU show up? | 47 |
| Orienting Gen Y to workplace realities – everyone on board? | 48 |
| Creating an unrivalled first impression | 48 |
| Designing training programs – shiny new tools for your toolbox | 50 |
| Diamonds in the rough – podcasts, vodcasts, and so much more! | 51 |
| Podcasts – get you headsets on! | 51 |
| Vodcasts – now I can see you! | 51 |
| Meet me online? | 52 |
| Once upon a time… | 52 |
| The polls are now open | 52 |
| Thinking outside the tank | 53 |
| Do you want to play a game? | 53 |
| Debate twister | 53 |
| Search and find | 54 |
| Mystery learning? | 54 |
| Upside down? Backwards? No, flip it! | 54 |
| Making transfer of learning "stickiest" | 55 |
| Forming sticky teams | 56 |
| Post-training collaborations | 56 |
| Evaluating your training – did you earn an "A"? | 57 |
| Reframing challenges as opportunities | 58 |
| Leaning in to change | 59 |
| Google it… | 59 |
| Meeting the Gen Y community | 60 |
| Summary | 61 |

**Chapter 4: Unlocking the Secrets to Awesome Conversations with Gen Y** — **63**

| | |
|---|---|
| So, what's burning? | 65 |
| Stretching the elastic band–a new role awaits you | 66 |
| Let go–getting out of your own way | 66 |
| Learning a new language–from crushers to connectors | 68 |
| Checking assumptions | 70 |
| Giving and receiving feedback–what to say and how to say it | 71 |
| What to say | 71 |
| What not to say | 72 |

How to say it 73

Navigating the super highway of conflict – potholes, puddles, and ditches 74

Shifting gears 74

Signaling a new direction 75

Seeing what's in the rear view mirror 77

Reframing challenges as opportunities 77

Leaning in to change 78

Google it 79

Meeting the Gen Y community 79

Summary 80

## Chapter 5: Inspiring Star Performance– Reaching Seriously for Sirius **81**

So what's burning? 83

Transmitting new messages – Why? What? How? 85

Exploring change within–an invitation to try something new 87

Tuning in to Gen Y's wavelength 87

Responding to Gen Y's input – are we clashing or collaborating? 88

Exploring new horizons for Gen Y – the galaxy beyond their jobs 89

Ideas that come from Jupiter, Mars, and Saturn 90

Responding to the pitch 90

Encouraging them to keep pitching! 91

Looking through the telescope 93

Falling stars – learning how to fall with grace and grit 94

Falling, falling, rising! 95

Morphing into a culture that knows how to fall 97

Reframing challenges as opportunities 98

Leaning in to change 99

Google it 100

Meeting the Gen Y community – introducing…Peggy Liu! 100

Summary 101

## Chapter 6: Performance Management– Becoming Hyperintentional About Sustainability **103**

So, what's burning? 105

Managing daily performance – the secret sauce for getting things just right 107

What's too much 108

What's too little 108

What's just right? 109

Developing performance appraisals – a new GPS for Gen Y 111

How to evaluate 112

Coordinate 1 – Blue sky dreaming: your head in the clouds again 113

Coordinate 2 – Developing a blueprint for success: getting from here to where? 114

Coordinate 3 – Contributing to Gen Y's success: YOUR GPS matters too! 115

Who evaluates 116

Appraisal interviews – from OH NO to OH YES!    118
Navigating the unexpected – when performance gets a flat tire    119
   Navigating the unexpected    120
   Deja vu – when the behavior recurs    122
   When it's time to say goodbye    122
Reframing challenges as opportunities    124
Leaning in to change    124
Google it    125
Meeting the Gen Y community – introducing...Abdulmohsen Almuhanna!    126
Summary    127

## Chapter 7: Rewarding Peak Performers – Goodbye Plaques, Trophies, and Recognition Pins    129

So, what's burning?    132
Incentivizing peak performance with financial rewards    133
   Performance-based reward system – rewarding superstars    134
     Identifying the superstars    136
     Fine-tuning our process – differentiating between low-end, middle, and top performers    138
     Determining fund size – how fat is your wallet?    138
   Rewarding team performance    140
Recognizing staff – possibilities beyond cash    141
   E-recognition – congratulatory messages go viral!    141
   Personalized recognitions – beyond another gold-plated watch    142
   Spontaneous bursts of caring – just because    144
Incorporating a few tantalizing workplace perks    145
   Work space – here, there, and everywhere    146
   Expatriate opportunities – pack your bags!    146
   A philanthropic generation    147
Sometimes, it's about doing nothing at all    148
Reframing challenges as opportunities    149
Leaning in to change    149
Google it    150
Meeting the Gen Y community – introducing...Victoria Kovalenko!    150
Summary    151

## Chapter 8: Mentoring the Next Generation of Leaders – Legacy Building, One Gen Y at a Time    153

So, what's burning?    155
Getting YOU primed for the mentoring journey ahead    156
   An invitation to get over ourselves    157
   Blueprint for your training – yes, training for YOU too!    158
Parachuting Gen Y into their future – their wish list and your map    159
   The great revelation – what's on Gen Y's wish list?    160
   Your map – guiding Gen Y to their career destination    162

Can I get a little support here? – mentoring the mentors    164
   Throwing a mentoring life raft to YOU    164
   Throwing a life raft to Gen Y too!    165
Reframing challenges as opportunities    166
Leaning in to change    167
Google it    168
Meeting the Gen Y community – introducing...Hande Gulsen!    168
Summary    170

**Chapter 9: Retaining Gen Y – What Else Does it Take to Keep Them?**    **171**

So, what's burning?    172
Putting your organization's culture on your radar screen    174
   The view under the microscope – one step back and two steps forward    174
   Parking one's ego for incoming messages    176
Developing your sixth sense to the noise around you    178
   Embracing the celestial sounds of whining    178
   Silence ain't golden    180
Oh no! They're leaving!... Let them    181
   Putting the stick down – don't beat yourself up    182
   Holding the door open for Gen Ys as they leave    183
Reframing challenges as opportunities    184
Leaning in to change    185
Google it    186
Meeting the Gen Y community – introducing...Dr. Ganesh Ramachandran!    187
Summary    188

**Chapter 10: Multigenerational Unity – Singing in Semiperfect Harmony**    **189**

So, what's burning?    192
Setting the right tempo for working together – maestro, please set the stage    193
   Singing from a value-based song sheet    194
   Establishing contractual agreements for our working relationships    196
     Welcome to your team charter!    196
     Checking in and checking out    197
   Zero tolerance for B'ing flat!    198
     Striking the right chord    199
     Striking a different chord    200
Multigenerational collaborations – singing an octave higher    201
   Leveraging the generational mix in unconventional ways    201
   Informal conversations – a cappuccino moment    203

Establishing community circles that keep us singing in semiperfect
harmony                                                                204
   Instruments of our success                           204
   How does feedback resonate with you – a prelude to success   205
Reframing challenges as opportunities                                  206
Leaning in to change                                                   207
Google it                                                              208
Meeting the Gen Y community – introducing...Gwen Hill!                 208
Summary                                                                209
Our last few minutes together...                                      209

# > Preface

Generation Y? Millennials? Digital Natives? The Net Generation?

Who are they? Where did they come from? Why are we having such difficulties managing them and keeping them in our companies?

In virtually every organization, the halls are buzzing with conversations about Generation Y (Gen Y)—the latest generation of workers that baffles us and leaves us with more questions than answers about how to manage and work with them. This book fills an important gap in the current academic and business literature by responding to the questions about Gen Y that keep you awake at night. It is a roadmap that helps you navigate through the uncultivated terrain of attracting, engaging, and retaining Gen Y talent in your organization en route to establishing a high performing and productive workforce that positions your organization for competitive advantage.

In my travels as a business practitioner, consultant, educator, and researcher over the past 20 years, I have been gratified and humbled by hundreds of your stories about Gen Y. You've shared with me those moments that caught you off guard and left you dazed: the candidate who showed up for a job interview armed with a reference letter from his mom, the market researcher who asked in disbelief, "What do you mean I can't use Twitter for my market analysis?", the employee who raised her hand in a staff meeting and asked if jeans and a t-shirt constitute business casual, and the employee—just shy of 3 weeks of service in your company—who, having been told by you that she wasn't eligible for promotion this month, text messaged you the next day to announce her resignation. The stories are endless and boundary-less.

My point in sharing these stories is not to disparage Gen Y but rather to heighten our awareness and honor the new realities in our workplaces. I'm hoping you will join me in suspending judgment about Gen Y so that we can begin what promises to be an illuminating trek toward discovering new possibilities to interact and engage deeply and meaningfully with the newest addition to our workplace complement.

## Why this book?

The main purpose of this book is threefold:

> - To chart proactive strategies to deal with the burning challenges you experience managing and working with Gen Y
> - To develop a toolkit of new techniques and practices you can use to enhance how you attract, develop, engage, and retain Gen Y
> - To dismantle myths about Gen Y and embrace a new mental model of who they are, which shapes, and how we build working relationships with them

The signature strength of this book is its practical and concrete tools, techniques, and practices that you can apply immediately. The proposed pathways are based on first-hand experiences, collaborating with organizational leaders, like yourselves, and members of the Gen Y community to unearth root-cause challenges and to chart proactive solution strategies. Offered are unique twists on solving the problems that you face, whether it is how to tap into the hidden talent bank to find qualified Gen Y candidates, how to communicate more effectively with Gen Y, or what motivates them to stay in your organization and work to their full potential. You will discover Gen Y's needs and expectations in the workplace and how you can channel these new insights into managing them.

The gold to be found at the end of this journey is:

> ➤ Better understanding of Gen Y (and perhaps, learning a little about yourself along the way)
> ➤ Building even stronger working relationships with Gen Y so that they want to join and remain in your organization, aspire to be your peak performers, and contribute substantially to the success and viability of your organization

Added to this, it is anticipated that you will gain confidence in your own leadership to air and resolve, in an open and constructive manner, the challenges that you currently experience with the Gen Ys in your life and lead by example in tackling the "us" vs. "them" battle that pervades many workplaces.

All the tools and practices move you closer to creating an engaging, high-performing, and productive workforce, especially at a time when organizations are racing to develop teams that position their organizations for competitive advantage in a fluid and shrinking global economy.

# What this book covers

In this book, you'll find the following chapters:

*Chapter 1, Generation Y – Who Are They?*, addresses questions about Gen Y's attributes and workplace needs and expectations and shatters common myths about the newest generation.

*Chapter 2, Attracting Gen Y Talent to Your Company*, explores social media in recruitment in order to surpass the competition in attracting Gen Y talent to your organization.

*Chapter 3, Acclimatizing Gen Y to Your Workplace – Training that is Sticky, Stickier, and Stickiest*, examines digital tools in training to engage a generation that leads the digital information revolution.

*Chapter 4, Unlocking the Secrets to Awesome Conversations with Gen Y*, explores how you can engage in more meaningful and productive conversations with Gen Y, tackle barriers to effective communication, and ultimately, build strong working relationships with Gen Y.

*Chapter 5, Inspiring Star Performance– Reaching Seriously for Sirius*, examines job enrichment strategies that you can use to foster work experiences, within and beyond the job, that inspire Gen Y to be and offer their best and become your star performers.

*Chapter 6, Performance Management– Becoming Hyperintentional About Sustainability*, charts a course of action to manage daily performance, developing and conducting effective performance appraisals and navigating the unexpected.

*Chapter 7, Rewarding Peak Performers – Goodbye Plaques, Trophies, and Recognition Pins*, proposes financial and nonfinancial rewards to acknowledge high performance and to give your organization the competitive angle in motivating Gen Y.

*Chapter 8, Mentoring the Next Generation of Leaders – Legacy Building, One Gen Y at a Time*, focuses on the leadership role you can play in mentoring Gen Y on their career-development journey and in developing the talent needed so that you have the right staff, with the right skills, in the right roles for your organization's future.

*Chapter 9, Retaining Gen Y – What Else Does it Take to Keep Them?*, provides you with a different twist on how to create and sustain a workplace culture that minimizes the probability that Gen Y will seek employment elsewhere.

*Chapter 10, Multigenerational Unity – Singing in Semiperfect Harmony*, traces how you can exercise your leadership to bridge generational differences in the workplace and foster a cohesive and cooperative workplace that contributes to sustainable organizational effectiveness.

In each chapter, you'll find the following unique features:

- ➤ *Meeting the Gen Y Community*. An interview with a member of the Gen Y cohort from around the world who unlocks the secrets of working with their generation
- ➤ *Reframing Challenges as Opportunities*. A description of a challenge typically experienced when managing Gen Y, followed by a recommended course of action that transforms the challenge into an opportunity for workplace success
- ➤ *Leaning in to change*. Questions posed to guide you in identifying and mapping out a change you would like to make in how you manage Gen Y
- ➤ *Google It*. Links to websites, articles, YouTube, and Ted Talks for those of you who are interested in exploring the topics further
- ➤ Practical applications and colorful examples and stories that inspire you to engage with Gen Y in new ways

# Who this book is for

This book is written for those of you in a leadership capacity who find yourselves intrigued and perplexed by Gen Y and who are eager to discover the buried treasure chest of approaches to managing and working with Gen Y that will put you ahead of your competition. The target audience for this book is new, experienced, and soon-to-be managers at all levels in the organization. The book is written in user-friendly, jargon-free language appropriate for managers in all professions, industries, organizational cultures, and at any stage in their leadership career.

# How to read this book

It is understandable that some of you may have little time to read this book cover to cover; hence, the book is organized so that you can skim through chapters or jump to the chapters that meet your needs. Others may like to read the book from start to finish, absorbing all the ideas that are offered. Feel free to read the book in whatever way you prefer. Regardless of your preference for navigating through the book, I hope you find the tools and techniques valuable and that you can spend time reflecting on how these new approaches can be applied to your organization as is or with a little tweaking.

# Conventions

In this book, you will find a number of styles of text that distinguish between different kinds of information. Here are some examples of these styles, and an explanation of their meaning.

**New terms** and **important words** are shown in bold.

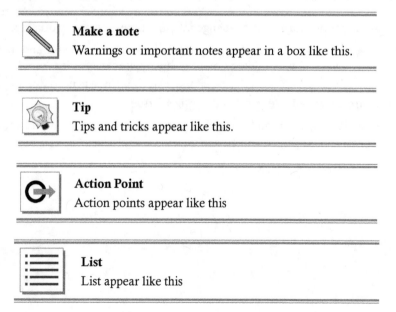

**Make a note**

Warnings or important notes appear in a box like this.

**Tip**

Tips and tricks appear like this.

**Action Point**

Action points appear like this

**List**

List appear like this

# Reader feedback

Feedback from our readers is always welcome. Let us know what you think about this book—what you liked or may have disliked. Reader feedback is important for us to develop titles that you really get the most out of.

To send us general feedback, simply send an e-mail to feedback@impacktpublishing. com, and mention the book title via the subject of your message.

If there is a topic that you have expertise in and you are interested in either writing or contributing to a book, see our author guide on www.impacktpublishing.com/ authors.

# >1

# Generation Y – Who Are They?

With hurricane-shattering force that broad-sided us unexpectedly, Generation Y (Gen Y), has descended on our workplaces. A new generation of workers—born between 1981 and 2000—is in our midst, and they are triggering the most radical workforce changes with their distinctive attitudes, behaviors, needs, and expectations. With their arrival, the organizational landscape will never be the same again.

This first chapter sets the context for the book by providing a portrait of Gen Y, so we have a common understanding of who they are before we launch into strategies. In this chapter, we will:

➤ Unpack the attributes of Gen Y

➤ Examine what Gen Y needs and expects from us in the workplace

➤ Shatter myths about Gen Y that can derail our working relationships with them

Before proceeding, there is a caveat to be mindful of. The description of Gen Y that is offered is not intended to label the entire generation with one sweeping brush stroke. In reality, not every member of Gen Y falls exactly within the parameters of the portrait—some less so than others. The purpose of the description is to familiarize you with the over-arching characteristics of Gen Y that emerged from research; specifically, how they experience and perceive the world and the events that influenced and shaped their values, expectations, and behaviors.

# So, what's burning?

In the preface, I mentioned that one of the goals of this book is to address burning questions you may have about Gen Y. So, what's burning?

As I stood in a packed theatre in Chicago, Illinois, a few years ago delivering a presentation about Gen Y, a senior executive from a multinational food company stood up and, with laser-precision, asked a question that likely was on the minds of many attendees and on your mind, as well: *"Why should we bother spending time on Gen Y?"*. It is one of the most crucial questions I've been asked—why should any of us invest time knowing about Gen Y and cracking the code for working effectively with them?

Quite simply, we can't afford not to. We owe it to ourselves, as organizational leaders, and to our businesses. If we choose not to acknowledge and explore ways to work with Gen Y, we risk losing out on the skills, gifts, and talents that they bring to our workplace. Much of this is sought-after expertise that can give our organizations a competitive advantage in an uncertain and unpredictable global economy. Gen Y brings the following elements to the table:

> ➤ Technological savvy (they are the most digitally wired and proficient generation in history)

> ➤ Industry knowledge attained from their post-secondary studies

> ➤ A new lens through which they view the world

With their distinct perspective on the world, Gen Y has the ability to awaken us to the realities of our workplace; that is, our practices, procedures, policies, and norms that we take for granted and may no longer serve us well in the new economy. They can shed light on how we can enhance our approach to business and, in doing so, better position us to meet the needs of our customers and clients—those savvy consumers who can freely take their business elsewhere if they aren't satisfied. Gen Y's perspective on consumer needs is especially advantageous if our customers and clients are Gen Ys themselves. If we are receptive, Gen Y can introduce us to a myriad of untapped possibilities that can transform the way we think about and lead our organizations, and can take us from being "in the pack" to "leading the pack" in our approach to business.

As well, how we attract and engage, not only with Gen Y, but with all of our employees, are the pillars upon which our reputation as industry leaders is built and sustained. At a time when we face a global labor force shortage, we are well advised to create and nurture workplaces that are characterized as respectful and collaborative in order to attract the shrinking pool of skilled employees that are available to us. If we don't figure out ways to work more effectively with Gen Y, and with all of our employees, we risk losing our best employees to our completion. How do you want to be recognized as a leader and what is the legacy you want to leave behind?

# Unpacking the attributes of Gen Y

*"I'll Google it and get back to you.…"*

*"What do you mean there isn't an app for that?"*

*"You want me to do… what?….fax it? Do fax machines still exist?"*

You likely have heard the preceding statements. They represent some of the ways Gen Y perceives and experiences the world. Let's spend time exploring the distinct attributes of this generation. As we proceed, please be mindful of the caveat presented earlier. The following descriptions are general insights that have been gleaned about the generation, as a whole, and by no means do they reflect the characteristics of every member of the Gen Y community. Also, the intent of offering the descriptions is not to label Gen Y, but to get us started in better understanding the newest generation in our workplace.

---

**Make a note**

Beside each characteristic that is listed below and throughout this chapter, you'll find references that you can consult if you'd like more information. The complete list of references appears in the *Google it…* section at the end of this chapter.

---

Overall, Gen Y is characterized as:

➤ The most ethnically diverse generation in history (Eisner, 2005)

➤ The most savvy technocrats (Howe and Strauss, 2000)

➤ The generation that is vehemently opposed to micromanagement (Martin, 2005)

➤ The cohort that places a higher price tag on empowerment, challenging work, and excitement than any other generation (Martin, 2005)

➤ The highest performing and most ambitious of the generations (Gilburg, 2008)

Gen Y was raised under the adoring eyes of parents, who encouraged them to have a crystal clear vision of their future and to pursue their goals with vigor and dogged determination. Parents of Gen Y are referred to as "helicopter parents" because of their strong presence in virtually all aspects of their children's lives, especially decision making, problem solving, and career planning (Howe and Strauss, 2000). Because Gen Y was under the umbrella of parental support and encouragement more than any other generation, they bring an infectious positive attitude, unwavering confidence, and high self-esteem to their careers. They are eager to take initiative and stretch into assignments and roles that appear to be outside their competency, because they believe they can accomplish anything they envision. Yet, at the same time, growing up in an environment where—for the most part—they received glowing feedback, Gen Y finds it difficult to accept negative feedback. We may even see a more vulnerable side of Gen Y, which can show up as insecurity and a fear of failure (Howe and Strauss, 2000).

Gen Y's have fewer siblings; hence, they had fewer experiences dealing with rivalry and competition at home (Strutton et al., 2011). They are referred to as "trophy kids"; those who rarely lost anything and are on the receiving end of everything, including recognition and rewards for effort as well as achievement (Alsop, 2008).

Gen Y has grown up thriving on the frenzied speed of technology, and this is mirrored in everything they do, including their relationships. Their multi-tasking, highly-stimulated world revolves around instant messaging, managing conversations in several chat rooms simultaneously, downloading, buying and selling online, blogging to get real-time reactions from their cyber network, engaging in wiki collaborations, searching Google for information—which is their primary source of information— and thriving on the instant gratification that comes with gaming and watching fast-paced videos and movies. The high-speed of their lives and the comfort with which they manage multiple tasks and relationships have left them with little patience for linear thinking, lengthy step-by-step instructions, analysis before action, and face-to-face meetings that follow a tightly scripted agenda.

Gen Y's core values include connectedness, collaboration, free expression, respect, creativity, work-life balance, and flexibility to move freely through life changing directions (Pew, 2010). Relationships are a high priority for Gen Y; hence, they gravitate toward online and face-to-face activities that promote interaction and collaboration (Howe and Strauss, 2000).

# Exploring Gen Y's needs and expectations

More than any other generation in history, Gen Y is coming into the workforce with more advanced academic credentials, greater technological competency than their supervisors and coworkers, higher expectations that their skills and talents will be rewarded, and higher expectations that others will accommodate their workplace needs and expectations.

# Can you live up to Gen Y's expectations?

From you, as their supervisor, Gen Y expects support and clear instructions on projects, yet they want autonomy to chart their own path and pace to achieve their goals (Yeaton, 2007). In your communication with them, they favor messages that are delivered with charisma and humor (Morton, 2002). They also expect regular and speedy feedback on their performance (Berkowitz and Schewe, 2011), which should take the form of objective methods of assessment and explicit guidelines on how to meet and exceed workplace expectations (Lowery, 2004). Gen Y wants to know immediately what they are doing right and wrong. However, they may be unprepared to handle negative feedback as they have been told often by parents that they are truly amazing in almost everything they do.

Since whirl wind speed is a way of life for Gen Y, they expect equally high speed performance from us (Junco and Mastrodicasa, 2007). Gen Y is perturbed by promises to "get back to them" with responses to their questions and concerns, and they are even more displeased by promises of distant pay raises and promotions (Lancaster and Stillman, 2002). They come into the workplace with expectations for fast-track promotions, raises, perks, and flexible work arrangements (Zemke, 2001).

Having been privy to the intense media scrutiny of corporate scandal and downsizing, Gen Y has become mistrustful and apathetic toward corporate cultures, traditional hierarchies, and authority (Martin and Tulgan, 2002). They question lines of authority, workplace protocol, and etiquette (Erickson et al., 2009). They do not conform readily to standards, and they confidently challenge the status quo, often expecting those in senior roles to explain why workplace practices make good business sense (Morton, 2002). Hence, they have earned the title of the "why" generation (Lyon et al., 2005).

# Can your organization live up to Gen Y's expectations?

Gen Y is attracted to careers that enable them to make contributions to the community, especially pertaining to environmental sustainability, and they value time away from work to pursue volunteer interests (Hewlett et al., 2009). Regardless of their chosen profession, the need for fun, excitement, and autonomy in the workplace are stronger in Gen Y than in previous generations and are regarded as workplace requirements (Lamm and Meek, 2009).

When they first join your organization, Gen Y is on heightened alert looking for evidence of alignment between their personal expectations and organizational realities. Gen Y does not spend much time contemplating how they will fit into an organization; rather, they spend their time hunting for answers to how an organization will be compatible with their lives (Espinoza et al., 2010), especially their commitment to work-life balance. They are able to size up an organization within the first three weeks, and if there is dissonance between personal and organizational expectations, they likely won't stay past six months. Gen Y's definition of long-term commitment is one year (Martin, 2005), and it is predicted that by age 38, Gen Y will have had 14 different jobs (Twenge et al., 2010). Even when there is high unemployment, Gen Y will exercise the right to leave, usually when frustrated with lack of, or denied, promotional opportunities (Beeson, 2009). This confidence, even during tough economic times, is the result of having a boundary-less view of their career and an awareness of their sought-after technological expertise (Zemke et al., 2000). Security is valued, but is defined as career security whereby they build a portfolio of transferable skills permitting them to change jobs freely (Twenge et al., 2010).

Gen Y is considered the most exigent generation for us to attract, as they prefer self-employment to working for others (Lipkin and Perrymore, 2009). With Gen Y declared as "the most entrepreneurial generation in history", we are confronted with the added weight of convincing them that working for a corporation has greater appeal than self-employment (Martin, 2005).

On the positive side of a ship that appears to be sinking, one in five Gen Ys anticipates tenure with the same company for six years or longer (Hastings, 2008). This is our lifeline, knowing there are Gen Ys considering long term employment in our organizations where they can hone their skills and advance their careers. Our challenge—and it is within our capacity to address—is to *create work environments that are even more alluring* than they currently are; hence, inspiring more Gen Ys to join us, to work at full capacity for us, to engage actively with us, and to stay with us.

Throughout this book, we'll explore the changes we can make in our organizations in order to create such a workplace, and, at the same time, position our organization to meet its overall objectives. Specifically, we'll explore:

> ➤ Job enrichment approaches for the current line-up of jobs in our organization

> ➤ Revisions to our human resources policies, practices, and procedures with Gen Y's input

> ➤ New ways to engage with Gen Y that inspire them to be even greater contributors to our organization

# Shattering myths about Gen Y

While traveling across North America and meeting hundreds of Gen Ys as part of my research, I was struck by Gen Y's deep-seated concern about the myths that others subscribe to about their generation. These assumptions cause Gen Y a considerable amount of angst; they feel both misunderstood and misinterpreted. As well, these myths are highly destructive. They have the potential to erode working relationships even before they begin, and they can sabotage opportunities to build high performing and productive work teams.

If our goal is to establish ourselves as leaders in our respective industries, that is, people want to work for us, customers and clients seek our services, and other companies pursue us as partners, then it is incumbent upon us to build a strong and stable workforce that is the pulse of success and viability. Specifically, this entails creating a climate of inclusion, respect, and compassion. As we reach toward this outcome, we can't afford to have misperceptions and misunderstandings about the newest generation in our workforce permeating the bloodstream of our organization and interfering with our efforts to develop strong work teams that ultimately position our organizations as industry leaders.

Presented in the following sections are five common myths that hover in the workplace about Gen Y, followed by responses to each. It's time to shatter our glass assumptions.

# Myth number 1 – Gen Y is entitled

*Entitlement? Can we reframe this as confidence?*

Gen Y hopes that we can put the term *entitlement* in abeyance and come to view them as confident. For Gen Y, this means we can launch working relationships on a much more positive note without the stigma attached to the concept of *entitlement*.

According to Gen Y, nothing punctures their eardrums and is more distressing than hearing that they are *entitled*. Where we see *entitlement*, Gen Y sees *confidence*, that is, self-assurance in their ability to declare who they are, what they stand for, and what they want in their personal and professional lives. They've been raised by their parents (that's us!) to have a compelling vision of their future and to persistently march toward their goals—slicing through anything that impedes their way. This confidence manifests itself in everything Gen Y does, including how they manage their careers. And we are on the receiving end of this tsunami of confidence! It shows up in our organizations as a "can do" attitude and sometimes as an overzealous game plan for career progression. To some degree, we might be a tad envious of the precision and persistence with which Gen Y communicates and pursues career goals. Their pathways and efforts are significantly more razor sharp in comparison to how many of us manage our careers.

Yet, at the same time, Gen Y is acutely aware that they face the same career struggles and daily setbacks as other generations: unemployment, difficulty securing their dream job, managing debt load, being sandwiched between raising children and caring for aging parents, and personal and professional disappointments that take a myriad of forms. Gen Y asks us to suspend the term *entitlement*, which divides the generations, so we can explore the similarities in our personal and professional lives that have the potential to unite us.

# Myth number 2 – Gen Y has no work ethic

*No work ethic? Can we reframe this as a different work ethic?*

Many managers speak of the apparent lack of a strong work ethic in their young staff and dismiss this as laziness. While this may be true in some cases, the majority of Gen Y is willing to work hard and aspire to great things, but they also place high importance on work-life balance. The work-life balance piece is where we hit a pain point. While we might be driven to work long hours and push ourselves beyond our comfort zone in ways that take a toll on our health and our relationships, Gen Y is not willing to do this. They have witnessed the side effects of unrelenting workplace demands and pressures on our generation, such as heart attacks, burnout, separation from loved ones, and divorces, and they aren't prepared to be on the receiving end of these outcomes in order to get ahead in their careers. Instead, they are starting their careers with firm commitments to work-life balance, which often means plans with friends and family trump work.

They value working hard, but they are committed to working differently. This generation is the strongest advocate for telecommuting. Working from home allows them to make maximum use of their day; that is, they are free from office interruptions that interfere with task completion, they save time in commuting, they don't fall prey to water-cooler conversations, which are colossal time killers, and they have the flexibility to work when they are most productive, whether this is 2 p.m. or a.m.

When we comprehend the work ethics of our youngest employees, we are better equipped to set mutual expectations for success. Here lies an opportunity for us to explain tasks to be completed and deadlines to be honored, and allow Gen Y to chart the pace and path for delivering final products. In *Chapter 8, Mentoring the Next Generation of Leaders – Legacy Building, One Gen Y at a Time*, on performance management, we will discuss approaches you can use to manage daily performance in a way that respects the organizational mandate and Gen Y's approach to work.

# Myth number 3 – Gen Y is disrespectful

*Disrespectful? Respect is one of Gen Y's core values.*

In reality, *respect* is a common thread joining all generations. The majority of us *value* respect, but each generation *defines it differently*.

While working in the hospitality sector on an initiative to enhance communication, I asked staff to provide examples of how respect should show up in the workplace. Senior employees replied that respect, for them, is evident in the following:

> Arriving on time for meetings

> Giving full attention to others when they are speaking by refraining from text messaging, gaming, and answering phone calls

> Wearing proper business attire

> Being in the office from 9 to 5

For the Gen Y contingent, none of these behaviors signaled respect. The following was on their list:

> Keeping promises

> Providing feedback

> Asking for their input

> The speed with which people respond to their requests, which is highest on their priority list

They added that respect is earned and not assumed; that is, Gen Y won't simply show respect to us because of our job title or role in the organization. Respect is earned predominantly by proving to Gen Y that we are willing to work alongside them, and that we wouldn't ask them to do a task that we, ourselves, would not be willing to do, no matter how unpleasant or difficult the task may be.

The preceding example is widespread in our organizations. We say that respect is valued, but we haven't taken the subsequent fundamental steps that are integral to creating a respectful workplace; hence, we remain frustrated, deflated, and irritated by the lack of respect around us. The important next step after declaring the importance of respect is to delve into what respect means to each of us and what we need from each other to create a respectful working relationship. This requires us to dig deep and do the heavy lifting that comes with identifying and agreeing on the specific and concrete behaviors that support working together respectfully. Once these behaviors are identified, we can then move toward demonstrating these behaviors in our daily interactions, and holding each other accountable to our new commitment.

# Myth number 4 – Gen Y is self-centered

*Self-centered? Gen Y actually has an altruistic streak running through their veins.*

We need not look further than the resumes we receive from Gen Y applicants in response to job vacancies for evidence of this. Their resumes are brimming with references that support their belief in and advocacy for social causes, and their remarkably strong sense of civic duty, environmental accountability, and community mindedness. Their covering letters also follow suit, by conveying their interest to work for organizations that care about how they affect and contribute to society. A number of studies show that Gen Y is volunteering at record rates at work, and in their local and global communities. Added to this, Gen Y's volunteer commitments appear to have started much earlier in their careers when compared to other generations.

Even though Gen Y is crystal clear and steadfast in declaring what they want, who they are, what they stand for, and what they envision as their career trajectory—at the core—they devote a considerable amount of time to community initiatives that are in their own backyard and in the global village.

# Myth number 5 – Gen Y wants to run before they can walk

*Taking the express lane to the executive suite? An invitation for us to restart our engine.*

I recall a story that a senior manager of a leading oil company in Alberta, Canada, shared with me: "We interviewed a Gen Y for an entry level position, but he appeared indifferent, except for his excitement asking me a number of questions about how he can get into my position and how long that would take! These young people today have no tolerance for entry level work. They all want to start their careers as managers."

Although Gen Y can create the impression that they are attempting to circumvent entry level work, Gen Y assures us this is not the case. They are aware that entry-level work is a stepping stone toward the dream job they aspire to have. However, Gen Y confesses that they can become disillusioned and disinterested in some of the entry-level tasks that we assign. Their disinterest stems from not having a clear understanding of how the work we have given them contributes to the organization. Specifically, they don't understand why they should work to their full potential when they perceive the tasks to be marginally significant to the organization.

To rectify this, a subtle change might be all that is needed. Along with communicating job instructions, goals, and expectations, perhaps we can spend time setting the context for Gen Y; that is, conveying the rationale behind what we expect them to do and underscoring the importance of their work to the organization. Even our most junior employees want to know how they can add value to the organization even if their work appears, on the surface, to be light years away from impacting the organization's strategic direction. A delicate change in the way we communicate the importance of their work can mean the difference between an employee who is slogging agonizingly though the day, and someone who is engaged, enthused, and working to their full potential.

Also consider giving Gen Y an opportunity to step outside the parameters of their entry-level accountabilities. This could take the form of inviting them to departmental meetings where they contribute to discussions and initiatives that would benefit from the input of younger workers. By encouraging their participation in new ways, Gen Y develops a richer understanding of the company's priorities, and they make vital connects between the company's mandate and their entry-level work.

Alongside their concerns about entry-level work, Gen Y questions the complexity of stepping stones in place to reach their career goals. Gen Y is eager to move their career expediently along. They want to complete the work assigned, master the skills required, and move ahead, without being told that they need to patiently wait for promotion. Perhaps this is a call for us to dust off and review our policies and procedures on talent management and succession planning. In consultation with Gen Y, we may find a way to fine-tune our career progression pathways to meet the needs of Gen Y and to fulfill our organizational mandate.

# Shattered myths? So what now?

Have the glass assumptions been shattered?

You may not be ready to wholeheartedly embrace all of the responses to myths about Gen Y, but I encourage you to take the first step toward eliminating, or at least minimizing, myths about Gen Y that pervade our organizations. At the starting gate, there are three invitations waiting for you:

> ➤ Recognize and confront your own assumptions, attitudes, and beliefs about Gen Y and how they manifest themselves in your interactions with young people

> ➤ Look beyond your assumptions to see Gen Y's talents, gifts, and potential

> ➤ Envision the working relationship you'd like to have with Gen Ys in your life; specifically, imagine what a new approach to supporting, mentoring, and collaborating with them might look like

In my years of being in the company of Gen Y as part of my research, teaching, and business practice, I've consistently found that Gen Y has enormous respect for other generations. The majority of Gen Ys want to be part of your team, they are keen to learn from your leadership, and they are eager to build strong working relationships with you and their colleagues.

As we progress through this book, each chapter will reveal a new set of tools and practices that bring you closer to the working relationship you envision with Gen Y. Leaders and organizations able to see beyond the falsely woven stories about Gen Y are en route to creating a climate of inclusion, respect, and compassion that is the heartbeat of prosperous and thriving organizations.

As mentioned in the *Preface*, space has been left at the end of each chapter for the voice of Gen Y to be heard. It only makes sense that Gen Y has an opportunity to weigh in on the issues that we'll be ruminating over as we reconfigure new pathways for working with them. At the end of each chapter, there is a section called *Meeting the Gen Y community*, in which a member of Gen Y shares a key message that is intended to further inform our thinking and approach to managing and working with the newest generation in the workplace.

In this chapter, we've been discussing the attributes of the Gen Y cohort, so we'll turn the narrative over to a member of the Gen Y community to discuss what he'd like us to know about Gen Y's workplace needs and expectations.

# Meeting the Gen Y community

*What would you like business leaders to know about your workplace needs and expectations?*

*–Ulusyar Tareen*

Ulusyar reflected on his work experience over the years, specifically, the many different leadership styles he has witnessed. A key message for us, as organizational leaders, is to remember to be "leaders, not bosses". Ulusyar encourages us to focus on coaching Gen Y toward performance excellence by:

➤ Communicating clear expectations, including the rationale behind the work that we expect them to complete

➤ Showing them exactly what is expected on the job

➤ Guiding them patiently as they strive to meet organizational expectations

➤ Keeping the work environment easy going, but still strict on performance standards

➤ Rewarding them for their achievements

According to Ulusyar, Gen Y does not respect or respond well to autocratic leadership, where the focus is on telling them what to do and controlling how the work gets done. This does not help Gen Y learn how to be their best and, as a result, pushes them away. Added to this, Ulusyar reminds us that team work is integral to our business operations, and therefore, we are advised to pay extra close attention to developing and sustaining teams. Time should be taken to train teams so they:

> ➤ Respect and welcome each other's differences

> ➤ Can bring their unique skills and backgrounds to the forefront

> ➤ Realize the importance of contributing as equally as possible to the end product

Ulusyar also invites us to reflect on the number of years of work experience that we expect from job applicants. According to Ulusayar, Gen Y becomes increasingly frustrated when they read job advertisements for positions that they are interested in—and they know they can do—but they don't have the years of experience that we are looking for. A growing number of Gen Ys choose to pursue graduate degrees right after their undergraduate studies in order to better prepare themselves to compete for the jobs they want; hence, they don't enter the work world with extensive work experience to their credit. Ulusyar asks us to consider reducing the work experience requirements and to take into consideration all the part-time work, internships, volunteer commitments, and extra-curricular activities that Gen Y brings to the workplace. Housed within these experiences are the transferable skills that we likely are looking for to get the job done. In the words of Ulusyar, "Give us a chance. You won't regret it."

**Make a note**

Ulusyar was born in Pakistan. He received his Bachelor's degree in Global Business from Coventry University, U.K., and he is currently working towards his Master's in Global Management at Royal Roads University in Canada. Ulusyar has 4 years of work experience in the banking sector. When he is not studying the global marketplace, Ulusyar enjoys reading books about psychology and human science.

# Reframing challenges as opportunities

*We haven't met, I don't know who you are, and we don't have any history together, but the split second you walk into the room, I've formed an impression—you are brimming with entitlement, overflowing with arrogance, saturated in confidence, bursting with self indulgence...*

Freeze this scene. Does this sound vaguely familiar? Have you found yourself in a similar situation where you've made a snap judgment about the younger generation? Perhaps it was when Gen Y entered the room for a job interview, stood up to speak at a meeting, took the stage to deliver a presentation, or walked into the office and was introduced as your new boss? Or perhaps, the Gen Y in front of you is your new financial advisor, lawyer looking after your legal issues, instructor teaching the night school course you signed up for, or doctor who is about to perform surgery on you. You can't help yourself; a torrent of first impressions flood your mind and it is difficult to concentrate on anything else.

When you are caught in the moment, be aware of your actions and reactions. Now, reframe. Change the message. In the moment when you are being held hostage by these first impressions, consciously lift those thoughts from your mind and transport them out of awareness. Replace the language of judgment and evaluation with *curiosity* about the person in front of you. Instead of leading with assumptions about them, what can you ask this person that shows your interest in getting to know them, and perhaps dismantling some of your initial first impressions? Start with a few questions that can enhance your awareness and appreciation of the person in front of you. This is the first incremental step in reframing challenges as opportunities to connect on a deeper and more meaningful level with others.

# Leaning in to change

Reflect on what you read in this chapter about the attributes of Gen Y, their workplace needs and expectations, and the myths associated with this generation. Identify one significant thing that surfaced for you. What did you learn? Describe what you plan to do differently in your interactions with Gen Y that reflects your shift in thinking.

Since *Leaning in to change* is featured at the end of each chapter, you may want to start a journal where you can record your thoughts and reactions as you read and respond to questions that are posed. This way, you can return to your notes at a later time to refresh your memory about the commitments you made to do things differently and to ascertain your progress in honoring new directions.

A chat room on my website (www.eyeofthetigerconsulting.ca) has been created for those of you who would like to discuss your workplace experiences, ask questions, and share resources. I'm looking forward to seeing you online.

# Google it...

For those of you who would like to continue exploring the Gen Y world, please check out the following resources:

> A video from 60 Minutes, the award-winning interviewers and broadcasters that showcased their research on Gen Y in the workplace: http://www.youtube.com/watch?v=owwM6FpWWoQ

> Alsop, R., *The Trophy Kids Grow Up*, San Francisco: Jossey-Bass, (2008)

> Beeson, J., "Why you didn't get that promotion", *Harvard Business Review*, 87(6), 101 – 105, (2009).

➤ Berkowitz, N. E., and Schewe, D, S, "Generational cohorts hold the key to understanding patients and health care providers: Coming-of-age experiences influence health care behaviors for a lifetime", *Marketing Quarterly*, 28, 190 – 204, (2011)

➤ Eisner, S., "Managing generation Y", *SAM Advanced Management Journal*, (07497075), 70(4), 4 – 15 (2011)

➤ Erikson, T., Alsop, R., Nicholson, P., and Miller, J., "GenY in the workforce", *Harvard Business Review*, 87(2), 43 – 49, (2009)

➤ Espinoza, C, Ukleja, M., and Rusch, C., "The millennial generation: recruiting, retaining, and managing", *Today's CPA*, Sept/Oct., 24 – 27, (2006)

➤ Gilburg, D., "They're gen y and you're not", *CIO*, 21(8), 40 – 43, (2008)

➤ Hastings, R., "Millennials expect a lot from leaders", *HR Magazine*, 53(1), 30, (2008)

➤ Hewlett, S., Sherbin, L., and Sumberg, K, "How gen y and boomers will reshape your agenda", *Harvard Business Review*, 87(7/8), 71 – 76, (2009)

➤ Howe, N., and Strauss, W., "Millennials Rising: The Next Greatest Generation", *New York: Vintage Books*, (2000)

➤ Junco, R. and Mastrodicasa, J., "Connecting to the Net Generation: What Higher Education Professionals Need to Know About Today's Students", *Washington, DC: Student Affairs Administrators in Higher Education (NASPA)*, (2007)

➤ Lamm, E. and Meeks, M.D, "Workplace fun: the moderating effects of generational differences", *Employee Relations*, 31(6), 613 – 631, (2009)

➤ Lancaster, L.C and Stillman, D, "When Generations Collide: Who they are, Why they clash, and How to solve the generational puzzle at work", New York: Harper, (2002)

➤ Lipkin, N. and Perrymore, A, "Y in the Workplace: Managing the "Me First" Generation", *Franklin Lakes*, NJ: Career Press, (2009)

➤ Lowery, J.W., "Student affairs for a new generation", In M.D. Commes and R. Debard (Eds), *Serving the Millennial Generation: New Directions for Student Services*, 106, 87 – 99, San Francisco, CA: Jossey-Bass, (2004)

➤ Lyon, K., Legg, S., and Toulson, P, "Generational cohorts", *International Journal of Diversity in Organizations, Communities and Nations*, 5(1), 89 – 98, (2005)

➤ Martin, C., "From high maintenance to high productivity: What managers need to know about GenY", *Industrial and Commercial Training*, 37(1) 39-44, (2005)

➤ Martin, C. and Tulgan, B, *Managing the Generation Mix*, New York: HRD Press, (2002)

➤ Morton, L.P., "Targeting Generation Y", *Public Relations Quarterly, Summer*, 47(2), 46 – 48, (2002)

➤ Pew Research Center, *Millennials: A Portrait of Generation Next*, Washington, DC: Pew Research Center, (2010)

➤ Strutton, D., Taylor, G. D., and Thompson, K, "Investigating generational differences in e-WOM behaviors for advertising purposes, does X = Y?", *International Journal of Advertising*, 30(4), 559 – 586, (2011)

➤ Twenge, J.M., Campbell, S.M., Hoffman, B.J., and Lance, C.E, "Generational differences in work values: leisure and extrinsic values increasing, social and intrinsic values decreasing", *Journal of Management*, 36(5), 1117 – 1142, (2010)

➤ Yeaton, K., "Recruiting and managing the "why" generation: GenY", *The CPA Journal*, 78(4), 68 – 72, (2007)

➤ Zemke, R., "Here come the millenials", *Training*, 38(7), 44 – 49, (2001)

➤ Zemke, R., Raines, C., and Filipczak, B, "Generations at Work: Managing the clash of Veterans, Boomers, Xers, and Nexters in your workplace", Washington, DC: American Management Association, (2000)

# Summary

In this chapter, we extinguished the flames of "what's burning", unpacked what the helicopter parents gave us, asked ourselves whether we can live with Gen Y's needs and expectations, and ended with shattering some glass. There is a great deal to ponder about the youngest generation that has arrived on our doorstep and that we have the privilege of working with.

Now that we have a better understanding of who Gen Y is, let's leap into how we can attract Gen Y talent to our organizations.

# >2

# Attracting Gen Y Talent to Your Company

*Now that we know who Gen Y is, where do we find them?*

This question nips persistently at our business heels. Over the next few years, we will find ourselves in a bleak and volatile labor market in which to recruit staff in general, let alone qualified Gen Ys. With the mass exodus of baby boomers from the workplace, which has already begun, the labor market will be earmarked by three core challenges:

> ➤ An overall shortage in the number of workers for the jobs that are available in the labor market—demand trumps supply
>
> ➤ A scarcity of workers with the right blend of skills, abilities, and knowledge to fill jobs that are currently available, especially at the leadership level
>
> ➤ Gen Y's preference for self-employment and their reservations about joining our organizations

Faced with these realities, we find ourselves ensnared in a vicious and relentless recruitment cycle. When we can't find the right candidate for the job, we bend our list of qualifications and expectations, expand our search by casting a wider net into the vast unknown, and even question whether we need to fill the job (perhaps it can be absorbed into the work done by others in the company?). From my conversations with Human Resources practitioners, many of them have already started to carry out a third or fourth round of recruitment for some jobs before they eventually find the right candidate. Indeed, we are in troubling waters. However, there is a beacon of hope. There are ways for us to turn this ship around and navigate to a place where we can reap the benefits we desire from our recruitment efforts. However, it calls on us to step away from recruitment practices that served us well in a more stable and abundant economy, and step into more creative and innovative ways in how we think about and approach the art and science of recruitment.

This chapter introduces you to the tools you can use to shift gears in your approach to recruitment and surpass the competition in attracting Gen Y to your organization. Added to this, you will get a glimpse into what Gen Y looks for when they job hunt and how you can leverage this knowledge to attract and ultimately select the "best fit" candidate for your company. Specifically, this chapter guides us through the following:

> ➤ Turbo-charging our job ads
> ➤ Tapping into social media
> ➤ Selecting the "perfect" candidate

As you can see, this chapter focuses exclusively on attracting Gen Y to your organization. Some of the courses of action proposed here might be equally as effective in recruiting job candidates from other generations to your organization. However, if you have recruitment approaches that are serving your needs, please don't abandon them. Simply consider adding a few approaches offered in this chapter so that you catch some Gen Y talent!

# So, what's burning?

Before we steer in new directions, some of you might be asking, *"Why should we invest in changing our approach to recruitment when Gen Y likely won't stay with us longer than one year?"* A valid question. It can be exasperating and disconcerting when Gen Y gets the one year itch (or sooner!) to leave our organizations. The mere suggestion in this chapter that we revamp our recruitment practices may be perceived as an act of futility and a blatant waste of precious time. However, before we discard the idea of re-strategizing our approach to recruitment, I remind you that twenty percent of Gen Ys *are* interested in working and learning under our leadership and are keen to establish long term working relationships with us. I encourage you to keep your collective focus on this catchment base as we progress through this chapter. Since Gen Y is connected to an extensive network, the word soon will spread that your organization is ahead of the curve in recruitment, and this will catch the attention of Gen Ys who have not yet had the pleasure of exploring opportunities with your company.

I'm anticipating that once you attract the right talent to your organization, you will also be interested in engaging Gen Y in ways that persuade them to stay with you and build their careers in your organization, which we'll address later in the book. The combination of transforming the way we recruit and creating a climate that is conducive to engagement and productivity will likely boost the number of Gen Ys who knock on your office door asking to join your team and ultimately deciding to stay.

Some of you may also be concerned about the sizeable investment of time, energy, and finances associated with breaking new ground in recruitment, especially when there are pressing operational and strategic matters vying for your attention. We sometimes neglect to appreciate the magnitude of the role that recruitment plays in the sustainability and success of our organizations. The additional stretch that we are prepared to take in order to find the best candidate for the job, and for your organization's culture, can mean the difference between effortless sailing and navigating abysmally treacherous waters. We've probably all experienced the reverberations from hiring "the wrong" person for a job. The distress caused by one person spreads rampantly throughout the organization until soon our entire staff falls prey to the symptoms. The grief shows up in disrupted working relationships with our staff, clients, and customers, and soon it creeps into the overall performance and productivity of our organization. It can rage through the bloodstream of our organization putting financial and non-financial strains on you and your organization. In the case where we opt to dismiss the individual, the costs associated with dismissal, initiating a search for a replacement, and eventually hiring a new employee can be exorbitant, let alone the forthcoming costs associated with orienting and training new staff. We can never prevent this situation from happening, but by adapting new recruitment practices, we can minimize the probability of hiring someone who isn't right for your company.

So why should we invest in changing our approach to recruitment? We want to:

> ➤ Minimize the probability of mistakenly inviting someone into our organization who wrecks havoc on our culture and productivity, which are the pillars of our reputation and success

> ➤ Hire Gen Y staff in the most effective and efficient manner possible

> ➤ Increase the likelihood of selecting the "best fit" Gen Y candidate for our organization

> ➤ Preserve time and energy for the other items on our "to do" list as organizational leaders

# Turbo-charging our job ads

I had the pleasure of partnering with a client in the pharmaceutical industry, who, at the time we met, was miffed by the lack of success in finding a Junior Medical Writer. They had been actively hunting for the right candidate for over a year, but to no avail. We spent a considerable amount of time ruminating over the facts and dissecting the situation from every conceivable angle. We eventually agreed that a change in how they recruit was inevitable. As you can appreciate, letting go of comfortable, past practices and embracing newness are difficult things. Change beckons, but we are tentative about whether the new beginning is better than what we currently have. After much deliberation and with a smattering of curiosity about where the path could lead, they stepped into the unknown with me and worked in the trenches to revise their approach to recruitment. In a few weeks, they went from receiving a hand-full of resumes from semi-qualified Gen Y applicants to a batch of resumes from applicants whose qualifications were spot on for the job. What did they do differently? They stopped following the same path as everyone else; it is probably a path you are familiar with.

You create what you think is an advertising masterpiece and marvel at what you've written. It includes:

> ➤ An impeccable description of your company's mandate and strategic direction

> ➤ A tantalizing array of competitive benefits

> ➤ A robust description of the job vacancy

> ➤ A precise list of qualifications and experience required

You post the advertisement in a few favorite places, such as newspapers or prominent magazines. Then, you wait. Resumes trickle in, or perhaps there is a deluge of resumes, but to your chagrin, few, if any, of the applicants spark your interest. You begin plotting what to do next.

Before we proceed, let's slam on the brakes and come to a complete stop. That familiar and comfortable path we've been following, regrettably, no longer differentiates us from the competition. It does not afford us the competitive edge that is needed when we are recruiting in today's labor market. What we need is to *turbo-charge* our job ads. We need to inject a little high octane gas in the recruitment tank to reach the finish line, that is, finding the "best fit" Gen Y candidates before they start entertaining job offers from our competition. What's the secret formula for doing this? It starts with revitalizing the first impression we make. Let's convert our ads from mild to sizzling hot and then, let's make them roar!

# Converting our ads from mild to sizzling hot!

What is the *overall impression* that your company conveys through job ads? Is the temperature of the ads mild or sizzling hot? That is, do your ads have the magnetism that lures Gen Y away from applying for jobs with the competition and entices them to forward their resumes to you?

The key ingredient in the recipe that transforms job ads from mildly appealing to highly captivating is our ability to paint a crystal clear and vivid picture of the *culture* of our organization. Specifically, we need to articulate the signature qualities of our culture that strikingly differentiate us from our competition. Just like individuals, each organization has a distinct personality that distinguishes it from others; no two companies, like no two individuals, have an identical personality profile.

In your ads, seek to play a video in the minds of potential applicants of what it is like to work in your organization. Describe a typical day in the life of your organization that captures:

> ➤ The spirit of the team and the working relationships

> ➤ The intrinsic and extrinsic value of the work your staff does

> ➤ The enthusiasm, fulfilment, and dedication experienced by your staff

Where some organizations fall short is by only *listing* their values—make an extra effort to communicate how your organization *lives its values*. This will be a welcomed addition to your ad and a key market differentiator. Also highlight a few of the more notable social events that speak to how you build and sustain community in your organization. Since social responsibility and making a difference in society are key considerations for Gen Y applicants, profile how your company contributes to the local, national, and international community.

In describing your organization, find phrases that are out of the ordinary, examples, milestones, testimonials, and stories from management and non-management staff, customers, and clients that speak to the distinctiveness of your organization. Again, we are presenting a narrative that is intended to set you apart from your competition.

Alongside the narrative, there is power in visuals. To reinforce the culture you've described, consider including some footage from your corporate photo album or attach a video that features your organization. The video can take many forms, but the ones that are most persuasive feature guest appearances by your staff, who are undoubtedly your best marketing tool for attracting job applicants. Record a few interviews with your staff that include them speaking about:

> ➤ Their careers in your organization
>
> ➤ What attracted them to your company
>
> ➤ What motivates them to stay
>
> ➤ Their career aspirations in the organization
>
> ➤ The key message they have for future employees

The visuals offer a twist on traditional job ads and a glimpse into your organization's culture, which rarely can be captured fully in written words alone. If you don't have a video, consider tasking one of your Gen Y staff to lead the production of one. They can exercise their leadership to pinpoint messages and images that have maximum appeal to Gen Y job applicants. A project of this nature gives Gen Y a sense of contribution to the organization, which is what they crave from our workplace.

In the narrative and your visual depiction of your company, underscore the aspects of your workplace that are fun, exciting, and fulfilling, which as we know, are Gen Y's values and workplace priorities. Since Gen Y is acutely attuned to the charismatic side of people and organizations, we more fittingly position ourselves to catch their eye when we convey the distinct cultural DNA of our company through stories and visuals.

# Putting the lion's roar in your content

You aim to create a job ad that—like the lion—will be king or queen of the "help wanted" savannah. You want the content to be majestic in its presence, carry a distinct prowess of leadership and charisma, and have the ability to strike a quick and precise with applicants. And similar to the lion's roar, which can be heard five miles away, you want your ad to cast a wide net of interest and resonate deeply with qualified Gen Y applicants.

As you recall from chapter one, Gen Y is attracted to workplaces where relationship building is a priority and where jobs are meaningful and add value to the organization. For the most part, Gen Y is interested in the "here and now" experience that your organization offers, and they can ascertain quickly whether an organization can deliver on their personal needs and expectations. Knowing this about Gen Y has implications for the content that we communicate in our job ads. We are encouraged to accentuate the role Gen Y will play in our organization and how the work they will do adds value to the organization. Even if the job entails lower-level and routine tasks, Gen Y wants to know how they can contribute to your organization. Invest some real estate in your job ad to set the context for Gen Y; convey the rationale behind what you expect them to do and underscore the importance of their work to your organization.

Added to this, speak directly to Gen Y's entrepreneurial spirit. Whet Gen Y's appetite about joining your organization by telling them about opportunities available to them outside the parameters of their job accountabilities. Reflect on what this might entail:

> ➤ Invitations to join committees, where they can contribute to discussions and initiatives that would benefit from the input of younger workers

> ➤ Leadership of, or assistance with, projects that are in departments that they aspire to be part of at some point in their career

> ➤ Collaborations with senior staff, who welcome the opportunity to mentor and coach them

Plant the seed of possibilities for a generation of workers who are looking for careers that are meaningful, challenging, and gratifying. At the core, if they are accomplishing, achieving, and contributing, they are more likely to stay with your company—this is what organizational loyalty hinges on.

To really capture Gen Y's attention and appeal directly to their penchant for interaction and connectedness with others in the workplace, consider going off the beaten business track and becoming uber creative. Encourage the supervisor, to whom the new recruit will report, to craft the job ad as a personal letter to job applicants. This not only kindles interest, but also gives job seekers a glimpse into the type of person they'll be reporting to. The tone of the message and the choice of words speak volumes about the supervisor's leadership attributes and the culture of the organization. Giving a voice to the supervisor will personalize the job ad and, in doing so, it appeals directly to Gen Y's need for connecting with others.

If the job vacancy requires applicants to be innovative and creative, which are high priority competencies in organizations who want the competitive edge in their industry, then consider shifting how you invite Gen Y applicants to apply for the job. In order to test Gen Y applicants' capacity for innovation and creativity, invite them to use alternative ways to present their applications for consideration. You can leave it to their discretion to ascertain the best way to do this, or you can offer a specific pathway, such as asking them to submit video resumes. An approach such as this will work only if you make it clear that, regardless of the presentation channel used, it is incumbent on the applicant to exercise due diligence in explaining how their knowledge, skills, and abilities align with the job requirements. This way, you get a chance to see how applicants present themselves and you can ascertain whether their espoused values align with your company before you invest time and money in face-to-face interviews. However, if you are proceeding with this approach, be vigilant about judging people based on first impressions. Minimize the probability of making snap judgments about candidates by:

> ➤ Organizing an interview panel to review applications

> ➤ Establishing crystal clear job qualifications based on a comprehensive job analysis

> ➤ Determining decision-making criteria and weighting used to identify which applicants will be short listed

# Tapping into social media – are you digitally networking?

*Did you know that in the majority of emerging countries, over 95 percent of Gen Ys own a smartphone? Text messaging is as natural as breathing and consumes upwards of 45 hours of Gen Y's time each week? A Facebook account is considered a networking imperative for Gen Y– it is a staple in their digital diet?*

*–Pew 2010*

This is Gen Y's reality. In the eyes of Gen Y, technology is not a tool to be used; it is their identity—an extension of who they are. Their world revolves around technology as their main source of information, entertainment, socializing, professional networking, and expressing who they are and what they stand for. Knowing the significant role that technology plays in Gen Y's life invites us to reflect on whether we are using social media effectively to connect with our future workforce. Are you digitally networking and collaborating? And, if so, have you maximized your online presence in ways that separate you from others?

If your recruitment strategy consists exclusively of posting job ads when vacancies arise, the probability of securing the right candidate for the job is dismally slim. Your future Gen Y workforce is engaged in a flurry of online activity; they are connecting, interacting, and collaborating online. If you aren't in the cyber playground with them, visibly and often, they likely don't know you exist. Searching for workplace talent begins long before you have a job vacancy. In an era of limitless digital connectivity, your recruitment strategy starts with developing a strong online presence; that is, building and sustaining a network—as widespread as possible—through a myriad of channels.

Time intensive? Definitely! Yet, in the long run, the extra effort we exert to establish and nurture our network of e-followers translates into an easier and more efficient and effective approach for finding qualified applicants. Our network of followers will likely be composed of people who have ascertained that there is something intriguing about us; hence, we are worth following. Usually, they become our followers because our organizational values and priorities align with their personal values, needs, and expectations—we tend to congregate with other like-minded folks.

When we circulate the news online that there is a job available in our organization, our followers likely will rise to the occasion; that is, they'll be quick to express their interest in the position, knowing they have already decided we are an organization they'd like to be part of. If they aren't qualified, they likely will share the ad with their circle of friends and colleagues, who they think would be qualified and interested in the position. If our followers have already identified themselves to us, they likely will refer someone from their personal network that will reflect favorably on them. Followers never want to put their own reputation at risk by recommending someone not suited for the job. Whether it is our immediate followers or referrals who apply for the job, we tap into our personal hidden market and, in doing so, get the word out faster and to a wider and more relevant audience, that a job is available in our organization.

Now, let's take a look at some of the tools that are paramount in establishing your online network and positioning you for greater success in the competition for talent—Twitter, blogs, and Facebook. Added to the list is a non-social media tool that is a useful first step in getting Gen Y to consider following you online—going back to school. They likely are familiar tools, but I've put a spin on them to heighten their advantage as assets in your recruitment strategy and building your online community.

# Tweeting away your time - #tellmeyourstory

Nothing captivates us more and draws us closer to one another than a personal story. We are riveted to every word and every twist in the storyline as we eagerly await the ending, which often imprints an enduring message in our minds and hearts long after the story is told. What is the power of the story? Through a story, we open the door that reveals to others the core of who we are—our values, our vulnerabilities, and our deep-seated hopes and dreams; we communicate our humanness. In doing so, we break down barriers and reveal to others that we are just like them.

Storytelling is equally powerful for organizations. Sharing your organization's story offers others a glimpse into the soul of your organization, which can intrigue them and endear them to you. With the right magic in your words, digital storytelling can bring an escalating stream of online Gen Y followers to you, which soon becomes a full-scale online community that is eager to network with you actively and often. Your prevalence in the minds of online followers is advantageous not only for talent acquisition, but it also makes them privy to breaking news in your business that situates you as an industry leader. If the thought of having an extensive online community that makes it their priority to follow your organization appeals to you, then let's take the first step in becoming digital storytellers.

*Hashtags? Retweeting? Tweeps?*

It's time to start tweeting!

To create the allure that draws Gen Y in your direction and inspires them to keep a watchful eye on what you are doing, consider messages that are markedly different than what your competition is communicating. For the most part, your competition's news stream is about product and service launches, branding and marketing initiatives, and company events. Take a more unconventional pathway. Create an intimate storyline for your network to follow, such as "a day in the life of...", which features snippets of the daily escapades of one of your staff members. This can take the form of a few postings during the course of the day that capture unanticipated happenings, near misses, unexpected guests, and sudden eruptions of fun that keep followers waiting in anticipation for the next posting. Keep the postings scattered throughout the day to keep followers on your trail, but not so frequently that your postings become nuisance reading and lose their charm. Focus on "the hook"; that is, the opening statement that grabs your readers' interest, and the final statement that leaves them wanting more.

Feature a new staff member every few weeks who can capture a different organizational vantage point. And who better to attract the Gen Y community, than your tweet-savvy Gen Y staff members! They know the Twitter language and etiquette, and they know the right spin to put on the events, achievements, and interesting happenings in your organization to attract their Gen Y peers.

The return on investment from the time devoted to fostering your online community will pay off significantly. When it's time for you to make a Twitter announcement that you have a job opening, the responses from applicants likely will be staggering. You will have a network of followers literally at your fingertips, who apply to the posting or refer you to applicants in their network who have the right mix of attributes, credentials, and experience for the job. Gen Ys that follow you on Twitter are the target audience you want to tap into when you have a job vacancy because they know what you represent, they are likely interested in your company, and have determined that your company is a place where they'd like to work.

# Blogging back to the basics

Since blogs are one of the primary sources of information for Gen Y, it is prudent to include blogging in our plan to create an online community. Blogging is a logical extension of the digital storytelling that we began on Twitter. Twitter, which limits postings to 140 characters or less, can be used as the appetizer that attracts followers to your organization, and your company blog can be used to host more robust conversations with followers. By developing your online blogging presence, you gain even more of the benefits that you reap from tweeting. Specifically, when a job becomes vacant, you can broadcast it on Twitter, and then direct your followers to the full job ad on your company blog. Your blog can also showcase additional information about the job, company, or industry that would entice qualified applicants to apply, and it can serve as a place to entertain questions that followers have as they ascertain their suitability for the position.

Once again, your Gen Y staff can be instrumental in championing the cause. For the most part, they have mastered the fine art of blogging, which comes from managing their personal blogs. Based on their own experimentation with postings and being on the receiving end of feedback about their postings from their own followers, they have first-hand knowledge of the essential ingredients of blogs that triggers favorable responses from readers and generates a loyal followership. A few Gen Y staff members who are charged with the task of being your company bloggers can lead the way in establishing and maintaining online dialog with followers that results in taking them deeper into the inner workings of your organization, and positions them to receive priority notice when jobs become available. Consider building the role of company blogger into a few job descriptions that are traditionally occupied by Gen Y staff members, perhaps jobs associated with marketing or human resources. In doing so, you signal that accountability for blogging is a high priority in your organization and deserves full attention.

As for the content, a modified version of the "a day in the life of..." chronicles from your Twitter postings could be a possible launching pad for your blog. This could include more in-depth narratives from your staff that depict your organization's culture. Anecdotes most likely to appeal to a Gen Y audience are about:

➤ Meaningfulness of the work they do, especially as it pertains to service to the global community, impact on environmental sustainability, and having fun in the workplace

➤ Staff's career progression and aspirations

➤ How staff perceive and experience the organization

Added to this, include a "guest appearance" slot, that is, a cameo appearance by a renowned client, customer, supplier, or partner who can speak about the magic of their collaboration with your organization, the glue that sustains the working relationship, and their vision of how the partnership will grow over the next few years. The added bonus is having a guest on your blog who is someone from the Gen Y community that speaks the language of the newest generation in the workplace and can inspire other Gen Ys to take an active interest in your company.

The invited guest could also be you or another member of your leadership team. As you recall from *Chapter 1, Generation Y – Who Are They?*, Gen Y values cultivating strong working relationships with their immediate supervisors; it is one of the top five values that attracts them to an organization. Specifically, Gen Y wants to know about the authentic person behind the leadership title, which includes triumphs and losses; dreams and worries; and confidence and brokenness. They aren't attracted to credentials, impressive leadership titles and roles, lengthy lists of credentials, or affiliations with prestigious committees and associations. They want to know that you, as their leader, have been in the trenches working alongside staff at all levels in the organization, and they want to hear about your strengths and imperfections that make you real to them. They are attracted to the authentic person who has a story. Having said this, are you willing to share your story and, in doing so, give Gen Y a glimpse into the person behind the leadership role?

As a final piece to add to the mix, toss in a question occasionally to canvass feedback from your Gen Y followership about newsworthy events in the media or to ask them questions about their generation. These could be general questions to help you better understand and appreciate Gen Y values and priorities, or specific questions that seek their input on initiatives that you are rolling out in your organization. Direct your followers to digital collaborating sites on your website, such as digital polling and digital questing to answer specific questions and to provide more detailed feedback.

The more novel you can be, the more likely you'll have a wave of followers with you every step of the way.

# Facebook – do you like me?

*Incoming message...thumbs up! Another one likes you!*

Imagine a wave of followers getting caught up in the excitement of being digitally connected to your organization and sending you the "thumbs up" sign that they are impressed with your organization! A thriving Gen Y community is at your fingertips. How can we create this online buzz? Facebook.

While tweeting and blogging capture the narrative of your organization, Facebook serves as your visual storybook. Since Gen Ys are, by nature, highly visual learners and communicators, a collage of pictures will grab their attention, have them sending you the "thumbs up" sign that they like your Facebook page, and keep them revisiting your website often. If your website evokes their curiosity more than other organizational Facebook pages, then Gen Y won't hesitate to text message their Gen Y friends and encourage them to check out your website; hence, almost instantaneously you increase your e-followership significantly.

The secret to a Facebook page that has massive Gen Y appeal is to create a photo gallery that provides a snapshot of how your organization lives its values, vision, and mission. Post photos that appeal to Gen Y's core values of connectedness, collaboration, free expression, respect, creativity, work-life balance, and flexibility. Show that your organization:

> ➤ Knows how to have fun
> ➤ Is an exciting place to work
> ➤ Provides opportunities for staff to engage in meaningful work that makes a difference in the global community

The litmus test to use to determine whether you've selected the right photos to feature on your Facebook page is whether each photo offers a glimpse into your organization's distinct culture and reveals the signature attributes that distinguish it from your competition. In order to determine if this is the case, consider showing your photos to a few members of the Gen Y community that are not familiar with your company to get their input on what is revealed.

Once you accumulate scores of photos on your Facebook page, you may want to find another way to preserve them for posterity; a way to have them serve as a tribute to your company's history, achievements, contributions, and progression throughout the years. All the photos that you have taken and collected represent the institutional memory of your organization. They speak to the niche you have carved out for your organization in the industry and in the community at large, and they serve as the legacy that you leave behind.

So what specifically do you do with this collection of photos?

I had the pleasure of working with a small, yet thriving consulting firm in San Francisco, California, that specializes in working with organizations to enhance their performance management systems. After years of collecting photos from special events, celebrations, parties, historic moments in the company's lifetime, and everyday photos of staff at work, they decided to publish a book that captures who they are. The book begins with a two-page letter from the leadership team that communicates the purpose of their book and includes a summary of their vision, mission, and values in a few statements. The bulk of the book is a collection of photos that capture the culture and progression of the organization over the past three decades. They are currently producing an e-book version that will be available through their Facebook page. This example might encourage you to explore ways that you can showcase your collection of company photos. Perhaps there is a book in your company's future?

In whatever way you wish to proceed at this point, here lies another opportunity for Gen Y staff to get involved. Developing and maintaining your Facebook page and taking the lead on a book are assignments that add value to the organization and also contribute to Gen Y's personal need for meaning. Consider inviting a Gen Y staff member to be your photo journalist. Again, build the assignment into their job description and allow them to take the reins in charting out a pathway to showcase your organization at its best.

# The ABCs of heading back to school

Even though it is outside the realm of social media, this last approach feeds into how we can connect with a wider Gen Y audience that could become our followers through social media, and eventually become members of our organization. In today's highly competitive job market where the demand for workers trumps supply and the number of qualified applicants is at a premium, we are scrambling to fill positions. If this is our new reality, and it likely won't change in the foreseeable future, then we are advised to start building our network of possible job applicants and scouting for talent long before they even enter the workforce.

Having said this, are you connected to the colleges and universities in your community? There are a number of students who are waiting to be introduced to you. Through your interactions with them, they will see the human side of your business, which is often one of the key selling points when they go job hunting. Hence, building these relationships early and often pays in dividends when it is time to recruit. Invite them to follow you on Twitter and on your blog and when you are recruiting they'll either apply for the job themselves or circulate the news of your job vacancy to their network.

Your involvement in building a network in the school system could include:

➤ Mentoring students through internships, field placements, or cooperative placements

➤ Offering to be a guest speaker, panel member, or judge for special events or classroom visits

➤ Partnering with the academic institution on a course assignment

For example, at Royal Roads University, in British Columbia, Canada, where I have the good fortune of being an Associate Professor in the Faculty of Management, I teach a leadership course in the Masters of Business Administration (MBA) program that relies heavily on community participation. In each offering of the course, an organization is invited to join us for the *Leadership Challenge*, a problem-based learning initiative that provides employers with an opportunity to present a workplace issue to our MBA students for the purposes of analysis and presenting a set of recommendations for their consideration. The workplace issue can either be an organization-wide or departmental issue that may be new, or it can be one that is persistent and troublesome, requiring investigation and resolution. The leadership team is invited back to Royal Roads in a few weeks to listen to presentations from the MBA students and to engage them in conversation about the recommendations offered. This not only allows students to explore the application-based potential of what they are learning in school, but also provides an opportunity for them to get to know employers and their organizations more intimately, which has great appeal to Gen Y when they start their job search.

Before these young people graduate, let's introduce them to who we are and the opportunities that await them in our organization. Plant the seed early.

# Selecting the "perfect" candidate

*Selecting the perfect candidate is comparable to squeezing toothpaste back into its tube. You'll consume an inordinate amount of time and energy doing it; yet, in the end, you'll likely be unsuccessful.*

That's the best way to describe our mission to find the "perfect" Gen Y employee for our organization. In our recruitment efforts, many of us chase the dream—searching endlessly—to find the "perfect" employee for the job, for our team, and for our organization. Breaking news—perfection is over-rated; it is a fallacy, especially when we are speaking about people. All of us come to the workplace with unique gifts and talents, but we also pack our fair share of warts and bruises, and struggles and limitations. There is no one who is an exception here. When we fully understand and appreciate this, we can begin to rethink how we approach our recruitment drive. Our challenge, and opportunity, is to shift our recruitment philosophy and mandate from selecting a candidate that is "perfect" to one that is "best fit".

In making this transition, let's set our sights on finding employees that are trying to be the best they possibly can be. Perhaps in our list of requirements for the job we can search for candidates who are stretching toward their full potential. We still need to be vigilant in finding candidates who have the core competencies that are fundamental to job success; however, there is likely some flexibility to bring in candidates that are aspiring into their own greatness, and who would benefit tremendously from your coaching to turn their limitations and underdeveloped skills into strengths. In staying open to possibilities, we may even discover that candidates also come with a portfolio of competencies that we didn't ask for, but are highly beneficial in propelling the job in refreshingly new directions and to unimaginable heights.

When we step away from "perfection" and embrace "best fit", we aren't lowering our standards; we are being more *realistic* about what we are searching for. Ultimately, this makes it less burdensome on our limited personal and organizational resources to find the Gen Y candidate who will truly complement our existing team.

We now turn the narrative over to a member of the Gen Y community who will share insights about what attracts Gen Y to apply to our job ads.

# Meeting the Gen Y community

*What motivates you to apply for a job in a company?*

*– Lingyan (Linda) Xu*

Linda draws on nine years of experience in the work world to answer this question. When she is on the hunt for a new job, Linda scours the Internet and consults her professional network. At the top of her wish list are large organizations that are well established in business, and they have a strong reputation for treating staff well and motivating them to reach their potential. Added to this, Linda looks for a workplace where the leaders live the organization's values. Specifically, she is interested in working for leaders who care about society and promote organizational initiatives that are motivated by a deep commitment to social responsibility. Linda's respect for an organization comes from knowing that its leaders model and promote the values that are important to the organization's culture,
and that they expect the same from their staff.

When reviewing job advertisements, Linda looks for:

➤ A challenging job that makes full use of her credentials, has projects that she has never done before, and provides her with an opportunity to experiment with different ways to solve problems

➤ A stepping stone in her career that will bring her job satisfaction

➤ An organization that will value and recognize her contributions and achievements

➤ A workplace culture that promotes teamwork. According to Linda, "*my eyes and mind are broadened by the collaboration that comes from different backgrounds working together*"

➤ A workplace that promotes her professional growth and development

➤ Attractive wages and benefits, including holidays, so she can balance her life and work responsibilities

Linda wants us to know the following about Gen Y when we are recruiting, "*We have a very strong work ethic, you can rely on us to get work done, we are flexible in how we work with you, and we have lots of experience with high technology that we would love to share with you!*"

**Make a note**

Linda was born in China and has nine years of experience in the import and export world. She has a BA in Economics and is currently completing her Master's in Global Management at Royal Roads University in Canada. She loves the world of work and hopes to some day occupy the seat of the Chief Executive Officer in a company. When she isn't working or studying, Linda enjoys movies. Tom Hanks in Castaway and Forrest Gump are two of her favorites!

# Reframing challenges as opportunities

*Look at this resume...she's had five jobs in the past three years! No company loyalty! This is a red-flag, triple siren alert for me! Who would hire this one? Next!*

Wait! Don't pass on this resume quite yet!

At first glance, this appears to be a problem. Her track record is far from stellar, so it is easy to make the decision to toss her resume unceremoniously into the "rejection" pile. Many of us do this; we judge an applicant's company loyalty by the number of years they've stayed with an organization. We scope the dates of the applicant's employment history, piece together their career path, and make assumptions about gaps in their employment. Any hint of job jumping sets off warning bells that this person has commitment issues and likely will not stay with us beyond a few months or a year. If this is the case, why would we consider them for the job?

Before we discard this applicant's resume, maybe there's another lens through which to look at the situation. Yes, this could be a case of someone who doesn't know what she wants, and some of the applicants that send their resume to us will fall into this category. Yet, let's try not to make this assumption about all candidates. Let's look beyond the job jumping and see what we discover. Perhaps we will find impressive academic credentials, an internship in a reputable organization, or service to the community both close to home and internationally. There might be a rare jewel of an employee right in front of us.

Perhaps it would be worth our time to at least bring her in for an interview and explore more deeply her reasons for staying only a short time with each company. There might be some legitimate reasons—beyond her control—for the erratic employment record that might cause us to shift our thinking about her. At the interview, we could also have a discussion about what she would specifically need from us in order to commit long-term to our organization.

So, before we rush to judgment and hurl her resume into the trash can, let's put our initial assumptions in abeyance long enough to explore this further. Maybe this isn't a "disloyal" employee as we originally thought, but a rare and golden jewel of a worker.

# Leaning in to change

Is your job ad generating a rich supply of star candidates? If it isn't as impactful as you'd like it to be, consider using this opportunity to revamp it using the tools and practices offered in this chapter. Start by taking a look at the ad itself and considering what approach you can take to convert your ad from "mild" to "hot" and to rework the content so that your ad casts a wide net of interest and resonates deeply with qualified Gen Y applicants. Now, test drive your job ad by circulating it to a few of the Gen Y staff in your organization for feedback. Would they apply to the position if they were in the job market? Why would they apply? Why not? Incorporate their feedback into the next iteration of the ad. When you finally have the right message, post away and see what happens!

An open invitation stands for you to post on my website (www.eyeofthetigerconsulting.ca) what you learned from this process, the feedback that Gen Y gave you, and new insights emerging from your reading. Also, feel free to share your recruitment experiences—whether they are best practices, works-in-progress, or efforts that fell flat. It is from our successes and misses that we learn and develop.

# Google it...

For those of you who would like to explore how to use Twitter and blogs more effectively, please check out the following resources:

Guidelines for using Twitter:

- ➤ http://mashable.com/guidebook/twitter/
- ➤ http://www.vegau.com/resources/how-to-use-twitter/
- ➤ http://www.hashtags.org/platforms/twitter/twitter-for-beginners-basic-guidelines-before-you-start/
- ➤ http://www.cnbc.com/id/43759244

Guidelines for using blogs:

- ➤ www.socialmediaexaminer.com/26-tips-for-writing-great-blog-posts/
- ➤ academy.hubspot.com/Default.aspx?app.../11...blogging-guide
- ➤ www.dummies.com/how-to/content/writing-a-good-blog.html
- ➤ www.quicksprout.com/.../a-simple-plan-for-writing-a-powerful-blog-post-in-less-than-2-hours/

# Summary

In this chapter, we explored how to turbo-charge our job ads by moving them from mild to sizzling hot and by putting the lion's roar in our content. We then discovered how to tweet away our time, blog back to basics, and reintroduce ourselves to the ABCs, but we need to be prepared to head back to school. We finished with selection criteria for finding the "perfect" candidate.

The new twist on recruitment offered in this chapter positions us to manage the complexities of the tough times that we face in the labor market and to put us ahead of our competition in attracting Gen Y talent to our organizations.

Now that we know how to attract Gen Y talent, let's head into the next chapter where we examine how to create training that sticks for our new Gen Y recruits.

# >3

# Acclimatizing Gen Y to Your Workplace – Training that is Sticky, Stickier, and Stickiest

*My research with Gen Y over the past few years has revealed that only 35 percent of content communicated in workplace training sessions is retained, barely 25 percent of learning from these sessions is transferred into workday practice, and approximately 70 percent of Gen Ys are dissatisfied with workplace training.*

I'm sure this knocks us off our swivel chairs when we hear this. Yet, this is how Gen Y experiences and perceives training initiatives in our organizations. From my conversations with Gen Y, an overwhelming number of them reported that training misses the target. It doesn't pack a powerful punch that contributes to the successful transfer of knowledge, skills, and abilities into workplace practice. They claim that our approaches to training are uninspiring, mind-numbing, and rooted in archaic practices that do not meet the needs of a new generation of workers in the labor force.

Mind-numbing? This can be enormously discouraging and frustrating to hear. Most of us invest a substantial amount of time, energy, and money into ascertaining the right complement of training programs to meet organizational needs, and developing and delivering training courses to close the gap between employees' current and requisite competencies. To be told that the return on our investment is neither favorably received nor yielding the outcomes we expect can send the most seasoned of us into a tailspin.

Here is our opportunity to improve the return on our investment. In the workplace, we refer to *training that sticks*; this is, learning and development initiatives that are compelling, retained, and transferred into workplace practice. It is the degree to which there is *training sustainability* that ultimately has an impact on our organization's bottom line. Our goal in this chapter is to explore ways we can design and deliver training that not only *sticks*, but goes beyond what the competition is doing. We aim to make your training *stickier* and *stickiest*.

This chapter introduces you to tools and techniques that can be used to design and deliver training that engages a generation of workers who are at the forefront of the digital information revolution. In doing so, your organization can be one of the few that claims:

> *"85 percent of the content communicated in our training sessions is retained and transferred into workday practice, and the same percentage represents the number of Gen Ys that are highly satisfied with our approach to training."*

You'll also notice that an investment in new approaches to training pays off for your organization in other ways, as well. This leads to:

> ➤ Increased retention
>
> ➤ Increased productivity
>
> ➤ A lower error rate on the job
>
> ➤ Enhanced employee morale
>
> ➤ Reduced training costs by getting new recruits up to speed and productive in less time

In order to achieve these outcomes, we'll unpack the following topics in this chapter:

> ➤ Revealing the learner within: The 360 degree request
>
> ➤ Orienting Gen Y to workplace realities: Everyone on board?
>
> ➤ Designing training programs: Shiny new tools for your toolbox
>
> ➤ Making transfer of learning "stickiest"
>
> ➤ Evaluating your training: Did you earn an "A"?

Even though this chapter is devoted exclusively to designing and delivering training for a Gen Y audience, consider how the tools and techniques can be adapted for use with other generations in the workplace. As a starting point, canvass feedback from older employees in your workplace to determine:

➤ Their perceptions and experiences with current approaches to training and development; specifically, search for the degree to which the design and delivery might be in need of a make over

➤ Their interest in having tools and techniques used for a more high-tech audience integrated into their own training programs

If they are not receptive, they will at least be appreciative that you are mindful of their learning needs and expectations and extended the offer. If they are interested, you open up a great opportunity for them to further hone their skills and abilities using a new set of tools and techniques. Added to this, you create an opportunity for Gen Y to mentor them in the use of the technology. In doing so, you make training *sticky, stickier, and stickiest* for everyone!

# So, what's burning?

I can hear many of you saying, *"You're going to expect me to completely dismantle my training program and revamp it to include technology that I'm not comfortable with! I don't know where to begin! I don't have the technological wizardry that Gen Y expects!"*. I hear you, and I can relate to your concerns.

Let me share a story. It isn't my proudest moment, but it seems fitting to share this with you considering the work we'll do together in this chapter.

A few years ago, I was sitting in my office frantically making last minute preparations for what was to be my first time facilitating a webinar—that magical, technological wonder that brings people together from anywhere to rally around a topic. I had designed a one-hour session on Awakening Creativity and Innovation in the Workplace to be delivered to Human Resources practitioners from across Canada, the U.S., Australia, and Europe. This was a new experience for me and, like most of us in new situations, I was a tad anxious. No—I was petrified. But, after polishing my script, engaging in a litany of positive affirmations and deep breathing to keep me from spiraling downward, I was primed to go!

Lights...camera...action! A brilliant start! A dazzling introduction followed by a crisp presentation of the outcomes, agenda, and expectations.

Then, without warning, it happened. No screen, no audio, no participants. Nothing. In a panic, I began pressing every button on my laptop in hopes that something would restore the screen. Along with button pushing, there were some colorful mutterings! There wasn't anything that I knew how to do in order to correct the situation. I begrudgingly surrendered and waited for what seemed like an eternity before technical support arrived to rescue me—my knight in shining e-armor!

To my chagrin and embarrassment, I was told that the malfunction was an "easy fix" and that, in a matter of seconds, I could have solved the problem on my own, instead of waiting twenty minutes for assistance. Between my online mutterings (which I later discovered were audible to my participants) and the public embarrassment that came with participants knowing I was a techno-neophyte, I wanted to crawl into a cyber hole! I was so shaken by the experience that I couldn't recover in the remaining time I had with my participants. The session was a wash.

You'd think after that horror I would never set foot on the webinar stage again. Yet, shortly afterwards, I put my headphones back on and launched into another webinar.

My reason for sharing this unflattering story is to let you know that I would not be advocating for changes in workplace training unless I was prepared to take the journey with you. Moving away from our traditional approaches to training evokes uneasiness on our part. Our traditional ways of training are comfortable, and they are ingrained in both our psyche and in the system as the staples of instruction. Some of you may even think that the technology will eventually replace us.

Our journey through this chapter isn't about overhauling everything you do (or replacing you!). It's about incrementally exploring new tools and building them into your repertoire; that is, slowly and thoughtfully examining how new instructional methods can fit with the outcomes you are trying to achieve in your training programs. As for technology, it's about searching for ways to position technology as a supplement to training, not a replacement for you.

By trying new approaches we not only expand our repertoire, but we also make an important connection with Gen Y by being inquisitive and exploratory in our own approach to learning. This is a connection that will serve us well as we continue to build our working relationship with Gen Y.

Take your time through the change process. If you make a few fumbles along the way, relax. Use these unsuccessful trial runs as learn opportunities. Getting stuck in the mud can be the hallmarks of our best learning. Imagine the possibilities that emerge when we are willing to take risks and make a few mistakes along the way.

Let's now head into a discussion about what Gen Y is burning to tell us about their learning preferences, and how they'd like us to be involved in their professional growth and development.

# Revealing the learner within – the 360 degree request

*Was the content meaningful?*

*Did they like the training activities?*

*Did the session inspire them to apply new learning to their jobs?*

Have you caught yourself asking these questions after delivering training to a Gen Y audience? Most of us likely have left training sessions with these questions swirling around in our brains. In this section, we'll explore Gen Y's learning preferences and the approach to delivery that best suits their learning style.

# Gen Y – who shows up for training?

*Slowly…slowly…nodding away…fast asleep…*

Nothing is more excruciatingly painful for Gen Y than sitting through lectures, following along in training manuals, watching an endless stream of PowerPoint slides, and being invited occasionally to ask questions. This is the generation that has grown up in cyberspace, where instant messaging, socializing in chat rooms, blogging, downloading, and gaming are natural, expected, and fast. Gen Y retrieves, processes, and works with information differently and faster than previous generations, which is evident when we see them bouncing back and forth effortlessly on various digital platforms retrieving bits of information that they need. No wonder they cringe at the thought of lectures and marching collectively in a linear fashion through the content.

For Gen Y, learning is meant to be organic, hands-on, experiential, and constantly stimulating! It is an ongoing trial and error adventure that can take place anywhere, anytime, and with anyone. Their best learning experiences are characterized as highly connective, interactive, and collaborative. This can be nurtured in an informal and relaxed environment, where they:

> ➤ Experiment freely and creatively with content
>
> ➤ Exchange significant learning with each other in the moment
>
> ➤ Are not constrained by inflexible practices and structures
>
> ➤ Have plenty of fun!

To support their development, Gen Y encourages us to develop and foster a *360 degree experience*—a full spectrum of diverse and colorful learning that expands and challenges their thinking. This includes:

> ➤ Extensive orientation when they join our organization in order to acclimatize them to job and company expectations, performance standards, and workplace culture.
>
> ➤ Training agendas that place a premium on communicating the rationale for content being covered.
>
> ➤ Opportunities to be autonomous, creative, and investigative in their learning.
>
> ➤ Cooperative activities and interactive media that challenge their assumptions and promote inductive reasoning.
>
> ➤ A blend of activities that accommodate multiple learning styles and closely resemble workplace accountabilities.
>
> ➤ Visually stimulating learning experiences, such as images, videos, demonstrations, and role-plays (Gen Y's visual literacy is acute and they prefer visuals instead of text). Make sure the photos and videos aren't from what Gen Y refers to as "the dinosaur age"; that is, visuals that are pre-1990!
>
> ➤ Quick interactions with content, which aligns with the speed that they thrive on (avoid belaboring points; keep the pace crisp and change it up every 10–15 minutes).
>
> ➤ Leave space for Gen Y to suggest activities and discussions that make the learning meaningful for them (they would like to be partners in the learning and have a voice in decision making).

Within this environment, they expect a technology-rich learning experience which goes beyond the use of PowerPoint presentations. Gen Y is not enamored with our slide presentations no matter how magnificent we think our graphics and photos are, or how grand we think our customized animations are that fade in, fly in, or spin in. Regrettably, that doesn't get a standing ovation at the end of the day. However, Gen Y is impressed with how we use technology to showcase the application of content to the work they'll be doing on the job. Training that engages them with the technology will win their hearts, gain their respect, and earmark your training as "star quality".

Many Gen Ys are concerned that there is little, or no, consultation with them prior to training to ascertain their needs and expectations. Consider making time before training commences to canvass Gen Y's feedback on content they'd like covered, the delivery format they prefer, and the post-training supports they'd like in place to enhance the successful transfer of learning to the workplace. You may want to ask them what they expect of you.

# Delivering training – how do YOU show up?

Our challenge and opportunity is to create a full spectrum learning experience, which includes an assortment of interactive activities and multimedia that are challenging, stimulating, thought-provoking, and fun! I realize, in saying this, that there is a risk of transforming learning into *edu-tainment*, that is, creating a circus-like atmosphere where there are so many flashy activities shoe-horned into the training session that entertainment trumps the learning that is integral to the success and viability of our organizations. I wholeheartedly agree that edu-tainment is not our goal. Instead, let's aim for crafting a few revisions that take us closer to meeting Gen Y's learning preferences, but also remaining grounded in the learning outcomes that are the foundation of our training architecture.

However, training goes far beyond selecting the best training activities. At the core, it is about the guiding principles that shape how you engage with others to create a climate that is conducive to learning. Having said this, how do you show up to deliver training? Are you the person who is the expert disseminator of information, the entertainer, or the overzealous motivator? No matter how you characterize your style, consider how your approach aligns with Gen Y's learning preferences. Does your delivery style engage and inspire Gen Y to move learning into workplace practice?

Gen Y weighs in on the discussion by encouraging us to shift from being *trainer-centered* to *learner-centered*. As much as they value the knowledge we've gleaned from years of experience, they'd prefer that we not dominate the learning by being expert disseminators of knowledge. They'd like us to be more *facilitative;* that is, guiding them toward *learning how to learn.* This means moving away from transmitting information and readily answering all their questions to encouraging them to discover knowledge on their own and to examining its relevance to their personal and professional lives. For Gen Y, this is achieved by:

> ➤ Asking thought-provoking and controversial questions that inspire critical thinking

> ➤ Challenging their mental models so they think about content in a new light

> ➤ Familiarizing them with reliable and credible sources of information so they can explore topics and hunt for answers to questions on their own

> ➤ Coaching, instead of rescuing, them when they struggle to navigate the complexities of integrating learning into practice

Gen Y also expects immediate feedback on their progress and ways they can improve. Yet, you may recall from our discussion in *Chapter 1, Generation Y – Who Are They?*, Gen Y can be sensitive to criticism, which means we are advised to cushion our feedback as constructive and offer support and guidance in how they can take corrective action. We'll tackle this in the next chapter when we unlock the secrets to great conversations with Gen Y, including how to give and receive feedback.

With background information about Gen Y's learning preferences in hand, we head into discussion about how we can create a learning environment that peaks Gen Y's curiosity and ignites their passion to transfer learning into practice. We begin with their first day on the job!

# Orienting Gen Y to workplace realities – everyone on board?

What do we do with them when they arrive? Our first training opportunity arises when Gen Y arrives for their first day on the job. As we discussed in *Chapter 1, Generation Y – Who Are They?*, the first impression we make after Gen Ys have been selected determines whether they stay with our organization or put their resumes back in circulation to find companies and jobs better suited to their needs and expectations. In order to avoid being another statistic in Gen Y's career trajectory and preventing our investment from flying out the door, let's chart our plan for creating a strong introduction to our organization.

## Creating an unrivalled first impression

Gen Y is expecting an orientation, also known as "onboarding", which socializes them to our workplace. The goal is to acclimatize new recruits to the workplace culture and to equip them with tools to *survive and thrive* in our organization, that is, to familiarize them with expected and rewarded behaviors, rules, practices, and performance standards so they can perform according to organizational expectations.

Common orientation practices include pre-arrival welcome packages, formal presentations, tours of facilities, buddy systems especially with fellow Gen Ys, and follow-up orientation meetings. These are admirable inclusions in our orientation program, but they aren't addressing a major concern that Gen Y has when they arrive on the scene.

In my conversations with Gen Y, they speak about the high levels of stress that they have on the first few days of the job. Even though they come into our workplace with an abundance of energy and confidence, they are shaking in their boots for the first while. The major source of their trepidation? It is the newness of the environment, people, and responsibilities, coupled with the many questions they face from virtually everyone in the organization about:

> ➤ Projects and committees they'd like to be involved in
>
> ➤ Networks they'd like to cultivate

> ➤ Long-term goals and aspirations
> ➤ Plans for how they'd like to contribute to the department, the organization, and even the industry at large

During these early days in a new job, Gen Y is often at a loss for how to respond.

Within the first few weeks, you have a rare and golden opportunity to lessen Gen Y's anxiety and create the unrivalled first impression that inspires them to build a long-term future with your organization. And here's where you can navigate your way to *stickiness*.

For the first few months of employment, schedule time in Gen Y's calendar for *an exploratory workplace lab*. Leave a day, or a few afternoons, each week for your new recruits to freely explore your organization; that is, roam where they please, have conversations where they feel inclined to do so, and engage in activities just for the sake of trying something new. Give them time to explore the uniqueness of your organization's culture and expectations as intuition guides them—a practice to be welcomed by Gen Y given their penchant for free-spirited experimentation and autonomy.

Experimentation provides an opportunity for them to test and reflect on what your organization has to offer. In doing so, new recruits gain insights, not only about the inner workings of your organization, but also their passions, talents, challenges, needs, and expectations. Armed with these new discoveries, they are in a better position to articulate their personal vision of how they'd like to be contributing members of your organization. With this clarity of purpose, the stage is set for you to mentor them toward achieving their goals and aspirations. Your willingness to collaborate with Gen Y, in these early days, to map out possibilities for them to contribute to your organization gives Gen Y a reason to remain with your organization.

The following are a few ways you can create an exploratory workplace lab:

> ➤ A job shadowing far and wide throughout the organization
> ➤ Attending cross-departmental meetings, so they can comprehend the company's mandate and priorities, and make connections between the company's direction and the job they've been hired to do
> ➤ Attending committee meetings of interest to get a sense of the group's accountabilities in the organization and to gauge whether they'd be interested in
> ➤ Interviewing staff at all levels in the organization about their organizational involvement and what sustains their passion and commitment to the organization
> ➤ Assisting with ongoing projects, whether or not they are directly related to their job
> ➤ Mentoring events with other Gen Ys in your organization
> ➤ Attending networking events with you to learn about organizational and industry issues and trends and to expand their professional network
> ➤ Informal conversations with other Gen Ys on staff to get a sense of their experiences in the organization and to receive a few survival tips for orienting themselves to a new culture

Once exploratory work is done, our attention turns to designing training programs that prepare Gen Y for job and organizational expectations.

# Designing training programs – shiny new tools for your toolbox

*Some shiny new tools are ready to join your collection of instructional methods. Is there room in your toolbox for a few more?*

In this next section, we'll introduce tools to jumpstart your exploration into ways of captivating Gen Y learners. The key is to build your repertoire of instructional methods one step at a time. Select one new tool you would like to test drive and experiment with it—make it your own by putting a creative spin on it or combining it with other instructional approaches.

However, as you know from experience, the road can be a tad bumpy when we try something for the first time. To make the task of integrating new instructional methods into practice a little easier, consider the resources that are available to you.

Look around. Right in front of us is the perfect resource—Gen Y! Consider asking them to collaborate with you as you navigate the maze of new instructional methods. They are positioned ideally to:

➤ Recommend which instructional methods are better suited for Gen Y, especially as it pertains to technology

➤ Give feedback on your instructional design

➤ Propose solutions to challenges you might experience as you integrate technology into your training framework

Better yet, consider asking Gen Y to join you as co-creators of instructional design and as co-facilitators of the delivery. A multi-generational training team not only creates an interesting and powerful synergy of skills and abilities that can enrich the overall training experience, but it also models the way for other multi-generational collaborations in your organization. As we'll discover in *Chapter 5, Inspiring Star Performance– Reaching Seriously for Sirius*, this is a critical step toward harmonizing multi-generational differences in the workplace en route to increasing employee engagement and productivity.

As we begin to examine instructional methods, especially those that are in the technology domain, there is a caveat we need to be cognizant of. The use of technology is not a guarantee that learning will take place. Like the nontechnology-based tools of our trade, they can be used well or poorly. It is incumbent upon us to exercise our due diligence in being crystal clear about our training goals and select the tools—technology-based or not—that are best suited to achieve desired outcomes.

With this in mind, let's take a peek at the instructional methods that Gen Y is hoping we'll build into training!

# Diamonds in the rough – podcasts, vodcasts, and so much more!

You eagerly await the great reveal, that is, the road-tested activities that will equip you to deliver training that is *sticky, stickier, and stickiest.*

In order to deliver on this commitment, I canvassed my personal network before writing this chapter to get input on what should be included. In this section, you'll find the *top ten* most memorable activities that have been well received by the Gen Ys that I've had the pleasure of learning with, and from, and the methods that my colleagues in the field of learning and development have identified as diamonds in the rough. These activities are not presented in any particular order. Your top ten list is explored in the following sections!

## Podcasts – get you headsets on!

These recorded narratives are a hit with Gen Y. Podcasts can be created for virtually any topic and are a great substitute for delivering content traditionally covered in lectures. Gen Y can listen to these recordings on their laptops or mobile devices at anytime and anywhere, making this a highly convenient and familiar way for them to be introduced to foundational content before they join an online or face-to-face discussion. There are also the added conveniences of:

➤ Being able to pause the lesson so they can learn at their own pace

➤ Listen to the recording during the time of day when they are most alert and motivated

Keep the narrative interesting by changing the pace and direction every ten minutes or so, by adding music, a colorful story, or a second speaker.

## Vodcasts – now I can see you!

The vodcast is similar to the podcast, but it takes podcasting to the next level with its added video feature. Vodcasts are ranked at the top of Gen Y's list of instructional tools. For a generation that thrives on visually stimulating learning experiences, the vodcast gets the award for excellence when built into our training design. Consider using vodcasts when you want to showcase best practices that you expect Gen Y to model in the workplace, such as customer service etiquette, responding to conflict, sales training, workplace health and safety, and training for staff that will work and live abroad. Gen Y is more willing and able to integrate new behaviors into practice when the expected behaviors are modeled and when the rationale for the behaviors accompanies the demonstration.

# Meet me online?

When you want an interactive and collaborative element to your training—that your podcasts and vodcasts can't deliver—then a webinar might be the route to take. Webinars allow you to convene online with your audience for a cyber space version of a face-to-face seminar. In a webinar, you can deliver a mini-lecturette and then either lead your audience in a plenary discussion or organize breakout rooms for small group discussions. Software packages on the market offer whiteboard and presentation features that can be accessed in breakout rooms and the main learning room. Webinars are especially effective for training virtual teams in your organization. They can be used to deliver an entire course, or they can be used after face-to-face instruction to check on trainees' progress and address questions that surface pertaining to the application of content. Webinars can be recorded, so trainees can review the session afterwards, or trainees who were unable to join the live session can get caught up on the learning.

# Once upon a time...

Since Gen Y not only searches for online information, but contributes to the online narrative, *digital storytelling* will be a hit in your training session. This form of online journaling captures Gen Y's learning experiences and can take the form of photos, audio, photos with audio, and video with audio, that can be posted on wikis and blogs. Consider giving trainees their own personal wikispace that can be used for reflections about the course and for creating a blueprint of their plans for moving learning into workplace practice. Encourage them to view each other's digital storyboards and to examine the themes that emerge from the learning. Software packages are available that allow two trainees, either sitting together or in different parts of the world, to co-create short stories of their experiences, including photos and videos.

# The polls are now open

Here lies a high impact activity that capitalizes on Gen Y's expertise in navigating social media networks. *Digital polling*, or electronic voting, allows trainees to collaborate with relevant and interested parties outside your training session and beyond your organization. During your training session, trainees invite an external audience to complete an online survey or answer an interview question that asks them to weigh in on the training topic that is being examined. It allows Gen Y to connect far and wide to get reactions, views, and experiences pertaining to the topic at hand and enables them to see the myriad of divergent perspectives that exist. This sets the stage for robust debate in your training session. Gen Y especially enjoys this activity when it is done in real time; that is, the questions are posed online during the training, and they check back later in the session to discuss the responses that were posted. In order to encourage Gen Y's ownership of the activity, invite them to generate a list of possible questions and then agree on the best ones for the survey.

# Thinking outside the tank

We know that Gen Y wants to take ownership and control of their learning, and the *think tank challenge* allows them to do this. In this live case study, trainees are presented with a real-time workplace problem—in your organization or the industry—and asked to analyze the situation and propose a viable solution. Trainees are encouraged to stretch beyond the status quo of thinking into the realm of formulating innovative solutions that demonstrate their strategic acumen. This activity, which can be facilitated online or face-to-face, is made even more meaningful for Gen Y if external stakeholders close to the problem are present for the presentation of solutions. This way, stakeholders can ask questions about the recommendations and give feedback on the merits of the pathways proposed. The think tank challenge is especially effective in leadership development programs to hone problem solving and critical thinking abilities, but it can be adapted to any training program where a live case study would be advantageous to learning and development.

# Do you want to play a game?

Talk shows, game shows, reality shows, and movies! Gen Y is the gaming generation who will be thrilled that you've included the entertainment world in the training design. You may want to canvass Gen Y to determine which shows they currently watch, and then build a learning activity around it. For example, you could show YouTube clips of popular shows such as *Mad Men, CSI,* or *The Big Bang Theory* in class and then ask teams to compete against each other to come up with the most innovative and creative solution to the challenge that was faced by the television characters. You would also have a group of staff, who are not participating in the activity, sit in as a panel of judges to determine the most impressive solution.

The most popular backdrops for training tend to be the reality shows and some of the regular features that appear on late night television. Interviewing guest experts also have appeal. The games that are focused on personal growth, development, and team collaboration tend to be better received than games and simulations that pin one trainee against the other in a competition. For maximum fun, Gen Y can create avatars that are the main characters in an unfolding drama, especially applicable for team development and customer care.

# Debate twister

The debate that lends itself to critically examining both sides of a controversial issue is a classic favorite for Gen Y. It allows them to bring forward their own opinions, experiences, and stories, and weigh them against the positions of their colleagues. For Gen Y, an opportunity to make meaning of their world is of the utmost importance to their personal and professional development. However, let's put a twist on this to further enhance its appeal. Allow Gen Y to support their positions by bringing multimedia into the discussion, such as videos, movies, blogs, digital stories, wikis, podcasts, and music. Suddenly, the narrative of the debate becomes further enriched by this layer of multimedia. If you explore this route, consider putting a caveat in place about the type of references that can be brought forward. We each know our own line in the sand on what is considered acceptable referencing.

# Search and find

Since Gen Y has impeccable search engine skills, let's capitalize on the use of search engines and research databases in our training design. Reflect on the content you traditionally deliver in lecture format and, instead of presenting all the information to your learners on a silver platter, develop a series of thought-provoking questions that inspire them to search and find the information, or interview experts in the industry to canvass their opinions. Also, design assignments or activities that require Gen Y to draw on their investigative skills. This is best suited for controversial topics (and sometimes ethically loaded issues) that allow Gen Y to explore the application of legislation and professional protocol in decision making in the industry. If you are asked a question during the training session for which you don't have the answer, ask a trainee to look it up online for you in the moment. The speed with which answers can be made available will also be a hit with Gen Y.

# Mystery learning?

Leave space in your agenda for learning activities that Gen Y proposes. Invite them periodically to recommend how they would like to experience learning around the content. This can be done formally through a needs analysis survey that is administered prior to the start of the training session, or it can emerge spontaneously during the learning. For example, I recall facilitating a leadership development workshop for a Gen Y audience and, in our first session together, I asked them to form triads and discuss their perceptions of leadership. They chimed in with requests to make this a video activity, whereby they find a video clip that represents leadership. The room erupted with activity, discussion, and laughter as each triad combed the Internet in search of the perfect visual representation of a leader. What emerged was the most astounding collection of videos that showcased their heroes, from all walks of life, demonstrating the qualities of exemplary leadership. I've now built the video activity into my introductory session. It remains a home run every time!

There you have it. The top ten instructional methods that hopefully spark your curiosity sufficiently that you'll want to begin experimenting with them. Again, the intent is to not to completely overhaul the way you facilitate training, but to encourage you to add one new tool at a time to your repertoire of instructional methods.

Before we leave this section on designing training programs, we'd be remiss if we didn't discuss the *flipped classroom*.

# Upside down? Backwards? No, flip it!

As we discussed earlier, Gen Y recoils at the thought of lectures. Yet, many of us, as facilitators, might be hanging on to the lecture format thinking that it is a staple in our training architecture. How else could be possibly deliver content and meet learning outcomes without a formal platform speech? There might be some smattering of appropriateness to the lecture—possibly in the form of a mini-lecture—but for the most part, those longer sermons from the mount no longer have a place in training.

The solution? *Flip the classroom.*

The content we traditionally deliver in lectures can now be disseminated through podcasts and vodcasts. By front-loading the training session with a podcast or vodcast, the salient lecture content about the topic gets delivered, and it is done in a way that aligns with Gen Y's learning preferences. They can now access the recorded narrative in chunks whenever and wherever they wish. As a result, they are more likely to come to the training session better prepared to discuss and apply the learning.

To encourage Gen Y to listen to your podcast prior to attending the training session, which increases the probability that everyone has the preliminary knowledge required so that you can move forward with the in-class lesson, consider building in an incentive. For example, I've often started the classroom portion of the training with a quiz that assesses participants' knowledge of the content that was covered in their homework. If they score 80 percent or better, their name is entered in a draw for a "hot item". This could take the form of gift certificates to popular restaurants or for online shopping, or tickets to attend a sports event or concert. Let them know ahead of time that there will be a quiz and a draw, and be creative in offering an incentive that will entice your group to prepare for class!

Flipping the classroom allows us to preserve the space in our online or face-to-face sessions for learning activities that engage Gen Y more deeply in the content. We can devote more time to hands-on and experiential activities that ignite Gen Y's interest in learning. We likely have more room in our training schedule to discuss transfer of learning into workplace practice, including goal setting and charting action strategies, which often gets squeezed out of our plans because we run out of time.

A victory for you and Gen Y!

# Making transfer of learning "stickiest"

In the previous section, we came to realize that a flipped classroom frees up time in our training schedule to delve deeper into activities that contribute to the transfer of learning into workplace practice. I'd like to introduce you to a process you can use to strengthen the link between learning and practice. It is part of a transfer of learning model that I developed and use to facilitate training, and one that has gone through an intensive 18 month study to ascertain its effectiveness as a transfer intervention. I won't share the entire model (it's too lengthy for the purposes of this chapter), but I'll present pieces that are relevant.

The structure of the model is based on a team approach to transfer of learning that is woven into the training design and filtered into post-training. Does the approach work? One month after training there was 80 percent on-the-job application of learning, 64 percent after six months, and 58 percent after 18 months. According to the trainees, these results are attributed to the application-centric design and delivery of training, and the team meetings that channeled learning into practice. Teams were continuously reflecting on, discussing, and steering action plans in the direction of personal relevance.

# Forming sticky teams

At the onset of training, assign trainees to teams comprised of approximately four members that remain together during and after training. It is best to assign teams randomly so that the diversity inherent in the team's composition will be reflected in conversations. Different views and experiences add a layer of richness to the conversation, especially when teams are formulating goals and action strategies.

Following the delivery of each learning module in your training session, allow time for *transfer of learning reflections;* that is, time for teams to discuss their significant learning and its applicability to their personal and professional lives. As the training progresses, encourage trainees to hone in on two or three specific goals they would like to set based on their learning.

During these transfer of learning meetings, team members serve in a coaching capacity, supporting each other in the following ways:

> ➤ They guide each other in making sense of key learning and its application to workplace practice

> ➤ They offer feedback on how to refine goals

> ➤ They recommend action strategies to support achievement of goals

> ➤ They counsel and encourage each other during transition

> ➤ They strategize innovative solutions to anticipated problems, such as barriers that could derail achievement of goals

> ➤ They challenge each other to set goals and action strategies that stretch them personally and professionally

# Post-training collaborations

Teams are encouraged to reconvene monthly, either online or in person, to continue their collaboration. The focus of their meetings is on reporting goal progress, sharing experiences, and seeking input on how to manage challenges that arise. By pooling their collective wisdom, trainees are empowered with an array of possibilities to take back to the workplace. Within this framework, teams engage in an ongoing process of formulating and experimenting with goal strategies, evaluating their effectiveness, and modifying directions to refine goal achievement. Teams are encouraged to continue meeting monthly until their targeted goals are reached or members are confident they can proceed on their own.

Extending team collaborations into Gen Y's work world was cited as a driving force mobilizing trainees into action and sustaining momentum and commitment for transferring learning into practice. Having journeyed together since the onset of training, teams emerged as the primary support system for transfer of learning. The collaboration fostered confidence in forging ahead with goal strategies and greater accountability for following through with proposed plans.

I hope you'll experiment with all, or a portion, of the model in your own practice. The power of teams can be instrumental in making training *stick.*

# Evaluating your training – did you earn an "A"?

Wait! Before you launch into your next training session or begin championing another workplace initiative, leave some space to gather feedback on your training session. From my own experiences working with organizations, few of us carve out time to evaluate the effectiveness of workplace initiatives, let alone training. Some organizational leaders told me they don't have time, some don't think it really matters, and some are apprehensive about evaluation because it might uncover a shocking reality that the initiative they championed did not have an impact on the organization. This would be bad for their career!

But...wait! Making evaluation a priority might be to your benefit more than you realize. Why? First, it conveys your strong leadership in determining the return on investment from the financial and non-financial resources allocated to training. Secondly, wouldn't you want to be the first one to step forward with the results of the training, before someone else does? If the results are positive, you have the opportunity to announce this (and bask in the glory of your achievement!). If the results aren't favorable, you can control what and how this is communicated to others, including your plans to rectify the situation. This would speak volumes about you—you chose to be proactive, instead of waiting for someone else to discover that the training was amiss and then having others question if you knew about this prior to the public reveal. I would think that someone else revealing how your training flopped would be *worse* for your career.

So, let's evaluate!

Evaluation of training is a complex art and science of its own and can involve detailed data gathering to ascertain whether the training had impact on key performance indicators that drive success in your organization. As we noted in the previous section, there is value in using a team approach to transfer of learning that is woven into the training design and filtered into post-training. This likely will result in favorable outcomes when you assess at the behavioral level (degree to which trainees are using new skills on the job) and at the results-based level (impact of training on organizational effectiveness).

In this section, I offer a few recommendations for canvassing feedback from Gen Y on their perceptions of the training; specifically, their satisfaction with the training and what they learned from the training that prepares them for on-the-job performance.

In my earlier days of collecting data from Gen Y about their workplace experiences, I came to discover that the traditional data collection tools, such as surveys and interviews, bore them to tears! For a generation that is visually wired, prefers engagement and fun, and expects interaction with the content, I can see why the traditional methods fall flat. Having said this, a few approaches to data collection that I found useful are as follows:

> ➤ **Visually pumped focus groups**: Either display a selection of photos, or ask Gen Y to find or take a photo, which represents their experience in training. The metaphors that are revealed through the photos allow Gen Y to speak deeply and specifically about their experiences.

> ➤ **World cafe**: An event whereby you can host multiple conversations about Gen Y's training experiences. Tables are organized in the room for group discussions. At each table there is a flipchart stand with a question written on it that would be helpful to the evaluation of training. Participants are asked to freely circulate to each table to discuss the question posed. Their responses to the questions are recorded on a tablecloth that has been spread across each table. Participants can use words, photos, graphs, and doodles to communicate their responses to the questions. The approach is ideal for a generation that is highly visual in its approach to communication. I've included a website reference in the *Google it...* section for those of you who would like more information about the process.

> ➤ **Online surveys (instead of paper versions at the end of training sessions)**: Various types of software are available to poll Gen Y's reactions to training.

> ➤ **Concept mapping**: Allows Gen Y to graphically depict the interconnection of the theories, concepts, and practices covered in training and explore the application of learning to workplace practice. The depth and breadth of the connections help you gauge how Gen Y made sense of content.

Regardless of the approach you use to gather feedback from Gen Y, consider framing your questions in three domains that will give you all the information you need to know:

> ➤ What do we need to *continue doing?*

> ➤ What do we need to *stop doing?*

> ➤ What do we need to *start doing?*

With these three questions in your back pocket, you are set for evaluating your training. Did you earn an "A"?

# Reframing challenges as opportunities

Have you ever noticed that Gen Ys are riveted to their smartphones and iPads feverishly connecting far and wide? This can be an unnerving sight when we want their undivided attention.

I recall the CEO of an oil conglomerate giving the opening address in a training session for new recruits who, midway through his speech, stopped abruptly. He glared at one of the new recruits who he thought was text messaging, and exploded in anger: "When you're done chatting with your friends would you like to rejoin us?!", to which the new recruit replied, "I wasn't online with my friends, sir, I was taking notes on your presentation." The new recruit showed the CEO the notes he was taking. The CEO was left speechless—completely taken aback by what had transpired in that brief exchange.

Likely, many of us would have responded in a similar way. We see Gen Y glued to a mobile device, with their fingers flying over the keyboard, and we immediately assume they are disrespectful and rude. It causes our blood to boil and compels us to immediately bring our annoyance to their attention and squash what we perceive to be inappropriate behavior.

The next time we are tempted to react like this, I encourage us to think about what might really be happening here. Some Gen Ys might be disengaged and shift their attention to texting friends, but some might actually be verifying information they've just received from you, seeking answers to questions they have about the content you've presented (they are inclined to search the Internet for answers before they ask for assistance), or taking notes.

Before we leap to conclusions, let's check our assumptions. It might surprise you to discover, like the CEO from the oil company, that we have an engaged and inquisitive audience in front of us. What happens if we don't have this audience? If this is indeed a case of behavior gone bad—no worries. We'll tackle *that* issue in *Chapter 8, Mentoring the Next Generation of Leaders – Legacy Building, One Gen Y at a Time, one Gen Y at a Time*, when we discuss performance management issues!

# Leaning in to change

Are you ready to give your training design and delivery a facelift?

Identify one of the training courses that you deliver in your organization that could use a makeover. If you aren't directly responsible for facilitating training, invite a staff member from your organization's learning and development team to work with you. Your task is to review the expected outcomes from the training and propose one change you can make to the course. This can take the form of making a change to your approach to facilitation in order to connect more effectively with a Gen Y audience, or selecting a new tool from the "shiny new tools list" that you would like to integrate into your training.

Write a statement of the goal you aim to achieve. Your goal should be clear, concise, and focused on a specific behavioral change you'd like to make. Once you have stated your goal, map out the specific actions you will take to reach your goal. Make sure to include consultation with someone on your Gen Y staff as part of your action plan.

Join me online (www.eyeofthetigerconsulting.ca) to share your training makeover. I look forward to chatting with you about how the content in this chapter informs your thinking and practice. See you online!

# Google it...

Please check out the following resources:

> ➤ J. Hofmann, *The Synchronous Trainers Survival Guide: Facilitating Successful Live and Online Courses, Meetings, and Events* (2003)
>
> ➤ S. Kozlowski, Learning, Training, and Development in Organizations (2009)
>
> ➤ P. Palmer, The Courage to Teach (2007)
>
> ➤ R. Pike, Creative Training Techniques Handbook: Tips, Tactics, and How-to's for Delivering Effective Training (2003)
>
> ➤ M. Silberman and C. Auerbach, Active Training: A Handbook of Techniques, Designs, Case Examples, and Tips (2006)

- ➤ P. Van den Bossche, Facilitating Learning in the 21st Century: Leading through Technology, Diversity, and Authenticity (2013)
- ➤ C. Wick, R. Pollock, A. Jefferson. and R. Flanagan, The Six Disciplines of Breakthrough Learning: How to Turn Training and Development into Business Results (2006)
- ➤ www.storybird.com
- ➤ www.mindmeister.com
- ➤ www.theworldcafe.com
- ➤ www.digitaltrends.com/how-to/how-to-make-a-podcast/

# Meeting the Gen Y community

*When you begin a new job, what signs do you watch for that indicate you've made the right decision to join the company?*

*– Shiho Itagaki*

For Shiho, the most important indicator is the working relationship between employees and the supervisor. She watches carefully to see how they relate to one another; that is, the informal banter between them, respect for diverse views, employees' comfort in being able to ask for the supervisor's assistance when needed, and whether they socialize with each other over coffee or tea. She also watches to see if work-life balance and gender equality are honored in the workplace.

Shiho mentioned that Gen Y does not work well under a top-down approach to leadership. Her generation wants to have a voice that is heard in the organization, no matter what position they occupy.

In the first few days on the job, Shiho is mindful of the degree to which others–that is supervisors and non-management staff—go out of their way to invite her to join them for breaks and lunch, and to encourage her to share her ideas at meetings. It builds her confidence and sense of worth in the organization, when others ask for her ideas on a project, genuinely listen to what she says, and then give her some praise for her contributions. It is also a huge confidence boost when her supervisor encourages her to ask questions often, regardless of how insignificant these questions might seem. For Shiho, a work environment where there is positive and unconditional positive regard goes a long way in helping her feel welcome in the organization.

Shiho used to be a supervisor and realizes how important it is to look after your staff. She spent a great deal of time coaching her staff and checking in regularly to see if they needed assistance. The most important task of a supervisor is to develop the confidence of your team so they can succeed.

*Shiho Itagaki is from Japan where she was the Sub-Branch Manager in the education sector. She has a BA with foci in English Pedagogy and Linguistics and Communication, and is currently studying in the Masters in Global Management program at Royal Roads University in Canada. Shiho's goal is to manage her own cosmetics or marketing company liaising between Canada and Japan. In her spare time, she enjoys watching comedies, swimming, and cycling.*

# Summary

We devoted this chapter to exploring how we can create learning and development opportunities for Gen Y that are *sticky*, *stickier*, and *stickiest*. We began with the 360 degree request, got everyone "on board", and then explored the diamonds in the rough that should be in everyone's training toolbox. We finished the chapter exploring how we can evaluate our training to determine if it made a difference.

Did you earn an "A"? I hope so!

Now that Gen Y is acclimatized to our workplace, let's head into the next chapter where we unlock the secrets to having great conversations with them.

# > 4

# Unlocking the Secrets to Awesome Conversations with Gen Y

*Hello?*
*Are you listening to me?*
*Did you hear a word I said?*

Have you caught yourself thinking or saying this in the middle of a conversation with Gen Y? Have your exchanges with Gen Y baffled you and left you at your wit's end trying to decipher what happened? You are not alone. Many of you have shared your stories with me about hanging onto a thread of patience during conversations with Gen Y with me. You've told me about blank stares on their faces as you convey important news; the ease with which they divert their attention away from you—usually while you are mid-way through a sentence—to answer incoming text messages, e-mails, or phone calls; late arrivals to meetings without an apology, remorse, or explanation; and, their oblivion to the fact that the headset super-glued to their ears isn't conducive to active listening! To inflame you even more, Gen Y doesn't appear to detect the changes in your tone of voice or shifts in your body language that signal you are becoming increasingly annoyed with their inattentiveness! These cumulative experiences have frayed your nerves and driven you screaming in another direction and vowing to steer clear of Gen Y as best you can.

I hear your frustration. It is discouraging to have conversations with Gen Y go sideways, especially after the time and energy you've invested in bridging Gen Y's personal expectations and organizational realities so that they remain with your organization and become key contributors. You've dedicated yourself to:

- ➤ Understanding Gen Y's attitudes, behaviors, needs, and expectations
- ➤ Revamping your approach to recruiting Gen Y talent
- ➤ Establishing meaningful work experiences for them
- ➤ Searching for new ways to create a culture of excitement, autonomy, challenge, and fun, which are at the top of their wish list

Now, communication starts to unravel. How can this be? Before you give in or give up, be assured that there is a way to salvage the situation.

The goal of this chapter is to equip you with the skills and abilities to have awesome conversations with Gen Y, so that you can build and sustain strong and long-term relationships with the newest generation in your workplace. In awesome conversations, you are able to masterfully:

- ➤ Set the right tone for dialog
- ➤ Initiate and hold meaningful conversations
- ➤ Manage tension points that unexpectedly pop up
- ➤ Leave the conversation knowing it was a worthwhile exchange

In order to increase the probability that you'll have awesome conversations with Gen Y, this chapter will examine the following topics:

- ➤ Stretching the elastic band—a new role awaits you
- ➤ Giving and receiving feedback—what to say and how to say it
- ➤ Navigating the super highway of conflict—potholes, puddles, and ditches

# So, what's burning?

A few years ago, I was contracted by the leadership team of an auto manufacturing company in the U.S. to roll out a plan for bridging generational communication differences in their organization. At the end of the meeting one of the senior members said, "Nothing's going to change around here. Gen Y is incorrigible, self-absorbed, and uncommunicative! They choose to communicate in ways that are vastly different, and we'll always be in a tug-of-war with them. Even if we lead the change, there's no guarantee Gen Y will follow suit."

I concur. There are no *guarantees* in this situation. However, I *can* guarantee that if we don't attempt to break free from the tug-of-war, then the frustrations we currently experience are likely to escalate and do irreparable damage to our working relationships. In turn, this diminishes our capacity to develop collaborative and high performing teams that are integral to achieving our organization's mandate, establishing our market relevance, and securing our competitive standing in the industry and in an open and global economy. Breakdowns in communication can seep into the bloodstream of our organization and affect key performance indicators, such as productivity, profitability, customer satisfaction, and employee turnover. Knowing that these risks loom in the background, I don't think it would be prudent to brush communication aside.

I also agree that Gen Y's communication preferences are different from our own and that this can problematic. At the core, Gen Y prefers a more relaxed and informal approach to workplace communication. This is evident in their use of text messaging, tweeting, blogging, and e-mailing as the dominant sources of their communication. Since their world revolves around the written word, Gen Y could easily spend an entire day having few, if any, face-to-face interactions. Knowing this, we can hardly blame them for not having the skills we expect in face-to-face engagement. Where would they have learned to refine face-to-face etiquette, including interpreting and responding to the finer nuances of tone and nonverbal messaging? Their interpersonal skills in this regard likely are a tad rusty for our liking, and this is one of the contributing sources of our frustration with Gen Y. As for answering incoming text messages, e-mails, and phone calls during a conversation, to Gen Y, this is not considered rude; it is part of being efficient with one's time.

In contrast, we prefer greater formality in workplace interactions, which shows itself as preference for face-to-face communication. Face-to-face communication is considered the height of business etiquette and respect for others, and it serves as the benchmark for measuring professionalism in ourselves and others. It includes a host of expected practices:

➤ Picking up the phone and speaking to clients and customers

➤ Walking to someone's office to have a discussion

➤ Meeting with new clients over lunch

➤ Attending business functions to build one's professional network

➤ Deferring respectfully to and listening uninterruptedly to people who have seniority or authority (or both)

Although we navigate proficiently on smartphones, iPads, and laptops, technology is not our favored tool for building and sustaining workplace relationships. For us, nothing replaces a solid handshake and looking directly into someone's eyes.

Even though we might be tempted to point fingers at Gen Y and accuse them of being the culprits in our communication debacle, there is little value in doing this. Casting blame on Gen Y doesn't move us closer to getting our conversations back on track, and it implies that culpability for derailed conversations rests with Gen Y. If we are being completely honest with ourselves, I think we would admit that we shoulder some of the responsibility here.

Both generations have some adapting to do. However, I'm asking you to be the first one to let go of the rope in the communications tug-of-war and to break free from the habitual ways that we've been communicating with Gen Y. I'm not expecting you to do all the heavy lifting, but I'm relying on you to take the lead and model the way.

This won't be easy. A change of this magnitude requires courage, openness, persistence, and risk-taking like no other. Are you up for the challenge? If so, let's fasten our seatbelts and get ready to steer in a new direction. Destination? Awesome conversations with Gen Y! Along the way, we might even uncover practices that are applicable to our interactions with others who are outside the Gen Y circle.

# Stretching the elastic band–a new role awaits you

Our working relationships with staff are the pillars upon which we build successful and viable organizations. Gen Y's willingness to work to their full potential, rally behind us on causes that shape the future of our organization, step outside their job accountabilities to champion initiatives that contribute to our mandate, and ultimately their decision to remain with our organization are dependent upon the quality of their working relationships with us.

During your conversations with others from this day forward, I ask you to make one promise, and one promise only. No matter how other people act and react and no matter what unexpectedly flies at you and challenges every iota of patience you have, remember to *remain grounded in respect for others.*

So where do we start? We start with ourselves. And just like an elastic band, I ask you to stretch in new directions.

## Let go–getting out of your own way

This seems like a bizarre place to begin, yet it is imperative if we want to set the right tone for conversations with Gen Y, and others. In this section, we will unearth and face a few truths that can radically shift our thinking and help us build a sturdier foundation for communication reform.

Our starting place is with ourselves and asking a critical question: *How do you show up as a leader?* I'm asking you to be completely candid with yourself here. Who are you and how do you show up in the presence of others, especially in your interactions with Gen Y?

When we reflect on all the great leaders of our time, there is one attribute that is the *magnet* that compels people to follow them. People will rally behind leaders, defend them, and engage wholeheartedly and honestly with them when these leaders reveal one key quality—their *authentic* self. Revealing to others who they truly are, what they stand for, and why they do what they do, is vital to leadership, especially to one's ability to connect with others, influence them, and build a community that is the bedrock of an organization's culture and prosperity.

Do you let others see the authentic side of you? Do you show your humanity, with its juxtaposition of strength and weakness, confidence and insecurity, and composure and fear? Some of you might be thinking this is the seat of demise for a leader. In actuality, it is the opposite. People are not attracted to, warm up to, or rally behind a leader who is infallible. They are attracted to brokenness; our willingness to unveil our humanity, with all our foibles and warts, as we push forward with our strategic vision and plans. It is in this brokenness that people find themselves standing beside their leaders and realizing they share more in common than they ever thought imaginable. Discovering the universalities that bind us, is where real and lasting connections with people are cultivated.

When I invite you to *let go*, I'm referring to letting go of who you think you are supposed to be. Let go of all the behaviors that might be keeping you from being your authentic self; hence keeping others at bay. This could be the words you use to express yourself, your tone of voice, or your actions and reactions that signal you might not be approachable and others should keep their distance.

What exactly do we need to start doing to become more authentic? Since each of us is extraordinarily unique, it would be inappropriate for me to prescribe a specific pathway for enhancing authenticity. I can't think of anything more unbefitting than giving you a checklist of behaviors that we collectively adapt. Instead, here are a few questions to guide your reflection that, hopefully, will inspire you to take your own first step toward greater personal authenticity:

➤ How much of yourself do you let others get to know?

➤ If you aren't revealing your true self, what are you holding on to and why? What would happen if you simply *let this go*?

➤ What is one incremental step you can take today that would reveal more of yourself to others?

➤ If you follow through with this, what do you envision might change for you and for others?

➤ How will you sustain your commitment to personal change?

When you commit to even slight changes, notice what happens. Suddenly, there is a shift in how others engage with you.

We now venture to ask, "What language are you speaking?"

# Learning a new language–from crushers to connectors

*Did he really just say that?! What a fool! What was he thinking? Doesn't he realize how embarrassing that comment was? Doesn't he realize the professional faux-pas he just committed? Doesn't he have a filter?*

We've likely all experienced moments when someone made a remark that instantly silenced the room and caused everyone to wonder: *What was he thinking?* What's more intriguing is what this situation reveals about *you*.

Before we proceed further, I invite you to ask yourself an important question. What percentage of your internal dialog today has been:

> ➤ Evaluative; that is, focused on judging or critiquing others and the world around you?

> ➤ Inquiry-based; that is, focused on being curious and genuinely interested in better understanding others and your world?

Being cognizant of our internal dialog is vital to understanding how we show up and interact with others. Our inner voice, with its intricately woven web of values, beliefs, attitudes, and assumptions, shapes not only our thinking, but also our speech and our behaviors. It is one of the primary determinants of whether connections with others will be short-range and arms-length transactions or long-term and meaningful alliances. For the most part, all of this happens on an unconscious level; we don't realize the domino effect that our private thoughts have on how we act and react to others, and how others experience us in conversation. Awareness of the power of our internal dialog helps us explain why some conversations with Gen Y disintegrate in front of us and how we can turn the situation around.

When we show up predominantly with an evaluative presence, we can potentially become a *conversation crusher*. We play the role of a critic who weighs in with judgment and criticism about the world around us. When evaluative people come together, the conversation tends to divide and disengage them because they focus on:

> ➤ Identifying gaps in thinking
> ➤ Finding faults
> ➤ Refuting the beliefs of others
> ➤ Finger pointing
> ➤ Seizing center stage periodically to showcase their personal expert knowledge, instead of leaving space for others to contribute

Evaluation *can* play a salient role, but only in moderation. Reserve it for occasions when it makes a constructive and critical contribution to organizational or personal change, for example, when an expert critique of a workplace policy or practice is required or when assessment of performance is expected. The evaluation that has the potential to be a conversation crusher is that which does not add value. It is simply commentary for the sake of voicing one's opinion, and it does more harm than good.

When we show up with an inquisitive presence, we are on target to becoming a *conversation connector.* We enter into dialog with inexhaustible curiosity about the world, and we strive to comprehend and appreciate others, regardless of how divergent their beliefs and values are from our own. Conversation connecting takes the form of:

➤ Asking more questions instead of having all the right answers

➤ Leaving space in conversations for others to share their stories rather than dominating with our own

➤ Actively listening to others in a way that shows genuine interest in getting to know them

➤ Listening deeply for that which binds us rather than focusing on what divides us

➤ Parking our judgment and being unconditional in our regard for others

So what is the language playing in your mind? Are you a conversation crusher or conversation connector? If it's time to hone the language of connection, I offer you a tool to help you make the transition. I've used this approach myself to turn down the volume on the evaluative messenger in my own mind and change how I show up for conversations.

For the rest of the day, I would like you to regularly take your *judgment temperature.*

**Action point**

Be mindful of the messages in your brain. Every time you catch yourself thinking evaluatively, follow it up by making three statements or asking three questions that are inquiry-based.

At first, this is awkward—it feels like you are speaking a foreign language. Yet, with persistence and practice you'll train your mind to shift from being *evaluative* to *inquiry-based.* Eventually, the shift in thinking transfers to your speech and how you act and react to others. What originally was awkward will, in time, become natural.

Imagine the presence you will have when you apply your learning about communication connectors with your learning about authenticity. This combination can leave an indelible mark on how you present yourself, how you are perceived, and how you model the way for others.

Now that we've turned the volume down, let's turn the volume up on *what you will hear,* possibly for the first time.

# Checking assumptions

Over the years, many of you have asked me, *"What did Gen Y mean when they said....?"*. You can fill in the blank with the countless interpretations I've been asked to make. To each of you who have asked this question, my response has been the same: *"Did you ask Gen Y what they meant?"*.

Although I'm flattered that you ask for my take on the situation, the person best suited to explain the meaning of anything that is said or done is the speaker. By consulting an outside source, we muddy the waters of communication. When someone is asked to be interpreter, judge, or jury for a conversation they did not participate in, or witness, they run the risk of making serious errors in judgment. Communication becomes more complicated than it needs to be when those of us who were not part of the exchange put words and actions under the microscope and play the game of *"he said, she said"*.

To minimize the probability of erroneous interpretations polluting the conversational landscape, let's return conversations to their rightful owners—the speakers involved directly. I encourage you to be proactive in your conversations—*check assumptions*. Seek clarification when you are unsure about anything in the conversation, whether it is the verbal message, the tone of voice, or the nonverbal message. As mentioned earlier in the chapter, Gen Y's communication patterns are different than ours, which reinforces the importance of checking assumptions. When you notice blank stares on Gen Y faces or their attention being diverted to a text message, stop the conversation and address your concern. In that moment, air what you heard or saw, how you interpret it, and ask for clarification.

Yet, in doing so, let's be mindful of our approach. Often, we climb the ladder of inference when we see certain behaviors, or we are on the receiving end of remarks that we perceive as unbecoming of an employee. In zero to three seconds we go from composed and confident to stark-raving angry! This is usually accompanied by a litany of evaluative remarks that back the speaker into a corner and cause the conversation to spiral downward into a messy puddle of disengagement and dislike for each other. This would not be one of those shiny examples of leadership excellence.

Here is where I'm going to push you gently beyond your comfort zone. It is in these moments of elevated anxiety (or seething anger) that the litmus test of communication awaits us. When you are ready to engage in a fight or flight response, I invite you to rethink your approach. As best possible, put your emotions in abeyance (I offer a way to do this in the upcoming section on managing conflict) and step into the conversation with the *inquiry-based* approach to communication that we discussed earlier. Bring your pure and insatiable curiosity into the discourse by asking questions to better understand the intended meaning. This way, you can put to rest the confusion, discomfort, or anger you are experiencing.

Don't let anything fester. Psychological distance from others begins when we don't voice our concerns and seek understanding. The sooner we attend to these matters, the sooner we get back to a collaborative and respectful dialog. However, in cases when anger is too intense and unbearable, and you are unable to come from a place of inquiry, then definitely take a break from the conversation and re-engage when calm is restored.

Consider having a discussion with Gen Y about checking assumptions. Set a new norm that it is acceptable, and expected, that both of you address irritants immediately when they arise. Hence, we pave the way for honest and authentic dialog.

If at first checking assumptions doesn't go as planned and your patience is tested severely, please remember the promise you made earlier in the chapter: *remain grounded in respect for others.*

# Giving and receiving feedback–what to say and how to say it

From *Chapter 1, Generation Y – Who Are They?*, we know that Gen Y values and anticipates receiving frequent feedback about their job performance, but they are somewhat ill-prepared to cope with negative feedback. As you recall, Gen Y has been raised under the watchful eyes of parents who sheltered them from feedback that was uncomplimentary of their efforts and contributions.

In this section, you'll find the essentials for facilitating all types of feedback conversations, including key ingredients of constructive feedback and approaches for establishing a positive tone. Our goal is to enhance our effectiveness in giving feedback to Gen Y and to demonstrate ways for them to give feedback in return.

## What to say

*Look back. Look forward.*

Feedback conversations encourage us to *look back* and *look forward.* If done well, it can mean the difference between Gen Y's performance skyrocketing or declining, and whether they stay or leave our organization. In *looking back*, we recognize Gen Y's extraordinary competencies and strengths, applaud their contributions and achievements, and identify areas for professional growth and development. In *looking forward*, we collaborate with Gen Y on envisioning their future with our organization—setting goals to enhance performance, stretching in new directions, and charting action plans to reach new milestones.

As we *look back* and *look forward* with Gen Y, let's keep the following guidelines in mind:

➤ Couple constructive feedback with a healthy dose of praise for work they have done

➤ Be specific and direct (speak in terms of concrete work-related behaviors that you want them to start doing, stop doing, and continue doing)

➤ Focus on performance standards (compare their performance to expected job standards; refrain from comparing their performance to that of another person, which builds resentment)

➤ Ask open-ended questions that encourage Gen Y to critique their own performance and to identify areas for improvement

➤ Collaborate with Gen Y in developing their personal action plan for professional growth and development

➤ Follow up after the meeting to discuss progress on action items and to offer support

➤ Trust them to reach their destination (let's not micromanage here—when they get it, get out of the way)

When constructive feedback is warranted, we have a golden opportunity to step into a coaching role. In these sessions, focus on the behaviors that need to change; specifically, what they are doing currently that needs to stop and what you want them to start doing. Avoid focusing on the *person*. We don't want the *person* per se to change; we want their *behaviors* to comply with workplace standards. For example, it would be counterproductive and arouse defensiveness to ask someone why they are lazy in returning calls from clients. Instead, reframe this to put the focus on *behavior.* Ask why the standard of returning clients' calls within one day is not being honored. Provide examples of critical incidents and specific suggestions of what you'd like to see them do and why. In any feedback session, remember to keep your comments objective and respectful, and try to avoid extremes in your language such as "always" and "never". We would be hard pressed to find examples where our staff are "always distracted" or "never on time".

Many of you tell me that after a feedback conversation, you occasionally doubt Gen Y understood your message. Even when they tell you that they did understand, you still feel unsettled. You aren't left with any warm assurance of *what exactly* they took away from the discussion. To put your mind at ease, consider asking these two questions at the end of your conversations:

➤ What did you understand from our conversation today?

➤ What have I not said that you need me to say?

# What not to say

What's the worst feedback you can give to Gen Y, or to anyone for that matter?

*Keep up the good work.*

I'm sure you are aghast to read this. As reinforcing and uplifting as you think this phrase is, advocating for your staff to *keep up the good work* is an invitation to *maintain the status quo.* You are encouraging them to continue doing what they've always done. In reality, no person, team, or organization thrives in a highly competitive and open global marketplace with status quo behaviors and performance. People, teams, and organizations that make the headlines and are leaders in our industry are constantly re-strategizing and taking audacious steps to reinvent themselves. To be in today's competitive arena requires you, your staff, and your company to embrace wholly the spirit of risk taking and rattle the chains of status quo behaviors and performance. To be ahead of the curve demands that there be an organizational norm that expects everyone to step outside their comfort zone and keep asking "what if...".

Yes, your staff should be praised and recognized for the excellent work they have done, and are doing, but don't stop there! Challenge them to reach beyond their current performance to set new goals and reach new performance heights. All of your employees–even your super stars–should have something significant to strive for. As we know, Gen Ys are highly ambitious and they are eager to move ahead in their careers. By giving them specific feedback on how they can improve their performance, you are guiding them to make changes that will position them for the jobs that they aspire to have. In doing so, you motivate and inspire them, and the results will benefit everyone.

# How to say it

The climate for giving feedback is equally as critical to the feedback process as the message itself. One of the most important things we can do at the onset is to ask the person who will be on the receiving end of our feedback when it will be a good time for a discussion. Giving feedback whenever it suits us can be highly problematic. If the person on the receiving end isn't prepared for the feedback, for whatever reason, it can land on defensive ears and be discarded. Engaging in a feedback conversation at a time that works for them will increase the probability that they will be more attentive and receptive to your message. It elevates the chances that feedback will be graciously and thoughtfully received and with the intent to take action.

Remember that you are in a two-way conversation here. Feedback is not a one-way dissemination of information from your end. To engage Gen Y fully in their professional growth and development, encourage them to join in the feedback conversation. Invite them to comment on:

➤ How they view their job performance

➤ How they'd like to change or enhance their performance

➤ How they would like you to support and guide them in their endeavors

Leave space for Gen Y to give *you* feedback as well. There is a great deal to be discovered about how we lead and how we interact with others if we are willing to listen to our Gen Y staff. If at first Gen Y is guarded about offering feedback (it can be a tad intimidating when first asked), you may want to coach them by asking a specific question that is niggling in your mind about how you work together. For example, this could take the form of asking:

➤ How you can support them better on projects

➤ What they would like to see you doing differently in your weekly meetings with them

➤ What you can be doing differently to support their career progression

➤ What feedback they have for you about...how you give feedback!

Alongside face-to-face feedback sessions, consider the power of technology to send a text message or e-mail that conveys your gratitude for what they did and acknowledge a job well done. By sending a quick e-message, you honor Gen Y's preference for regular contact with you.

# Navigating the super highway of conflict – potholes, puddles, and ditches

Road trip! Pack your bags, fuel your vehicle, find the map, point the compass due north, and away we go! Hold on; it isn't that easy! Along the way, anything can happen. Our route can be unexpectedly marred by inclement weather, road closures, accidents, incidents, gridlock, fast drivers (slow drivers!), and then potholes, puddles, and ditches! We are thrust into the quagmire of decision making: swerving to avoid collisions, taking detours when roads are closed, speeding up then slowing down, and sometimes just pulling over to the side of the road to breathe and reassess the situation. It takes proficiency, patience, and perseverance to navigate the intricacies of the highway. And the same is required of us when we navigate conflict that surfaces in our workplaces. Without warning, we face communication breakdowns not unlike those potholes, puddles, and ditches on the highway that cause us to swerve, detour, change our speed, and sometimes pull over.

In this space, we explore new tools we can use to manage communication gridlocks more effectively so that the end result is constructive, results in outcomes that both Gen Y and you can live with, and honors our earlier commitment to *remain grounded in respect for others*.

## Shifting gears

When we hear the word "conflict", many of us cringe. It ignites a barrage of negative thoughts and sends a chill through our veins. At the mere hint of conflict—whether it takes the shape of something subtle in Gen Y's body language or a derogatory comment—we position ourselves to do battle. We don our armor, raise our shields, and defend ourselves and our ideas unrelentingly against the opponent.

Is this really the best way to manage conflict?

If we continue to view conflict as a battleground, then we risk isolating our workplace allies, arm twisting others to agree with our ideas (which may not always be the best course of action), and damaging our reputation as leaders that Gen Y wants to work with.

In order to reap positive outcomes for both parties and preserve our working relationships, we need to shift gears; that is, reframe our thinking about conflict. This means a paradigm shift in which we move away from viewing conflict as being volatile, destructive, and focused on win-lose outcomes, toward viewing conflict as healthy, natural, and productive. Here are a few tips for how we can begin to reframe conflict:

- ➤ **Remind ourselves that conflict is part of life**: At some point in time we'll disagree with something that is said or done.
- ➤ **View conflict as a relationship builder**: Authentic working relationships develop when we share candidly what we think and feel.
- ➤ **Think of conflict as a problem that we are invited to solve with Gen Y**: Imagine the possibilities when we start brainstorming!

> ➤ **Keep the focus on issues**: Be tough on issues, but gentle with your Gen Y staff.

> ➤ **Stay grounded in respect for others**: Be cognizant of how our words, tone, and body language affect Gen Y.

> ➤ **Engage in deep listening**: Be curious about new information and perspectives that are different than our own. Don't rush to judgment until we've heard the full story.

> ➤ **Have faith in Gen Y**: Collectively, we can find a solution to problems.

> ➤ **Don't forget to breathe!**: The anxiety we experience in tense situations will pass!

I also encourage you to rethink how you handle those tense moments when our emotional triggers have been activated; that is, our internal radar sends us a signal that we are troubled by an incoming verbal or nonverbal message. An emotional response of any kind has the potential to cloud our ability to remain calm, logical, and grounded in preserving the dignity and respect of others. When emotions surface, they usually send off warning bells that we should politely excuse ourselves from the conversation and return when calmer heads prevail. But, when these emotions come to visit, I'm going to suggest we fight the little demons head on!

When an emotional gremlin invades your ability to concentrate, take a moment to acknowledge it; identify exactly what it is, label how it makes you feel, and then literally send it to the back of your brain where it belongs. Lock it up! At first this is difficult to do, especially when there is an emotional volcano exploding in your consciousness. Yet with practice, you can quell the emotional triggers that threaten to sabotage your ability to be present and to think and respond cogently in the heat of conflict. It is unrealistic to think we can eliminate our emotional triggers; they will always remain a part of who we are, and they can creep into our awareness at any time. However, we can develop a strategy for managing them when they land.

# Signaling a new direction

*Will you meet me in the middle?*

This is a question I ask when I'm at the bargaining table negotiating a collective agreement, in a meeting with a client discussing the details of a contract, or in a conversation that is derailing and crumbling at my feet. *Will you meet me in the middle?*

Our focus is on joining with Gen Y, in the spirit of collaboration, to resolve the conflict we find ourselves in and to come out relatively unscathed on the other side. A collaborative approach invites us to be consummate problem-solvers, who are able to put personal differences aside and merge the best of our thinking in order to reach an amicable decision that benefits both of us. It demands that we are mindful of finding a solution that minimizes the probability that the same conflict surfaces again.

The following principles serve as the guidelines for how we can enter into and sustain a collaborative spirit during conflict:

> ➤ Promote openness and transparency
>
> ➤ Safeguard mutual respect and dignity
>
> ➤ Commit fully to addressing each other's concerns
>
> ➤ Empower each of us to stand in our strength and be heard
>
> ➤ Seek integration and find a solution that we can both live with at the end of the day
>
> ➤ Preserve the best of who we are

However, when we are in the grips of conflict, these principles are tested severely. At some point in the discussion, it is not uncommon to find ourselves at a crossroads, and unsure of how to proceed. Each side declares its position, provides exhaustive explanations to support their stand on issues, but we don't know how to move towards a solution. We are stuck, and neither side knows how to break the uncomfortable stalemate.

Here lies the opportunity to *meet in the middle*.

> ➤ Convey that you understand Gen Y's position.
>
> ➤ Communicate genuinely and specifically why you are unable to honor or satisfy their request.
>
> ➤ Encourage them to join you in co-creating a new possibility; that is, finding a solution that has not yet been tabled. Shred the rules! Move away from archaic templates, processes, and protocols and begin blue sky brainstorming that takes you to a solution that is novel, ground-breaking, and precedent setting.

For example, in my *meet in the middle* collaborations with staff at the auto manufacturing company mentioned earlier, we launched *Technology Go Wild Zones* and *Technology Free Zones* throughout the facility. These are clearly demarcated areas in the organization (including two new high tech staff lounges) where technology is, and isn't, welcome. There are new guidelines in place for workplace etiquette too, including employee-initiated and led mentoring in technology and face-to-face business etiquette. A committee called the *Zone Trackers,* which consists of a healthy cross-generational mix of employees, was struck to oversee the zones, address questions and concerns, receive recommendations for improvement, and coordinate mentoring. Two years later, the zones are still celebrated as the pivotal change that led to decreased conflicts around generational communication in their organization.

Using this as an example, where are their opportunities to ask a staff member or your entire staff to *meet in the middle?*

And when all is said and done, what do you see in the rear view mirror?

# Seeing what's in the rear view mirror

There is a teachable moment in every conflict. In order to grow to be effective in managing and resolving conflicts, take time to reflect on what transpired in your exchanges. Without reflection, we steer blindly into the next conversation not knowing what we need to do differently; hence, we run the risk of repeating the same unproductive behaviors. Added to this, we miss the opportunity to celebrate everything we've done that is constructive, kind, and compassionate.

During your reflection, ask yourself the following questions. When faced with conflict, what do I need to:

> ➤ Continue doing, because it is constructive and supports collaborative problem-solving?

> ➤ Stop doing, because it is counterproductive to finding win-win solutions?

> ➤ Start doing, because there is still more for me to learn about the process of managing and resolving conflicts?

On a final note—if, at any point in the conflict resolution process, it is evident you made a mistake; don't shy away from it. The worst thing you can do is ignore the mistake, make excuses for your behavior, or blame others. By not owning up to the mistake, you put your credibility in peril, and you likely will lose the respect of your staff. It is a long and arduous road to earning people's respect, but it doesn't take much to lose it.

In reality, your staff cares less about the mistake you made, and more about how you respond after the mistake is exposed. Do you take ownership for your mistake as soon as it is brought to your attention? Do you convey genuine remorse for what you did and communicate your understanding of the damage done? Do you offer a concrete pathway for how you will rectify the situation? How you recover from the mistake is the focal point of their attention.

# Reframing challenges as opportunities

*I'm not defensive! I'm just being honest! It's not my fault those reports don't get done. With everything I'm expected to do and all the added duties that come across my desk every day, I can't get to the reports. I don't have any help around here. I can't do everything on my own.*

As painful as it is to be on the receiving end of defensiveness, it is a familiar human response; it is the way some of us choose to protect ourselves when we feel blamed. When a person is accused of poor performance, there are many possible reactions:

> ➤ Denial to avoid having to question personal incompetence

> ➤ Anger and aggression, which helps them let off steam and postpones confronting the immediate unpleasantness of the problem until they are able to cope with it

> ➤ Retreating into a shell in hopes that the entire incriminating situation will vanish

When you face defensiveness from your Gen Y staff, or others:

> ➤ Recognize that defensive behavior is normal (someone is actually trying to communicate something to you).

> ➤ Refrain from attacking a person's defenses. Try to concentrate on the behavior (reports are not generated) rather than on the person (you aren't getting your work done on time).

> ➤ Allow the person to vent (reschedule the conversation for another time, if required. Given time, a more rational reaction usually prevails).

> ➤ Empathize with the person's situation and offer support to achieve workplace standards and expectations.

> ➤ Remember that they own their emotional responses, and they are responsible for their actions and reactions.

Whatever you do, stay calm. Two people getting defensive will not contribute to solving the problem. Let the person vent and if you see that it is safe to proceed, instead of rescheduling the conversation, then move further into the discussion. Consider asking, *"What can we work on together to remedy the situation that we face?"*. This question sets the stage for collaborating on a solution, and gives you and your staff permission to share what both of you need to repair the situation.

# Leaning in to change

Is there an *awesome* conversation waiting for you?

Reflect on a conversation you want to have with a Gen Y staff member. Perhaps it is a conversation you've been deferring or a follow-up discussion after a conversation that went astray. Take time to chart the approach you'll take to increase the probability that it becomes an *awesome* conversation. Consider the following in your planning process:

> ➤ What do you hope to achieve by having the conversation?

> ➤ How do you want to show up as a leader?

> ➤ What is your approach for leveraging praise and constructive feedback?

> ➤ How will you create a climate that is conducive to joint problem solving?

Join me online (www.eyeofthetigerconsulting.ca) to share your experiences applying content from this chapter to your workplace practice.

# Google it

If you are interested in learning more, please consult the following resources:

> B. George, P. Sims, A.N, McLean, and D. Mayer, D, "Discovering Your Authentic Leadership", *Harvard Business Review*, *85*(2), 129-138, 2007.

> R. S., Kaplan, "What to Ask the Person in the Mirror", *Harvard Business Review*, *85*(1), 86-95, 2007.

> John, Maxwell, *Everyone Communications Few Connect*, Tennessee: Thomas Nelson, 2010.

> K., Paterson, J., Grenny, R., McMillan, and A., Switzler, *Crucial Conversations: Tools for Talking When Stakes are High*, New York: McGraw Hill, 2012

> D., Tjosvold, "The conflict-positive organization: It depends upon us", *Journal of Organizational Behavior*, 29, 19-28, 2008

> Ted Talk: Itay Tulgam's "Lead Like the Great Conductors".

# Meeting the Gen Y community

Introducing Cherishka E. G. Isebia (better known as Erika)!

*What advice do you have for business leaders who would like to enhance how they communicate with Gen Y?*

Erika advises business leaders to be aware that Gen Y views their work and career differently than other generations. Gen Ys consider themselves highly creative and capable of charting their own directions for developing themselves personally and professionally. Erika encourages leaders to be open when approaching Gen Y and to avoid putting boundaries on what Gen Y can do or say. It is also important to be honest when we communicate with Gen Y; don't "beat around the bush; always tell things like they are".

Erika stresses the importance of treating everyone equally. Do not give more attention and privileges to employees with different jobs and titles in the organization. Communicate respectfully and equally with everyone.

As much as Gen Y appreciates honest and constructive feedback, they also appreciate compliments when things are going well. Acknowledge Gen Y's efforts—"it gives us a push to go on!".

Erika's final message to us: "Being open-minded, honest, straight to the point, and especially being yourself are most important for good communication with our generation."

*Erika lives in Curacao, an island north of Venezuela. Erika and her father worked tirelessly to transform their small family business into an E&R consultancy. Erika now serves as the owner of the company and studies Human Resource Management at the University of Curacao. Her career goal is to continue being a business owner and to contribute to her community by being a mentor for young people. She wants to empower them with the skills, abilities, and attitudes to become the community leaders they aspire to be. When Erika is not working and serving her community, she enjoys time with her two daughters and reading novels by her favorite author, Paulo Coelho.*

# Summary

In this chapter, we examined the approaches we can use to move towards having awesome conversations with Gen Y. We stretched the elastic band in new directions by getting out of our own way and exploring the power of *crushers* and *connectors* so we can become the masterful communicators we aspire to be. We also discussed managing potholes, puddles, and ditches on the super highway of conflict; specifically, how to *shift gears, signal a new direction*, and make time to *see what's in the rear view mirror*.

No matter what happens in your conversations, remember your promise!

Armed with communication strategies, let's head into the next chapter. It's time to reach for the stars!

# 5

# Inspiring Star Performance– Reaching Seriously for Sirius

*Cast your eyes up into the night sky and there you will find Sirius; the brightest star in the heavens with luminosity that is the envy of all the other stars in the universe. We watch from a distance in awe of its spectacular beauty flickering in a rainbow of colors.*

Ever since Gen Y arrived at our doorstep, we've been searching for ways to create the right work experiences, with all the trimmings, that can inspire their star performance. We've engaged in a number of pursuits, including inquiries into the following:

➤ What does Gen Y specifically need from our organization as it pertains to meaningful work experiences?

➤ What can we do during the early days of Gen Y's employment that grabs their interest, inspires them to reach their full potential, and plants a strong and compelling vision of their future in our organization?

➤ How do we keep Gen Y for longer than a few years and hopefully long enough for them to join our leadership ranks and become the driving force in the next phase of our organization's evolution?

Despite our best efforts to answer these questions and put in place work experiences that are attractive and fulfilling, Gen Y continues to experience low levels of job satisfaction and a diminishing sense of job meaning. We are falling short of delivering experiences that are inspirational for our Gen Ys. Faster than any of the other generations, Gen Y becomes disillusioned with our workplace systems, practices, and protocols. Soon afterwards, they become disengaged and start scanning the marketplace for new jobs. We face an urgent need to address this situation given the rising number of Gen Ys who are resigning and seeking employment elsewhere. In a few short years, the Gen Ys who once were our rising star performers but left for greener pastures could become the leaders of companies that are in direct competition with us.

As discussed in *Chapter 1, Generation Y – Who are They?*, Gen Y size up an organization soon after they've been hired. This means we have a small window of opportunity to ignite their interest and convince them that our organization can fulfil their needs for job satisfaction and job meaning. In this chapter, we'll discuss the approaches we can use to foster work experiences that inspire Gen Y to:

- ➤ Be and offer their best
- ➤ Become our star performers
- ➤ Envision their future as leaders in our organization

In order to achieve these outcomes, we'll cover the following topics:

- ➤ Rethinking the work we hired Gen Y to do—the big bang theory
- ➤ Exploring new horizons for Gen Y—the galaxy beyond their jobs
- ➤ Falling Stars—learning how to fall with grace and grit

Although the job-enrichment practices discussed in this chapter are tailored to the needs and expectations of Gen Y, you may find that some of the ideas can be adapted for use with employees in the other generations in order to inspire their peak performance, as well. By being aware of job enrichment for Gen Y and the adaptability of the approaches to other generations, we balance the scales of equity and fairness in how we work with the entire staff. This will help us enhance job satisfaction, which is at an all time low across all generations in the workplace. Ultimately, our goal is to create a workplace that our best Gen Y staff could never imagine leaving!

# So what's burning?

> *I've tried everything to help our Gen Y staff become peak performers in the company,*
> *but it isn't working. Employees become star performers with hard work, and Gen Y*
> *doesn't know the meaning of working hard. They expect everything to be handed to*
> *them. This is a lazy generation!*

Over the years, many of you have voiced similar frustrations to me. After you exhausted every feasible avenue to provide your Gen Y staff with enriching work experiences, you eventually pulled away. You simply didn't know what more you could do to support their professional development. Repeatedly, you've cited Gen Y's lack of commitment to working hard and laziness as root cause challenges that were difficult for you to overcome. These challenges ultimately caused you to walk away in exasperation and with a healthy assortment of unflattering opinions about our younger workers.

As I reflect on the experiences that leave us bruised and fatigued, I'm wondering if we've misconstrued the situation. Perhaps, there is more to this than simply a lazy generation in our midst.

Perhaps, what we perceive as *laziness* in Gen Y is not an inherent trait, like many of us believe. Conceivably, it could be a *by-product* of how Gen Y perceives and experiences the workplace. There might be something in the way we conduct business that triggers a reaction and zaps Gen Y off their energy and enthusiasm to be, and become, fully participating and contributing citizens in our organizations. This in turn causes us to perceive them in a less than favorable light. For us, an older generation with a different set of workplace priorities and expectations, we may not see or experience anything untoward in our organization's work expectations, protocols, and structures, but this isn't the case for the youngest generation in our workplace.

If Gen Y is experiencing declining levels of job satisfaction and it is becoming painstakingly more difficult to attract and retain them in our organizations, then maybe it's time for a workplace tune-up. This is our wake-up call to the reality that current approaches to structuring work for Gen Y are in need of a partial or complete overhaul.

Don't misread the message here; I'm not hurling all the blame and responsibility into your arms. The solution—or at least part of the solution—rests, not exclusively with us, but in how we can collaborate with Gen Y in new ways to transform our workplaces into ones that provide job satisfaction for younger workers. Our Gen Y staff is ideally positioned to give us first-hand insight into the following:

➤ Strengths in the design and structure of work

➤ Aspects of the work that disengage them and contribute to job dissatisfaction

➤ Opportunities to enhance work experiences that capitalize on their strengths and deliver to their need to be involved in work that has a true business impact

As we move through this chapter, we'll step out on the ledge and explore how we can do the following:

> ➤ Partner with Gen Y to evaluate the current landscape in which we work
> ➤ Co-create experiences that inspire Gen Y to reach their full potential and become *star performers* and future leaders in our organizations

So, where do we start from? How can we create the right mix of workplace experiences for Gen Y?

It's time to rethink what we've always done.

Rethinking the work we hired Gen Y to do – the big bang theory

You arrive at your office to find the following letter waiting for you:

*Dear Supervisor,*

*The intent of this letter is to inform you of my resignation. After 3 weeks on the job, I've come to realize that what I need in my career is not what this company can deliver. My last day of employment is... (the letter continues).*

You never saw this coming. You aren't sure what meteorite just hit you. Your mind begins to race with the following questions as you attempt to make sense of what led to this unexpected resignation of one of your Gen Y employees:

> ➤ What did we do?
> ➤ What didn't we do?
> ➤ What should we have done differently?

To the best of your knowledge, there were no red flags that signaled a concern or a looming problem that would warrant a resignation. You thought he was acclimatizing well to his new job and that everything was progressing as it should. You saw tremendous potential in him, even during the short time that he was with your organization.

*Why didn't he come to me and discuss his concerns? We could have worked this out. He didn't have to just get up and resign!*

The more questions you ask, the deeper you fall into the black hole of confusion.

In this section, we'll explore ways to reinvent work experiences for Gen Y so that a resignation letter won't be waiting for you on Monday morning. We employ the *Big Bang Theory,* that is, we aim to wipe out some of the status quo practices that no longer serve us well and replenish our approach to how we structure work for Gen Y with some refreshingly new ideas. We won't completely annihilate everything you do, as you likely have some practices that are appealing to a Gen Y audience. Our goal is to blend new approaches with the existing ones to help us navigate our organization's priorities and mandate with the needs and expectations of Gen Y. Our anticipated end results are that Gen Y:

➤ Wants to contribute their best efforts to the work at hand

➤ Experiences a sense of accomplishment and gratification along the way

➤ Feels like contributing members of our organization's community

➤ Remains with our company longer than 3 weeks

As we've discussed in *Chapter 1, Generation Y – Who are They?*, Gen Y works differently than you and me. Though, at first, this can be disconcerting, it can actually be to our advantage. As we go through this chapter, keep an open mind and see how the universe unfolds.

# Transmitting new messages – Why? What? How?

As we know, Gen Y places high priority on knowing the sound business reasons behind *everything* we do in our organization. This curiosity extends to their jobs; specifically, they want to know the purpose of the work that has been assigned to them. However, it isn't enough to simply provide a justification; we need to pay attention to *where* we position the rationale in our message to Gen Y. In this section, I'm going to introduce you to a twist in Simon Sinek's work, *Start with Why*, which can be adapted for use in our engagement with Gen Y.

Our usual script for communicating messages is *What? How? Why?*

We tell our staff:

➤ *What* we want them to do

➤ *How* we want them to complete the task

➤ *Why* we want the task done

However, the *order* in which we communicate our messages can be problematic. If we begin with *what* we want Gen Y to do, we'll lose their attention. They may never hear the *how* and *why!* Typically, as soon as they hear *what* we want them to do, their minds shoot into space. They become consumed with their internal dialogue and mentally drift away from you while you are outlining the details of *what* and then segueing into a discussion of *how* and *why*.

Questions, concerns, and thoughts that race into their minds include the following:

➤ Why are we being asked to do this

➤ How am I supposed to do that

➤ This is too difficult

➤ This is too easy

➤ This is ridiculously boring

➤ This doesn't make sense

➤ That can never be done

> ➤ Where will we get the resources to do that
> ➤ Seriously—who has time to do that

As a result, there is an increased probability that the all-important rationale behind the work we expect Gen Y to do is not fully heard, even though we may have communicated it. Hence, the following outcomes are imminent:

> ➤ Enthusiasm and commitment begin to wane, because they don't know why they are doing what they've been asked to do.
> ➤ Shortcuts are taken in task completion, because the complete set of steps we asked them to follow doesn't make sense. This could increase the error rate and diminish the product or service quality.
> ➤ There is disengagement and lethargy to get tasks done and meet deadlines.

In order to minimize these outcomes, let's amend our script to *Why? What? How?*

Position the *why* ahead of the pack, that is, communicate the rationale for completing tasks or projects ahead of the explanation of *what* you want them to do. Paint a crystal clear picture of the specific problem or gap that is faced and the benefits that likely will follow for them, the team, and the organization when the problem or gap no longer exists. When Gen Y comprehend that they will be part of solving a problem or closing a gap, there is an increased likelihood that they will complete tasks according to expectations and with heighted commitment and satisfaction, because they know their efforts are contributing to bottom-line effectiveness. To further enhance their commitment and satisfaction, leave space for Gen Y to do the following:

> ➤ Ask questions about what you said or didn't say that needs to be said
> ➤ Weigh in on how the rationale, specifically your explanation of the problem or gap, is being perceived
> ➤ Add any commentary they feel is relevant to the *why* discussion

When it appears that all questions and commentary have been extinguished, proceed with an explanation of *what* you are expecting them to do and *how* you propose the work to be done. Yet, be mindful that if we prescribe every detail in the pathway to complete a task, we might strip Gen Y off their autonomy and decision-making power and rob them off the opportunity to contribute their unique spin on how tasks get completed. Encourage Gen Ys to figure out some of the pathways for task completion on their own.

After you unveil *what* and *how*, consider leaving space for Gen Y to ask questions, raise concerns, and offer input, just like you did after the *why* discussion. You likely will find that your staff are more attentive to each stage of your message when you give them time to have a dialogue with you about what has been conveyed. Also, you'll earn their respect. It will become evident to Gen Y that you are cognizant of their need to know the rationale behind tasks and that you are sensitive to the importance of transitioning slowly into new work assignments. In the end, you are likely to see more satisfied Gen Ys, and you will be on target to get the departmental work done.

We are on target, but there's more work to be done. There's a change in the sky overhead...

# Exploring change within–an invitation to try something new

We know that in order for our organization to compete and thrive in a world of unrelenting and unpredictable change, we must challenge the status quo throughout our organization—at the individual, departmental, and organizational levels. This entails inviting each employee in our organization to be vigilant, agile, and receptive to doing things differently in their own job domain.

An opportunity like this is highly attractive to our Gen Y staff; it satisfies a key need for them to be involved in initiatives that have a true business impact. However, getting Gen Y involved might be a tad more complicated than we think.

## Tuning in to Gen Y's wavelength

Generally speaking, Gen Y wants to be more involved in contributing ideas to enhance the work they've been assigned to do. However, they are hesitant to do so. According to Gen Y, the current organizational climate has not made it easy for them to openly and transparently offer their feedback and recommendations. In the past, they've attempted to exercise their leadership in this regard, but they haven't been received well. They faced, and continue to face, a wall of resistance that usually takes the form of the following:

➤ Why would we change when this is the way we've been doing things around here for the past 10 years?

➤ You've been here less than a few months, and you already want to change things?

➤ In my day, you were lucky you even had...

➤ There are too many risks involved with the changes you propose.

➤ That will never work.

Sound familiar? These common retorts have left Gen Y feeling disempowered and defeated and have discouraged them from coming forward with their ideas. Not having their voices heard in our organizations is one of the main contributors to their low levels of job satisfaction.

Yes, some of the ideas that they propose might be radical, impractical, and costly; yet, with some tweaking, the ideas that they bring forward might be worth considering. They might be just the shake-up that jobs and departments need in order to enhance efficiency and effectiveness.

As organizational leaders, we are in a key position to turn this situation around and, in doing so, heighten Gen Y's job satisfaction. If you are ready for the challenge, make a commitment to your Gen Y staff that you are receptive to their feedback and open to work with them to explore how their recommendations can be integrated into practice.

At the starting gate, invite them to hone in on their specific job and the changes they'd like to make. Invite them to do the following:

➤ Critique the effectiveness and efficiency of current practices, processes, guidelines, and systems in their jobs and in the department

➤ Recommend changes to the aforementioned, without censoring the feasibility of the ideas at this concept stage

➤ Propose new projects that contribute to the organization's strategic direction

➤ Advise on resource allocation to better support the work they do

➤ Propose ways in which they can personally and professionally contribute to their jobs

## Responding to Gen Y's input – are we clashing or collaborating?

When Gen Y comes back to you with their ideas, how will you respond? Here, you stand with a definite view of what Gen Y's job entails and how the assigned work feeds into departmental and organizational mandates. In front of you stands your Gen Y employee with a handful of freshly picked ideas for your consideration.

This is a pivotal moment. We can make considerable gains in enriching Gen Y's work experiences and increasing their levels of job satisfaction and job meaning if we are willing to do the following:

➤ Engage and support them genuinely and wholeheartedly in their quest for change

➤ Keep the dialogue open and resist the temptation to hastily dismiss their ideas

➤ Remain open minded to ideas that might be unconventional and take you outside of your personal comfort zone

Here are a few suggestions to manage the conversation. Inherent in these conversations might be the answers you've been looking for to nagging questions and concerns that your department has been wrestling with. Take the lead to:

➤ Listen deeply to proposals and consider the validity of each idea thoughtfully

➤ Ask for clarification if you aren't sure what is being proposed

➤ Paraphrase your understanding of recommendations to ensure you understand the message and to communicate to Gen Y that you really are listening

➤ Engage Gen Y in a discussion about the implications of moving their ideas into action

    ➢ Discuss the logistics of implementing their recommendations

    ➢ Share your concerns about possible impediments to implementation and canvass their feedback on how to minimize or overcome obstacles

    ➢ Discuss the role you and your Gen Y staff can play in moving recommendations into action

If there is even a shred of confidence that an idea has wings, consider giving it a test drive by implementing it for a trial period. You might have a few reservations upfront about the logistics of the implementation, but put Gen Y in charge of working out the details. By allowing them to play a lead role in the implementation, you further enhance their levels of job satisfaction and job meaning.

Monitor the initiative along the way and collect data at the end of the trial period to ascertain the contributions of the change and to determine if it is worthwhile moving the initiative more permanently into the job.

In *Chapter 8, Mentoring the Next Generation of Leaders – Legacy Building, One Gen Y at a Time,* we'll discuss rewards and recognition systems that support the efforts, contributions, and achievements of our Gen Y staff in this area.

# Exploring new horizons for Gen Y – the galaxy beyond their jobs

So far, our focus has been on ways to enhance Gen Y's work experiences *within* the jobs they were hired to do. However, our work is only partially done. There remains an entire domain *beyond* their jobs that offer Gen Y opportunities to:

➤ Fully enhance their level of job fulfilment

➤ Stretch further into their full potential

➤ Increase the likelihood of their long-term commitment to our organization

The next section invites us to step outside our traditional ways of organizing and assigning work. It takes us to a place where we are encouraged to release the reins of leadership to an even greater extent and provide Gen Y with more:

➤ Autonomy in charting their work day

➤ Ownership in decision making and problem solving

➤ Visibility and prominence in our organization

For some of us, this might be disconcerting as Gen Y has not been employed in our organizations for very long; hence, they may not have the institutional and industry knowledge to manage tasks that involve more autonomy and ownership. It is true that Gen Y might be a tad wobbly on their feet in these areas, but there likely are pockets of opportunities throughout our organization where they can flex their intellectual muscle and contribute their existing repertoire of skills and abilities.

We certainly need to be cognizant of the work assignments that we can realistically give to our Gen Y staff; yet, we also need to be willing to take a few risks to stretch with Gen Y into new horizons. In doing so, we contribute to Gen Y's personal and professional growth and development, and we might also set in motion our own personal reflection on how we lead and support our Gen Y staff to be successful. With eyes wide open for that which is practical and doable, yet propels us into the unknown where the richest learning awaits us, let's *explore the galaxy beyond* the jobs that Gen Y had been originally hired to do.

# Ideas that come from Jupiter, Mars, and Saturn

Every once in a while, a shining star comes into our lives with a significant lesson that we are meant to learn.

A few years ago, while on an assignment in a food manufacturing plant in the U.S., I was introduced to a spunky and fearless young lady. She was a true entrepreneurial spirit with bold ideas and an extraordinary ability to tell and sell.

She had a story to share.

Within 5 months of her employment, this self-assured Gen Y knocked on her supervisor's office door and pitched an idea for a new product line, which included a comprehensive **SWOT (strengths, weaknesses, opportunities, and threats)** analysis and detailed sales and revenue projections. She was hoping her supervisor would lead the initiative and invite her to be part of the implementation team. In response, her supervisor cast the idea aside without reading the proposal. He claimed that someone who had less than 1-year seniority in the company couldn't possibly comprehend the inner workings of the business well enough to propose anything of substance. A few days later, the Vice-President of Operations, getting wind of this proposal, called her to his office to hear the plan (ironically, on the afternoon she was composing her resignation letter).

To get right to the salient point, today, this Gen Y super star is the youngest supervisor in the company overseeing a team of 34 employees and managing the most successful product line in the organization's history. According to the Vice President, her knowledge of the organization was limited and her experience in the industry was dismal, but her progressive and quirky thinking, raw will power, and emerging leadership skills were exemplary. He surrounded her with a team of veterans who knew the organization and could provide her with the strategic intelligence she needed to make smart business decisions. The Vice-President admitted this was a huge risk for the company, but his instincts told him to proceed. Coupled with ongoing mentoring, a deluge of leadership support and resources, and heaps of courage and patience, they set sail on a new product line.

How do *you* respond when Gen Y knocks on your office door to pitch an idea?

## Responding to the pitch

Like the aforementioned example, are you willing to at least take into consideration those ideas that, on first blush, appear *to come from Jupiter, Mars, and Saturn*? That is, are you able to get past initial assumptions and attitudes that a generation of workers who have limited organizational and industry knowledge can't possibly offer ideas that have a true business impact? Even though not all of the ideas that Gen Y brings to you will be strokes of genius worthy of a supervisory role or organizational backing, there may be a few uncut gems that are the answers to burning challenges you face or could lead to the debut of new products and services that set your organization apart from others. In fact, the most innovative and creative ideas often come from our youngest generation in the workplace. Looking through a different set of glasses, Gen Y often sees what we've been missing. For some of us who have been in our organizations for a while, we can become so entrenched in the minutiae of daily operations that we are unable to objectively see the opportunities in front of us.

Gen Y can shed light on what we aren't hearing, seeing, or experiencing in our organization.

Here are a few suggestions to kick start the conversation with Gen Y the next time they knock on your door with an idea. The conversation is meant to be a high-end preliminary discussion to gauge the merits of the proposal and to propose further steps. The conversation will vary depending on the nature of the proposal, but the general framework is the same:

> ➤ Catch yourself prematurely dismissing an idea and refocus your attention
> ➤ Listen intently to the pitch by putting evaluative thoughts and commentary in abeyance
> ➤ Inquire about the origin of the idea
> ➤ Ask how they envision the idea being implemented in the organization
> ➤ Ask who they think can lend expertise to the initiative
> ➤ Ask for their high-end thoughts about strengths, weaknesses, opportunities, and risks of the idea, as they relate to the organization's mission, values, and strategic direction

If the idea peaks your curiosity and there appears to be merit in the proposal, work with Gen Y to roll out a more formal proposal that fleshes out the financial and nonfinancial details of the initiative. You are then ready to move the ideas forward through your organization's established channels for further consideration. The possibilities are endless!

In this section, our focus was on the *reactive* role you play, that is, how you can *respond* to your Gen Y staff when they pitch an idea. Equally important is taking a *proactive* role, that is, *encouraging* your Gen Y staff to actively search for ways to enrich their work experiences beyond the scope of their job.

## Encouraging them to keep pitching!

Do you encourage Gen Y to explore their work world beyond their assigned job? Yes, the jobs they were hired to do must get done, but this shouldn't ground them to a halt in exercising their curiosity about the organization and the industry from which ideas that solve problems or spark new initiatives might surface.

Gen Y thrives in a work environment that capitalizes on their strengths and engages them in projects that have a bottom-line impact. Along with heightened job satisfaction, these experiences contribute to the following:

> ➤ Higher performance and participation rates
> ➤ More volunteerism within our organization
> ➤ Greater loyalty to our organization
> ➤ An increased likelihood that they will remain with us

As these are the outcomes that we are striving for, it makes sense that we devote time to find out more about their backgrounds and how we can capitalize on the gifts and talents that they bring to our organization. Consider making time to explore the following:

➤ Breadth and depth of their skills and abilities developed from previous jobs and volunteer positions

➤ Subject matter expertise from their formal education

➤ Projects they've been involved in and what inspired and deflated them

➤ Extracurricular activities that ignite their excitement

➤ Knowledge, skills, and abilities they have developed from all walks of their life that they would like to hone as they progress through their careers

➤ Subject areas that ignite their curiosity and that they'd like to explore further

From here, encourage Gen Y to think about how they envision bringing their personal and professional experiences, knowledge, and training into the organization and industry. Inspire them to reflect on the infinite possibilities that exist far beyond their current jobs. They might not have an immediate response, but plant the seeds of curiosity and encourage unrestricted exploration. They may uncover a skill from their extracurricular activities that has relevance to your organization. For example, many extracurricular activities from snowboarding to video games have been capitalized on as fundraising and marketing initiatives in organizations.

Some of you might be questioning:

➤ How do we shoehorn these new ventures into a packed workday agenda?

➤ Aren't we just making more work for Gen Y and contributing to their burnout?

These are valid questions. At all costs, we want to avoid any workplace changes that contribute to employee burnout. Along with the physical and emotional toll that burnout takes on our employees, there are a host of organizational consequences with hefty price tags, such as the following:

➤ Increased error rates

➤ Decreased productivity

➤ Increased use of benefits such as prescription medications

➤ Higher levels of absenteeism

➤ Long-term disability leaves

In order to avoid these consequences, it is critically important to meet with your employee to discuss how space will be carved out in their current job in order to fulfil the responsibilities associated with new projects. Before adding any activity, discuss what can be streamlined, delegated, or removed from the employee's current job portfolio to make room for a new initiative.

Also, consider how dedicated space can be reserved during the work week or every other week for Gen Y to pursue initiatives that are outside the scope of their jobs. Consider allocating a half day or a full day each week where Gen Y—and actually everyone in your organization—can take part in activities beyond their assigned tasks. This could include the following:

> Reflection time that is the incubator of creativity and innovation

> Brainstorming pathways for an idea that is bubbling

> Collaborating with other staff on an initiative that merges their skills and interests

> Volunteer work in the community that strengths your organization's community presence and commitment

> Working on initiatives

By having this dedicated time to pursue interests that ignite passion and excitement, we reap the benefits discussed earlier, namely, increased Gen Y job satisfaction and their commitment to the organization.

# Looking through the telescope

*Cassiopeia? Orion? Polaris? All I see is a bunch of stars!*

To the best of your knowledge, everything is progressing well in your department. Your Gen Y staff appear to be engaged fully in the work they are doing; they are industriously seeking ways to enrich their jobs, and they are participating energetically in new ventures, outside of their jobs, that capitalize on their skills and abilities.

You *see a bunch of stars*; yet, your Gen Y staff see *Cassiopeia, Orion, and Polaris*, that is, your view of the workplace can be very different from that of your Gen Y staff. During any given day, we can be so consumed with our work that if we don't hear of any troubles underfoot, then we assume everything is progressing well, and we carry on with business as usual. Yet, in the deep silence, an issue could be lurking. It may intensify under the cover of night without your awareness to the point where a staff member becomes so distraught and frustrated that the only solution in their mind is to resign. As we know, Gen Y tends to not be very forthcoming in sharing that which troubles them. They tend to harbor a great deal inside, and if they don't see change on the horizon, they likely will search for employment elsewhere. Soon, the resignation letter is on your desk.

As you know, resignations are costly for an organization. They put us back on the treadmill of recruitment, selection, reference checking, orientation, training, and patiently enduring higher than usual on-the-job error rates as new recruits are in the learning curve. If we have high turnover in our organization, it plays havoc with our attempts to build a strong and stable workforce, which is the essence of our viability. Also, when Gen Y resigns, we are never certain how far and wide they will share their views and opinions of us with their personal and professional networks. This becomes worrisome and incalculable cost.

In order to be fully aware of how our Gen Y staff is thinking about their workplace experiences with us and to resolve issues before we are served with a resignation notice, consider periodically checking in with them. Check-ins are especially critical when substantial changes have been made in their work lives, such as the launch of new projects and initiatives beyond the parameters of their jobs. Schedule an informal conversation with each staff member to check in on how things are progressing. Use this as an opportunity to get a glimpse at what they are thinking, how they are thinking, and what questions and issues are brewing. For example:

> Highlights of their work experiences

> Aspects of their work experiences that invite change

> What they can commit to do differently to enhance their work experience

> How you can join them in enhancing their work experience

If we apply the skill, which we learned in *Chapter 4, Unlocking the Secrets to Awesome Conversations with Gen Y*, on how to have awesome conversations with Gen Y to our check-ins, then we likely will receive feedback about Gen Y's work experiences that is plentiful and meaningful. By asking our Gen Y staff *what they see when they look through the telescope*, we do the following:

> Keep the lines of communication open

> Find out what is too much, too little, or just the right amount for them in their work experiences

> Join them in co-creating work experiences that have value for them

> Minimize the probability that you receive their resignation letters soon after they've been hired

This might be a meeting request that you extend to everyone, not only to your Gen Y staff. There is value in checking in with everyone to inquire about their work experiences along the way.

# Falling stars – learning how to fall with grace and grit

Recently, I had lunch with a former student of mine who, over the course of 7 years, launched five businesses—one failure after another until finally, his current business has some teeth and is starting to show a profit. He declared bankruptcy, hooked up with the wrong business partners, invested in ventures that weren't lucrative, and chased entrepreneurial dreams that had no market relevance. As he recounted his harrowing tale, I was in absolute awe of his resilience, determination, and ability to maintain his sense of humor.

In those 7 years, he learned the most salient of life's lessons—how to fall with grace and grit. This is an integral lesson not only for Gen Y, but for all of us.

We've spent a considerable amount of time in this chapter discussing approaches we can use to encourage Gen Y to critically think about changes in their jobs and ways in which they can lend their skills to initiatives throughout the organization. In both cases, this requires risk taking, and with risk taking comes an increased probability of failure. If we are going to encourage our Gen Y staff to be adventurous in how they contribute to our organization and step outside their comfort zone to test drive new skills and abilities, then it only make sense that we provide them with a guiding hand in how to fall—just in case it happens. If we don't provide them with some fundamental survival tools in this regard, then we increase the probability that, when they experience a blow to their ego, they retreat to the comforts of their job routines. Once they return to creature comforts, job satisfaction and job meaning will likely wane, and from there, it is a short distance from making a decision to leave our organization. Added to this, if Gen Y becomes risk adverse, then our organization suffers; the incubator of ideas dwindles because Gen Y is no longer willing to take risks that mobilize change in our organization.

In this section, we'll explore how we can guide Gen Y in developing one of the most important skills that they will need in their personal and professional lives and one that will set them apart as star performers in our organizations—managing how to fall with grace and grit. Specifically, we'll explore how to shift attitudes toward failure and tackle it head-on when it happens. In the journey that unfolds, I'm thinking—and hoping—there might also be a few lessons for all of us, not just for our Gen Ys.

# Falling, falling, rising!

Many of us, including Gen Y, cower when we hear the word "failure" and recoil even more when we personally experience it. The word can echo incessantly in our ears and weigh heavily on our hearts. We replay the scenario that led to our demise over and over, envisioning everything we did wrong in graphic detail and narrating the story with some potent self-deprecating commentary. The more we revisit the story in our mind, the more likely we spiral downward into a puddle of pity and depression, which can crush our self-confidence and self-esteem. Failure can be one of the most debilitating life experiences.

Why is that? Why can failure bring us to our knees? For most of us, we never learned *how* to fall and, more importantly, how to rise from our failure. Amongst the subjects we learned in school—Math, Science, Geography, English, History—learning how to manage failure wasn't part of the curriculum. For many of us, including Gen Y, we grew up learning that failure is bad; it is to be avoided, and we must steer clear of taking risks that could potentially lead to failure. Added to this, Gen Y, for the most part, was raised in a safe and secure home environment where they were sheltered from failure. As a result, they likely have less experience responding to and managing life's letdowns.

Whether we are the older or younger generation in the workplace, failure is considered a death nail in our careers. Yet, it doesn't need to be. We have the capacity to stop it from being our ruination and to transform it into our asset. Failure can be a golden learning experience; it is from failure that our most significant learning comes. We don't learn when things are going well, that is, we hardly give a second thought to our actions and reactions when everything is progressing well and when a shower of accolades is bestowed upon us.

In such cases, nothing triggers a need to be reflective about what we are doing, how we are doing it, or why. We graciously acknowledge the praise and recognition, and we proceed to the next item on our to-do list that requires our attention. Failure, however, abruptly stops us in our tracks. It is when we fall in a hole that we become cognizant of a new reality. We replay a video in our mind, trying to find out what went wrong. More importantly, we come to realize our fallibility and what it reveals about us.

Gen Y's capacity for personal and professional growth and development lies in how they make sense of failures and use the insights gleaned from the experience to minimize or eliminate the probability of falling into the same hole again. Learning how to fall is an exercise in building character. It strengthens one's resolve and confidence to continue taking risks, knowing that we might fall again, but next time, we are better equipped with skills to cope and move onward.

Learning how to fall is a more organic journey than a linear one, that is, there is no step-by-step approach that will take us to the promise land of falling with grace and grit. However, will discuss some ways to think about failure and reframe it so that Gen Y can grow from the experience personally and professionally. Here are a few life lessons to share with Gen Y as they reconcile falling with the person they aspire to be.

Reframing Gen Y's thinking about failure:

➤ **Failure is inevitable**: You can't escape it, but you can learn how to respond to it

➤ **Separate the failure from the person**: We are not defined by our failures

➤ **Be gentle with yourself**: We are incorrigible when it comes to self-criticism

➤ **Reframe failure as an opportunity to learn and develop**: It is an asset in disguise

➤ **Process it and then let it go**: Stop the insanity of replaying it in your mind

Moving through failure:

➤ **Vent your emotions**: Put the intensity of the pain into words.

➤ **Articulate what happened**: Describe your actions in detail.

➤ **Process why it happen**: Dig into the root cause of why you fell.

➤ **Plan to minimize a reoccurrence**: Describe what you will do differently to minimize the probability of a reoccurrence.

➤ **Keep taking risks**: If failure arises again, lean in and learn.

➤ **Be in your grace and grit**: When you fall, brush yourself off, put a bandage on your skinned knee, and walk forward with grace and grit. Do not let the event define who you have yet to become.

➤ **Go through it, not over it, or under it**: Tackle failure head-on. Never avoid it!

It is easier to state these life lessons than it is to embrace and live them in our daily lives. It requires discipline to constantly be reframing one's views about failure, from that which paralyzes us to that which can be our greatest ally. Keep working with Gen Y as they develop skills to respond to and manage failure, and be prepared to pull them out of the dark hole if they appear to be struggling along the way. Keep reminding them of the messages mentioned earlier until that which is uncomfortable for them to think about and deal with becomes their strength in their personal and professional presence.

# Morphing into a culture that knows how to fall

As important as *risk taking* and *learning how to fall* are to the personal and professional development of Gen Y, they are equally important to the entire organization. If our goal is to brand and situate our organization as cutting edge apart from others, then advocating for a culture of risk taking and learning how to fall is integral to reaching that goal. It is only when our staff lean into the unknown and dare to think and act in bold and grand ways that the crystals of creativity and innovation gel and thrust them in unimaginable directions that can position us as industry trend setters.

However, many organizations baulk at the thought of taking risks where the potential for failure awaits them. They air so much on the side of caution by making predictable moves to avoid failure, that they simply don't know how to respond to and manage them. The play-it-safe mentality that we spoke about earlier permeates our organizations. Yet, if we truly aspire to be progressive and sustainable, we need to break free from thinking that failure is our demise. If you speak to people who are successful (in whatever way you define success), you'll likely discover a litany of stories about their toils and tribulations en route to their current success.

In order to become a culture that is willing and able to take risks because it is comfortable responding to and managing failure (if and when it surfaces), we start by setting the following in motion:

➤ Openly and transparently discussing failure

➤ Embracing the inevitability of failure that comes with risk taking

➤ Establishing guidelines to respond to and rise above failure

The messages we communicated to Gen Y about responding to failure, which were summarized in the previous section, are relevant for all staff and can help establish a norm of acceptance for failure. Also, consider how you can integrate risk taking and learning how to fall into the fabric of your organization's culture in areas such as the following:

➤ Value, vision, and mission statements

➤ Strategic plan including guidelines for how to manage failure when it arises

➤ Forums, such as town hall meetings, that put failures on the table and invite staff to discuss lessons learned and to chart pathways forward

➤ Performance evaluations that include risk taking as a performance criteria

➤ Goal-setting initiatives that promote stretching beyond the comfort zone

➤ Reward and recognition systems that honor risk taking

- ➤ Recruitment and selection that include risk taking as a hiring criteria

- ➤ Inclusion of risk taking in employees' job descriptions and job specifications

- ➤ Learning and development workshops that help staff reframe their thinking about risk taking and failure and develop tools to manage forward when they fall

Having said this, there is a note of caution to be added. We can accept mistakes that arise occasionally, but if someone keeps making the same mistake repeatedly, this is of concern. It calls on us to have a performance-management conversation with them, which we'll cover in *Chapter 6, Performance Management– Becoming Hyper-Intentional About Sustainability*.

# Reframing challenges as opportunities

One day, a few weeks or months after they've been hired and when you least expect it, one of your Gen Y staff will come into your office and announce, *I'm ready to be a manager.*

They hammer a stake in the ground and declare confidently that they want a management role …now. We shake our heads in gobsmacking disbelief. Our youngest generation in the workplace just arrived in our organization a short time ago, they barely understand our organizational landscape, and now they want to be promoted to the ranks of management? Seriously?

This is a common declaration coming from our youngest generation soon after they've joined us. In response, we immediately don our shield of resistance. We tell our new Gen Ys that it just isn't possible. That's just not the way we do things around here. You have to earn your way into these roles by doing the following:

- ➤ Working really hard to get noticed

- ➤ Establishing credibility in the organization and industry

- ➤ Honing an exemplary track record of achievements and contributions

- ➤ Learning at the heels of those who are more experienced in the business

For good measure, we might even add:

> *In our day, you had to prove you were worthy of a leadership role by displaying your burgeoning list of credentials, accomplishments, and contributions before anyone would give you a nod for the coveted management roost. Added to this, you had to wait your turn as others before you with more seniority, more experience, and more education were considered. Sometimes, you just had to wait until someone finally retired or resigned from the company so that you could claw your way through the competition for the job. That's the way it works in business!*

We go on and on and on….

With each passing word, we lose Gen Y…

Let's rewind the conversation. Let's think about how we can keep the channels of communication open and, perhaps, reach outcomes that are desired by you and Gen Y.

Instead of responding with a slew of reasons why Gen Y can't be managers this early in their careers and dismissing their request, consider asking them to roll out a more detailed proposal of their request that includes the following:

➤ Managerial role they envision for themselves

➤ Accountabilities to be entailed in this role

➤ How the role aligns with and contributes to the organization's mission, vision, and strategic direction

➤ Skill set they can bring to a managerial position, including their ability to influence and lead change

➤ All the brilliant reasons why you should not turn down the opportunity to promote them to a leadership role

A formal proposal might reveal a legitimate contribution that they can make to your organization and how they plan to fill an important gap in your organization's strategic direction. With support such as mentoring or placing them in an assistant leadership role as a trial run in place, this could possibly work. If there isn't merit in continuing the discussion about how you'll be promoting Gen Y into a leadership role at this point in their career, then the proposal provides the basis for you to discuss with Gen Y your specific reasons to decline the invitation. Rather than focusing on the fact that they are too young and inexperienced to join the leadership ranks, the focus is on whether another leadership role is warranted in the organization and what specific needs it can fill as it relates to the organization's future.

# Leaning in to change

Is there an emerging Gen Y superstar in your team?

What is the approach you can take to inspire this person to reach their full potential in your organization with all the benefits of job satisfaction and job meaning for them and heightened job performance for you and your organization? How might you:

➤ Invite them to think about their own job and changes they'd like to make

➤ Encourage them to reflect on how they envision bringing their skills from their personal and professional experiences into the organization

➤ Encourage them to keep lines of communication open as you explore with them opportunities to expand their talents in their current jobs and in projects beyond the scope of their job

➤ Inspire them to be risk takers and be bold in the face of falling

When the time is right, sit down with your staff for a conversation about how you can collaborate with them to become the rising star performer in your organization. I'm eager to read about your experiences and respond to your questions about the content we've explored in this chapter. I'll watch for you online (www.eyeofthetigerconsulting.ca)!

# Google it

If you are interested in reading more about the topic, please consult the following resources:

➤ R., Benincasa, *How Winning Works*, Harlequin, 2012

➤ T., Erickson,. *Plugged In: the Generation Y Guide to Thriving at Work*, Harvard Business Press, 2008

➤ C., Martin, From high maintenance to high productivity: What managers need to know about Generation Y, *Industrial and Commercial Training.* 37(1), 39-44, 2005

➤ John C., Maxwell *Sometimes You Win, Sometimes You Learn*, Center Street, 2013

➤ T., Schwartz, *The Way We're Working Isn't Working*, Free Press, 2010

➤ S., Sinek, *Start with WHY: How Great Leaders Inspire Everyone to Take Action*, Penguin Books, 2009

# Meeting the Gen Y community – introducing...Peggy Liu!

*What can organizations do to create and sustain a workplace that:*

➤ *Gets the best from its Gen Y staff*

➤ *Supports rising star achievers*

➤ *Is proclaimed as a place where people want to work*

Peggy insightfully spoke about Gen Y's *"pursuit of happiness"* that entails finding not *"just a job"*, but *"a career they can truly be passionate about"*. According to Peggy, if we really want to get the best from our Gen Y staff, we begin by taking initiative to break down hierarchical barriers that exist in our organization, especially restrictive channels of communication. This way, staff—regardless of the position title—can dialogue and get to know each other. As Peggy noted, *"creating a friendly, open, and informal environment where everyone gets to see and know the individual fully sets the right climate for work"*. Adding to this, Peggy says that Gen Y wants to work for an organization that cares about corporate social responsibility. She encourages us to provide opportunities for Gen Y to get involved in volunteer initiatives that contribute to the good of society.

In order to support rising star achievers, Peggy suggests mentoring programs where Gen Y can have one-on-one learning exchanges with seasoned staff. Mentoring offers the guidance and support that Gen Y is looking for, especially when they are tackling new projects and when something goes wrong. Gen Y wants to know that there is someone there who can guide them through the challenges they'll face as they go through their careers. In the mentoring relationship, Peggy urges us to be transparent, provide clear objectives and expectations on projects, and give them the space to figure out how to contribute to the organization.

Peggy's final message to us is about the importance of paying attention to our organization's culture if we want to be known as the place where people want to work. This starts with realizing, communicating, and engaging in decision making that conveys, "*our employees are our asset*". Creating a collaborative work environment where everyone is treated the same, diversity is honored, and there are no structures that prevent us from being equals is far more important than pursuing money. When we treat employees respectfully and fairly, they likely will be happier, and this translates into high performance and profitability for the company. As Peggy says, "*Notice who we are ahead of the profit we can make for you.*"

> *Peggy is studying Hospitality Management at Royal Roads University in Victoria, British Columbia, and she aspires to be a general manager by the time she is 30 years of age. The hospitality industry appeals to Peggy because of the many opportunities it gives her to interact with people from diverse backgrounds. Peggy would like to be known in her career as a successful person who is grounded in caring for and giving back to the community. When Peggy isn't studying, she enjoys hiking, trying out the latest restaurants —she loves the diversity found in food—and being in the company of good friends.*

# Summary

In this chapter, we focused on approaches we can use to develop star Gen Y performers in our organization in order to increase job satisfaction and job meaning for them and to heighten job performance and increase Gen Y retention rates for us. We started with the Big Bang Theory, where we explored how to transmit new messages and promote change from within. When gamma-rays were firing on all cylinders, we explored new horizons for Gen Y, beyond their jobs. We learned how to respond to and encourage ideas that appear to come from Jupiter, Mars, and Saturn. We then concluded with a discussion about falling stars and how to embrace a partial eclipse of the Sun.

Keep looking through the telescope—what do you see and what do your Gen Y staff see?

Chapter 6 is next. It's time to untangle how we manage day-to-day performance in a Gen Y world.

# 6

# Performance Management– Becoming Hyperintentional About Sustainability

*They arrive at the office, coffee in one hand, smartphone in the other.*

*They send a few text messages, chat with colleagues, and then they're off and running! Ahead is an action-filled day of Skype meetings with clients, think-tank sessions to brainstorm new marketing ideas, and spontaneously erupting talks between meetings that will ignite the next best collaboration when least expected. The day is full of possibilities.*

*And you? What are you doing while Gen Y settles into this new workplace reality that we've co-created with them on the heels of coming out of Chapter 5?*

So far, we've trekked a long distance together, and we've navigated some rugged terrain. We have foraged for answers to niggling questions about working with Gen Y, and we have pored over ways to create the awesomeness that Gen Y looks for in our workplaces. The journey has demanded a great deal from us as organizational leaders. We've been called to do the following:

> ➤ Refresh recruitment and selection initiatives to secure the best Gen Y talent

> ➤ Rethink onboarding and training to acclimatize Gen Y to our workplace

> ➤ Master new skills in order to have great conversations with Gen Y

> ➤ Revamp job designs so that work experiences for Gen Y are powerful and memorable

Yet, we risk losing ground on the progress we've made unless we are willing to hike one more mile and climb over one more rock. The success and survival of our workplace initiatives for Gen Y as well as our organization as a whole are dependent on our appetite and commitment to invest in measures that enhance the *sustainability* of what we've ardently put in place. As you likely know, scores of organizational initiatives plummet to their demise despite best intentions to keep them alive. The reasons for their collapse are vast, but the solution tends to point to a common denominator— sustainability management. If we devoted so much time to acquire, develop, and create satisfying work for our Gen Y staff, then why wouldn't we map out a sustainability strategy that protects our investment and takes us further toward the organizational rewards of high performance and productivity?

Sustainability hinges on *performance management*. It is the enduring and unwavering commitment that we make to gather, analyze, evaluate, and communicate information to Gen Y about how their job performance, workplace conduct, and results relate to our organization's mandate and goals. Its breadth is expansive, ranging from informal conversations to formal performance appraisals. As you noticed, the title of this chapter invites us to be *hyperintentional*. This is not just another task that sits on our daily to-do list that may or may not get done based on the myriad of duties we are accountable for. This is a priority item that requires us to exercise our due diligence to put in place the right checks and balances to manage performance in our units.

In this chapter, we'll hone in on performance-management approaches you can use in your daily interactions with Gen Y staff. It also focuses on how you can develop and conduct effective performance appraisals. Our travels take us into the following three topics:

> ➤ Managing daily performance—the secret sauce to get things just right

> ➤ Developing performance appraisals—a new GPS for Gen Y

> ➤ Navigating the unexpected—when performance gets a flat tire

Our goal is to develop a trademark approach and style in performance management that fosters high performance and strong employee relations. We might even become the envy of other organizations and establish a new benchmark standard that others aspire to achieve.

# So, what's burning?

While riding the subway in New York a few years back, I found myself sitting next to a distinguished executive from a law firm. He noticed that I was reading a book on managing workplace performance and he struck up a conversation with me. He asked my opinion of the topic, but before I could finish my highly enlightening little sermon from Mount Carolin, he grimaced, shook his head incredulously, and said:

> *As I see it, performance management is a waste of time. I'm a business person, and my priority is to attend to my existing clients and acquire new ones. Clients are the source of my revenue and the reason why our firm remains viable in a cutthroat industry. Every minute is a billable minute, and I'm not going to waste it meandering around the office, asking if the staff is happy today. How would you explain this to our management board?*

> *This is my advice to my staff: you've been trained—now do your job. If you need me—ask. If you are doing something wrong—I'll tell you. Get on with it.*

Oh bliss! The lessons to be learned on the tracks winding through the Big Apple!

I often hear similar skepticism from organizational leaders who are already burdened with the daily complexities of managing a business. They question how going the extra distance to manage performance is a strategically smart business maneuver, especially given the mind-boggling unpredictability and volatility of the global marketplace in which we operate. Yes, time is money, and the bottom line of every activity needs to be justified. Yet, can I persuade you to listen for one billable minute, if I tell you we can actually *make more money* if we invest in performance management?

If we fumble through the performance management process or fail to exercise our leadership in managing its intricacies, we risk a host of time depleting human resources issues. By not managing performance proactively through informal and formal means, we run the risk of appreciably increasing the amount of time we spend listening to, ruminating over, and determining resolutions to employee-related problems. This can result in a considerable financial drain on our organization's coffers. Specifically, costly problems stem from this spiraling downward chain of events:

> ➤ Employees who feel that they are not receiving enough quality performance feedback become job dissatisfied and disillusioned, and they soon work below their potential and your standards and expectations.

> ➤ Escalating substandard deliverables and increased errors resulting from work that is below standard.

> ➤ An increased number of complaints from clients and customers about substandard service, which can lead to cancelation of their contracts with you.

> ➤ A burgeoning number of employee grievances for you to address about decisions made based on staff performance, which they claim you rarely take notice of. This is especially the case as it pertains to merit and promotion decisions.

> ➤ Increased employee absenteeism that results from reprimands about lackluster performance.

> ➤ Likelihood of dysfunctional turnover, that is, losing star Gen Y performers to the competition.

Performance management is of considerable strategic importance to today's organizations, because the most effective way to differentiate a business in a highly competitive, service-oriented global marketplace is through the quality of its employees. A well-designed and well-facilitated performance-management system represents a largely untapped opportunity to improve company profitability.

If designed and managed effectively, a performance-management process can have far reaching benefits for you, your staff, and the entire organization. The benefits include the following:

> ➤ Early detection of ineffective performance so that remedies can be sought before it becomes increasingly more problematic and costly

> ➤ Revelation of systemic barriers that inhibit Gen Y from reaching peak performance that you may not be aware of and are hurting your business

> ➤ More valid and reliable information on which you base salary and promotion decisions, which will increase perceptions of fairness and equity and cut down on employee grievances about decisions in these areas

> ➤ Provision of more accurate information about their capabilities and aptitudes, which:

> > ➢ Highlights specific training and development needs they may have, which creates a culture of continuous learning in the organization

> > ➢ Supports talent management and succession planning for the next generation of leaders in your organization, which we will cover in *Chapter 8, Mentoring the Next Generation of Leaders – Legacy Building, One Gen Y at a Time*

> ➤ Creating a high-performance culture when Gen Y knows you are invested in their careers by engaging often with them to do the following:

> > ➢ Acknowledge and celebrate their contributions and achievements

> > ➢ Pinpoint performance improvements that are needed

> > ➢ Offer resources to guide them through troubled waters and to support their ascent to new professional plateaus

Overall, your business runs smoother, and it is more likely to soar when employees are aware of how they are performing, and they have access to resources that support their job performance and career aspirations.

One final thought. Our New York subway companion asked an astute question: *How would you explain that to our management board?* I'd like to know how you explain to the management board why you *aren't* paying closer attention to performance management.

# Managing daily performance – the secret sauce for getting things just right

I recall a situation in a manufacturing plant when one of our Gen Y employees chose not to complete the required paperwork on health and safety incidents, because he deemed the documentation of "near misses on the worksite" to be unnecessary. He didn't consult with his supervisor or his colleagues; he just stopped filling out the form. Others caught wind of this, saw no attempt by the management to correct the situation, and followed suit. It was unanimous across the unit that the document served no purpose. Eight months later, the Manager of Health and Safety was in need of a paper trail of health and safety incidents to make a case for improvements to workplace safety. To his amazement, there were no written records of any incidents even though he was privy to many stories about close calls in the plant. Without solid evidence, he was unsuccessful in making a persuasive argument to the upper management for change in workplace practices; hence, his attempt for safety reform was aborted. The decision by employees to sidestep a performance requirement, coupled with the management not catching this sooner, were to the detriment of the employees who would have benefited from enhanced health and safety coverage. To this day, the management and staff maintain that the additional benefits likely would have been instrumental in minimizing a number of serious accidents that happened in the months that followed.

This example highlights the role that we, as organizational leaders, play in managing daily performance. Specifically, it reinforces our role in making the link between their performance and conduct and the organization's performance criteria and overall objectives explicit to our employees. When we make the connections clear, we better position our employees to hold themselves accountable for their own workplace behavior, which is one of our key goals.

Along the way, however, there might be times when our employees question the significance of performance standards, and they may decide to change or outright ignore the standard. Like a slow intravenous drip, seemingly minor wanderings away from performance standards that go undetected, unaddressed, or ignored can escalate and give way to more serious performance disruptions. These have dire consequences for you, your team, and your organization. Our leadership is integral in keeping performance standards and expectations at the forefront of employees' consciousness. Yet, at the ground level and on a daily basis, what exactly are we expected to do? What specifically is the *secret sauce*, that is, the right amount and the right intensity of daily performance management?

*What's too much? What's too little? What's just right?*

# What's too much

*He's hovering, again…*

*You are sitting in your office absorbed in writing a report, and your supervisor wanders in and hovers over you. He is literally looking over your shoulders and reading as you type. Quietly, he reads, and then, in a blink, you are pelted with a hailstorm of questions: Why did you take that approach? Are you missing a key reference? Does that sentence make sense? Did you set the right tone?*

If *you* were in this situation, how would you react?

Affectionately known as the *helicopter supervisor,* supervisors like the one described above contribute to one of Gen Y's more distressing experiences in the workplace. For Gen Y, scenarios like this will result in the following:

➤ Stripping them off their autonomy to chart their own direction and make decisions

➤ Depriving them off the enjoyment and challenge of trudging through the early stages of a project in search of a linear pathway that eventually reveals itself

➤ Signaling a lack of trust in their capabilities

➤ Eroding self-confidence in their abilities, because we signal that our close supervision is needed

➤ Diminishing job meaning, which we've been trying to create for them

➤ Disrupting their concentration

Along with the evils of micromanagement, Gen Y offers us the following list of equally distressing experiences that are under the dome of *what's too much*:

➤ Inconsistent messages about performance standards, which usually manifest themselves when there is more than one supervisor overseeing a unit.

➤ Preferential treatment of some staff members, which is a hot-button topic for Gen Y who are acutely aware of it.

➤ Detailed accounts of how *you* would complete an assignment if it were assigned to you, which usually clashes with how Gen Y would tackle the task.

➤ Stepping in, more often than appreciated, with advice on how they should improve performance. Gen Y feels suffocated by the well-intentioned input about what they *should* and *need* to do.

Conversely, let's not slide to the polar opposite side and start doing *too little* as it pertains to managing performance. This can have equally unappealing consequences for Gen Y.

# What's too little

I was struck by the candidness of a Gen Y employee who I had the privilege of meeting while conducting research on Gen Y's plans for the workplace when they assume leadership roles. She shared the following with me that speaks to the impact of *too little* performance management and a sentiment that was more widely held by Gen Y than I expected. This was her message to her supervisor:

> *I remember our conversation when I started the job. You told me that if I don't hear from you, I can assume that I am doing a good job. At first, I thought I could live with this. As time went by, I realized I can't, and I shouldn't have to. I don't want to assume anything. I want someone to go out of their way to tell me I'm doing a good job. I need to hear it from you. I need you to affirm that how I perceive my successes are appreciated by you and this company.*

This punctuates the importance of daily interaction with our Gen Y staff. Yes, they value independence, but they don't want to be left completely to their own devices during the course of the day. Not engaging with Gen Y often diminishes the credibility of the feedback that we occasionally give them, and it undermines the value of performance-improvement initiatives that we recommend to them during their annual performance appraisals.

Also included in Gen Y's lineup of agonizing experiences under the category of *what's too little* as it pertains to performance management are the following:

➤ Standards that are irrelevant and unrealistic, that is, they are based on our assumptions of acceptable performance instead of being derived from job analysis

➤ Poor measures of performance standards, especially performance appraisals that are poorly executed, and focus on the person and not on the outputs expected from the job

➤ Lack of feedback on their achievements and areas for improvement that are grounded in performance standards

➤ Perception that some supervisors choose to ignore poor performance from some employees, or they choose to give higher than deserved praise to these employees in order to avoid confrontation and to be viewed favorably in everyone's eyes

➤ Orientation and training that does not go far enough in explaining performance standards and how they align with organizational objectives

In the end, one question remains for us to answer: *what's just right?*

# What's just right?

This is about finding the *right balance* between Gen Y's need for autonomy and our obligation to manage performance. It would be easy to simply advise you to do the opposite of what Gen Y experiences as *too much* and *too little*, but I'd like to offer something more nourishing. However, you are welcome to return to the previous sections and pledge allegiance to *not* advocate for, espouse, or soldier on with practices that appear on the hit list of being *too much* and *too little*.

Striking the *right balance* provides the right mix of encouragement and advice to support achievement of performance standards, and it doesn't cross the line in being over bearing in Gen Y's development. At the end of the day, the *right balance* conveys our faith in Gen Y to reach and exceed performance standards. This goes a long way in building Gen Y's confidence, job satisfaction, and a sense of belonging to our organization.

In order to achieve the *right balance*, here are a few guidelines to manage daily performance. Before integrating these guidelines into practice, please keep in mind the importance of custom fitting them to your needs and the needs of Gen Y. Every Gen Y staff member is a unique individual, and this needs to be respected in how you engage with them. Having said this, here is a general framework to manage daily performance:

➤ Dialog with Gen Y about their job description and performance standards and appraise their performance relative to the aforementioned aspects.

➤ Replace vague generalities such as "great work" with examples of specific, observable behaviors that speaks to efforts, contributions, and achievements.

➤ Keep the perils of rater errors on your radar screen in order to minimize the probability that they affect how you give feedback:

➢ Recency effect: Commenting on recent behavior only and not referring to how recent and past behavior are connected and changing over time

➢ Similar-to-me bias: Projecting your values onto others and assessing their behavior as *right* or *wrong* based on your code of conduct

➢ The halo or horn effect: Inability to differentiate between someone's strengths and limitations, hence making sweeping generalizations that their performance is entirely positive or negative

➤ Be consistent in how you give praise and constructive feedback to your staff. You may want to review the guidelines on giving and receiving feedback in *Chapter 4, Unlocking the Secrets to Awesome Conversations with Gen Y*.

➤ Refrain from leaping in with advice for Gen Y on how they *should* improve performance. Facilitate their critical thinking and problem-solving skills by asking questions that guide them through the following situations:

➢ Brainstorming possible courses of action for improved performance

➢ Weighing up the strengths and shortcomings of each option

➢ Choosing a course of action that is best for them and your organization

➢ Proposing and committing to how they will improve performance

➤ Recognizing and celebrating milestone achievements in their career, and as a vehicle to determine the next phase in their career

➤ Often underscoring the integral role your Gen Y staff collectively play in achieving your organization's mission and objectives; this conveys to them that they are valued contributors to your organization

Some of you might be questioning how managing performance, as suggested earlier, can be executed in a culture of telecommuting. Working from home during part of the week is a growing trend in the workplace and can make performance management more complicated, but it is still manageable. For staff working from home, establish guidelines that require them to be available for consultation by Skype or other videoconferencing capabilities. In doing so, you can achieve much of the performance management agenda mentioned earlier. Also, you have the advantage of face-to-face discussions that allow you to notice nonverbal cues and respond to them if required.

Whether you are working with Gen Y in person or from a distance, how will you know if you are on target? According to Gen Y, *ask them*. Be willing to ask them about whether the conversations are truly helpful in solidifying their understanding of job expectations and motivating them to perform accordingly and beyond.

In our daily efforts to reinforce the interdependence between Gen Y's performance and our organization's goals, we move closer to building an organizational culture that is collectively mindful of this connectivity and channels their efforts accordingly. With this shared stream of consciousness, we create the most solid and enviable organizational culture that can weather unforeseen storms, which threaten the viability of our organization.

We now head deeper into the topic and explore systems to appraise performance.

# Developing performance appraisals – a new GPS for Gen Y

Many of the performance-appraisal systems used in organizations today miss the target, especially for our Gen Y workforce. I learned this the brutally tough way.

Five years ago, one of my clients in the high-tech sector asked me to design a performance-appraisal system for her predominantly Gen Y staff. I designed an assessment grounded in **behaviorally anchored rating scales (BARS)**, which consisted of scales that were quantified with specific behavioral examples ranging from poor to exemplary performance. This means that instead of standalone rating scales from 1 (poor) to 5 (outstanding), there was a description of behavior at each point on the scales. This reinforced the key tasks and performance standards expected at level 5.

At the end of the first round of evaluations, I invited the staff to participate in a focus group to get their feedback on the performance-appraisal system. The Gen Y jury returned a unanimous verdict—"guilty of crashing and burning". The process neither inspired them to do their best work nor guided their professional development. It was a human resources nightmare on the grandest of scales.

Armed with their feedback, I scrapped BARS, went back sheepishly to the beginning, and started to envision a performance appraisal more befitting of Gen Y and one that would meet the needs and expectations of the organization's leadership team. The next offering was radically different from the BARS format proposed. I presented the new framework to the team with trepidation; I wasn't sure if the proposal would be butchered or blessed. The verdict? In the words of Gen Y, "it rocks!". The approach that was endorsed by Gen Y and the executive 5 years ago continues to be used with great success in their organization today.

In this section, I'll share with you the approach we used and pass along the lessons learned. By no means am I advocating that this is the only way to evaluate Gen Y's performance; there likely are many routes yet to be discovered. I merely offer a few ideas based on my own experiences in the trenches as a starting point in hopes that you will tweak and massage the process and create something uniquely refreshing and relevant for your own organization.

We begin by exploring tools we can use for evaluation. Specifically, the spotlight is on establishing a system that serves the following purposes:

> ➤ **Formative or developmental**: This acknowledges Gen Y's productivity and strengths, coaches them through performance improvements, and encourages them to envision their future with the organization through goal setting

> ➤ **Summative or evaluative**: This serves as a basis for making valid, reliable, and fair promotion and salary decisions

Grounded in these two orientations, our performance evaluations are positioned to make explicit the link between individual performance, quality improvement, rewards, and our organization's mission and priorities.

# How to evaluate

In the story above, I spent 6 months working with the team on job restructuring even before I began developing a performance appraisal for them. Many of the practices for job design from *Chapter 5, Inspiring Star Performance– Reaching Seriously for Sirius*, were put in place. In hindsight, I should have known better than to design a performance appraisal that clashed with the job restructuring. My key learning was the importance of developing a performance appraisal that is consistent with a company's philosophy, values, and objectives and is aligned with the nature and type of work performed.

Overall, BARS is a good standard approach to evaluate performance, but in this case, it fell short of meeting the team's needs, because it didn't recognize and honor the unconventionality of the work redesign that was put in place for Gen Y. A performance appraisal that works best for a Gen Y workforce is one that reaches toward the following:

> ➤ Reflects the distinctiveness of each Gen Y's project-based portfolio

> ➤ Measures and evaluates the full and diverse gamut of competencies that Gen Y is using on the job and contributing to the organization's strategic direction

> ➤ Is flexible and adaptable to changes in job responsibilities

> ➤ Accentuates clear objectives and standards by which performance is appraised

> ➤ Minimizes rater errors discussed earlier

> ➤ Allows Gen Y to reflect on their aspirations within and beyond their current jobs

These outcomes are more realizable when we shift toward an outcome-based approach to evaluation that does the following:

> ➤ Draws you and Gen Y into the performance-appraisal process

> ➤ Helps you and Gen Y collaborate on charting a path for successful performance and to envision Gen Y's career aspirations

> ➤ Underscores action, results, and the importance of ongoing skill development

> ➤ Straddles the need for structure and flexibility

I'd like to share with you the outcome-based approach that I used with the client featured in the story mentioned earlier and an approach that I offer to other clients. As mentioned earlier, I'm not implying that it is the *only* system that should be used in evaluating performance. It is *one* approach that you can adapt as is, modify to suit your organization's needs, or use as a starting point to create your own unique evaluation system that meets the needs of your organization.

Offered is the GPS (*Goals* and *Pathways* for *Success*) system to evaluate performance!

It consists of three *coordinates*, or navigational stages, for Gen Y's professional growth and development. Also included is a central role that involves your own GPS.

Let's unpack each of the three coordinates to reveal how they contribute to a collaborative and results-based experience for Gen Y.

# Coordinate 1 – Blue sky dreaming: your head in the clouds again

My mentor and dear friend often says, "Give yourself permission to dream the biggest dream ever, where your heart races faster than your mind with the excitement of what could be."

This is blue sky dreaming, that is, envisioning what we aspire to be and to be doing in our careers when anything and everything is possible. It is in this magical moment that the direction we are meant to pursue reveals itself and everything begins to fall into place. The benefits of a crystal-clear vision of our career destination are many. Some of them are as follows:

> ➤ Position us to make conscious and thoughtful decisions about what we want and should do in our career instead of simply falling in and out of jobs and leaving our career to chance

> ➤ Keep us focused, inspired, and motivated, especially during the difficult times in our career when we feel like we have lost our way and we question whether we are "doing what we are meant to be doing"

> ➤ Empower us to ask for the right set of support from others, because we know exactly what we want in our career

> ➤ Enable us to hone the right network of professional contacts that can mentor us through our career

> ➤ Increase our ability to confidently decline tasks and assignments that are not aligned with our career destination

In this first coordinate, take Gen Y into *blue sky dreaming* where they can picture a compelling vision of their multiple careers over the course of their working lives. Specifically, encourage them to carve out a space for personal reflection, whether this takes the form of journaling, meditation, music, art, or conversations with others. Inspire them to do the following:

> ➤ Reflect on their personal values, attitudes, strengths, and motivations that are the bedrock upon which they build their career

> ➤ Reflect back on the story of their life to times that were most exhilarating and fulfilling; these images might reveal clues as to what they need to pay attention to as they go forward in their career

> ➤ Shut down the niggling voices in their mind that put constraints on visioning by telling them what is realistic, reasonable, logical, and responsible

> ➤ Remain in an uber-positive space, that is, keep dreaming about all the fabulous possibilities that weren't imaginable yesterday

> ➤ *Let their hearts race faster than their minds* and envision on the grandest scale *the excitement of what could be*

> ➤ Ask the most fundamental question: *At the end of the day, what would really make me happiest and most fulfilled?*

We now turn to explore how Gen Y's personal vision statement becomes the compass for leading them to their career destination.

## Coordinate 2 – Developing a blueprint for success: getting from here to where?

In coordinate 2, we work with Gen Y to develop their blueprint for success, which houses all the key ingredients of their journey from *here* to *wherever* they want to take their career. Specifically, this includes using their career vision statement crafted in coordinate 1 as the over-arching umbrella under which they chart the pathway to translate hopes, dreams, and good intentions into career reality. By positioning Gen Y's career vision prominently in the document, it serves as a reminder of their commitment. It also stands as a reference point to ascertain whether the goals that they set are aligned with their career vision and—let's not forget—aligned with our organization's strategic direction as well.

Below are the key ingredients of the blueprint to be completed by you and your Gen Y staff. Gen Y brings their vision and ideas about their future and you bring your expertise in facilitating a coaching conversation to help them chart a manageable and achievable action plan to execute their vision.

> ➤ **Declaration of personal career vision**: A clear and concise statement of Gen Y's career destination

➢ **Goal #1**: This includes the following:

> ➢ **Goal statement**: What do you hope to achieve this year?
>
>> Identify a specific goal they'd like to work on over the course of the year. Much of the work you did in *Chapter 5, Inspiring Star Performance– Reaching Seriously for Sirius*, which involved exploring new work experiences for Gen Y within and beyond the scope of their jobs, gets synthesized and recorded here. Keep the goal specific, measurable, feasible, and timely as it relates to the achievement of personal and organizational goals.
>
> ➢ **Action pathway**: How will you get there?
>
>> Chart the action strategy to achieve the goal. It is best to hone in on a few key actions in order to keep the process manageable over the course of the year. The action strategy section should include the following:
>>
>> ➢ How Gen Y will achieve the goal
>>
>> ➢ Resources required
>>
>> ➢ Assistance from you and others
>>
>> ➢ Targeted completion date
>
> ➢ **Outputs**: What awaits you? Yet, be prepared to be surprised as well!
>
>> Describe the anticipated outcomes from their efforts with focus on how the achievement of goal aligns with vision, mission, and strategic goals at the individual, team, and organizational levels. Also include how outputs will be measured and documented. Even though there are anticipated outcomes, stay open and receptive to the benefits that are least expected!

When you write up the second and third goals, please follow the format described above – goal statement, action pathway, and outputs.

We now shift the focus onto you!

# Coordinate 3 – Contributing to Gen Y's success: YOUR GPS matters too!

In coordinate 3, you are invited into a role that is not customarily part of the evaluation process, but one that has several benefits. By taking on this new accountability, you:

➢ Support and increase the probability that Gen Y will reach their goal

➢ Build collaborative and collegial working relationships between you and your Gen Y staff toward departmental and organizational mandates

➢ Earn the respect and admiration of your Gen Y team when you commit *in practice* to their career development

You are asked to identify a specific goal that you are prepared to commit to, and work towards, that will help Gen Y achieve their goals. So what goal will you set that is directly related to your responsibility as a leader to support the professional development of your staff?

As it is physically impossible and impractical to declare and achieve a specific goal related to each and every one of the developmental plans produced by your Gen Y staff members, consider finding a theme that threads its way through all of the GPSes that year. This way, you declare and work toward achieving one or two universal goals that have far-reaching implications for the team. Once the goal is identified, give thought to a few action strategies that will demonstrate your commitment to the achievement of the goal. Communicate the goal and corresponding action strategies to your team so that they can be on the lookout over the course of the year for the support you have promised them.

The specific contribution you make to the development of your Gen Y staff is at your discretion. As long as an effort is made to offer something substantial that clearly complements the initiatives that Gen Y is committing to, you are on the right track.

The entire GPS, with all three coordinates, serves as a tool to guide performance throughout the year and will be the centerpiece of your performance-evaluation review with your Gen Y staff in the following year.

# Who evaluates

Your ratings are still the heart of the appraisal process, because you are in the best position to observe and evaluate the performance of employees who report to you. Yet, you may want to expand the sphere of influence here, especially if you don't see your Gen Y as often as you'd like because of your own busy schedule or because of your Gen Y staff working on projects in other departments, or them or you working from home.

Alongside your assessment, consider implementing an internal 360-degree feedback process in which employees who have worked with Gen Y most closely over the course of the year are given an opportunity to offer feedback. This evaluation can be immensely valuable since it does the following:

> ➤ Captures Gen Y's many roles, contributions, and achievements in teams across the organization that you may not be aware of.

> ➤ Presents multiple viewpoints, opinions, and recommendations for performance improvement that can't be captured in the feedback from one person.

> ➤ Provides an opportunity for Gen Y to compare their self-assessment with the views of others.

> ➤ Has a high degree of reliability, especially when similar feedback is given by several colleagues.

➤ Has a high degree of accuracy because they work closely with Gen Y; thus, they see them at their best and worst. By nature, people tend to reveal more of their authentic selves to colleagues at the same or similar level in an organization than to more senior-ranking staff.

➤ Can have a positive impact on perceptions of open communication, motivation, and group cohesion and satisfaction.

The intent is to structure the feedback session as a formative, instead of a summative, process. A formative approach allows employees to have open dialog about performance and to focus exclusively on how they can support each other in their careers. Conversations that are grounded in summative outcomes tend to be more competitive in nature. This means that harsher than warranted criticism seeps into summative feedback sessions because performance results are tied to promotions, transfers, and salary increases, and the staff are acutely aware that they are competing for limited access to each.

To further enhance the formative nature of the process, consider facilitating the feedback session as a focus group instead of using the traditional survey approach. Each employee takes the center stage to share their goals from the previous year with colleagues, who in turn do the following:

➤ Acknowledge their contributions to the organization's goals, with specific examples of what they saw the employee doing that contributed to success

➤ Offer advice on snags that surfaced in the execution of goals and how to improve performance

➤ Strategize about new goals and action plans that align with the employee's career vision

➤ Challenge each other to stretch into new skills and knowledge domains

➤ Identify new collaborations between staff who share similar interests

Alongside the 360-degree feedback process, the performance-appraisal cycle creates the perfect opportunity for each staff member to engage in self-assessment. In doing so, they develop the capacity to be *reflective practitioners*, that is, to be mindful of who they are and who they aspire to be and the importance of taking time to think deeply about how their past and present informs their future. Specifically, it allows them to reflect about the following:

➤ How their professional lives align with their personal values and vision

➤ Their story over the past year, with all its successes, misses, contributions, and achievements

➤ Lessons learned from their story

➤ What's next, personally and professionally

Encourage your staff to engage in self-assessment prior to the 360-degree feedback. In doing so, they can bring their reflections about their past, present, and future into the conversation to enrich the discussion even further.

# Appraisal interviews – from OH NO to OH YES!

Any meeting with the words *appraisal* and *interview* in the same breath are bound to send many employees into a full-blown and feral-like panic attack weeks in advance of the fateful day. Since the beginning of time, appraisal interviews have been causing electric shockwaves of terror through the bodies of even the most highly lauded employees in our midst. Why? The causes are varied, but for most of us, we fear the criticism that might be lurking behind the ominous door that leads to our supervisor's office. For many of us, criticism is equated with rejection, that is, *someone doesn't like me*. Even though the rational, highly cognitive, and super-smart frontal lobe of our brain tells us, no, *demands* us not to take feedback personally, we hastily usher criticism from our ears to our hearts, where it lays indefinitely like an insufferable wounded bird. No matter how hard we try, it is tough *not* to take criticism to heart. This is the never-ending curse of the appraisal interview.

Yet, it doesn't need to be like this. Here's a golden opportunity to be one of the few supervisors who erases many of the apprehensions that employees have about appraisal interviews and creates a refreshingly new perspective on what these meetings can and should achieve.

In reality, there should be no surprises in an appraisal interview. It should be relatively straightforward and predictable; hence, no need for apprehension. If there is a problem with an employee's performance, address it at the time of the incident instead of storing it for retrieval during the review.

In order to begin minimizing any free-floating anxiety that our Gen Y staff might have about the impending interview, it might be helpful ahead of time to do the following:

> ➤ Communicate the goal of the meeting, that is, have a dialog committed to honoring their performance over the year and a coaching conversation about how to strengthen performance and plan for the next stage in their career with the organization.

> ➤ Distribute the agenda for the interview so that they have an understanding of the topics to be discussed. We'll cover the specifics of this shortly.

> ➤ Reinforce that there will be no surprises during the interview.

> ➤ Encourage them to contact you if they have any questions or concerns that they'd like addressed prior to the interview.

> ➤ Treat this scheduled meeting as critical. Do not reschedule it based on other priorities.

As *Chapter 4, Unlocking the Secrets to Awesome Conversations with Gen Y,* covered the guidelines for giving and receiving feedback—what to say, what NOT to say, and how to say it—we'll jump right into the topics that you might want to cover in your conversations with Gen Y during the appraisal interview. In order to make the discussion meaningful for Gen Y's professional development, consider including the following pieces in your agenda:

- ➤ How Gen Y viewed their past year
- ➤ Review the GPS report they produced last year, and provide your feedback on their achievements, contributions, and overall success over the year
- ➤ Review your GPS contribution from last year, asking Gen Y for feedback on your contributions to their goals
- ➤ Ask for Gen Y's impressions of the 360-degree feedback they received:
  - ➢ What was affirming and in what way
  - ➢ What was surprising and why?
- ➤ Review their self-assessment, specifically how the past year has informed their thinking about the upcoming year
- ➤ Strategize about the next phase in their career development and what goals they'd like to set en route to reaching the next career milestone
- ➤ Agreeing to how you will follow up after today's meeting to review progress

Wherever possible, encourage Gen Y to take the lead in responding to each of these agenda items. This way, you get their insights, perceptions, and experiences that are untainted by your interpretation of events.

Also, be vigilant of any nonverbal and verbal cues, which surface signally that they might be uncomfortable in the conversation. This could take the form of breaking eye contact, changes in tempo, volume, or tone of voice, and shifts in body posture. If you notice a change, check your assumptions by sharing what you observe. If they are uncomfortable, ask them how they'd like to proceed. Heightened uneasiness during the interview is never a recipe for success in a meeting that requires both parties to be open, transparent, and fully present. If you misread the signs, don't worry. You likely communicated that you care enough about making the appraisal interview a positive experience for them to stop and check in.

All is well, until performance gets a flat tire.

# Navigating the unexpected – when performance gets a flat tire

We now press forward into a delicate topic that can unnerve even the most iron-willed of us—managing performance problems. For the sake of this discussion, our focus is on corrective action required when the work done by our staff does not meet performance standards and expectations. Employee wrongdoings such as theft, disobedience, insubordination, intentionally defying rules and regulations, and legal infractions are outside the purview of this book. Violations of this nature require us to activate more formal systems of progressive penalties, such as suspensions, demotions, and dismissals, in our organization's disciplinary policies and procedures. For those of you who are interested, there is a book on the **Google it** reference list about managing more serious breaches of behavior.

No matter how diligent our employees are and how hermetically sealed our performance-management policies, practices, and procedures appear to be, *performance gets a flat tire* on occasion. Even our star Gen Y performers are going to fumble and make mistakes, misinterpret what we've asked them to do, get into workplace skirmishes with others, and lose their footing for a variety of foreseen and unforeseen reasons.

As awkward and unsavory as it may be, we are obligated to step in and take corrective action. Yet what specifically does this entail?

# Navigating the unexpected

Let's be completely honest here. By nature, we don't like to confront our employees with their performance weaknesses and wrongdoings. We struggle with how to do the following:

> Set the right tone for corrective action

> Broach the topic

> Frame messages in a way that the staff will be amenable to changes in their behavior

> Manage the myriad of emotions that could arise—theirs and ours

> Recuperate from the potential strain on everyday working relationships resulting from this discussion

We would rather dodge the conversation bullet entirely instead of coming across as the formidable and crotchety workplace ogre who is clutching the good book on performance standards and expectations and wielding a big stick! The vision of this burns a hole in our cornea and sends chills down our spine.

To avoid having these conversations, some of us might rationalize the undesired performance or conduct as only a minor lapse in judgment that isn't integral to workplace operations, and therefore, it doesn't need to be addressed. Consequently, we might choose to ignore the behavior when it surfaces and bypass a discussion about it during performance appraisals. In some cases, we might even reward all employees in our unit with the same or similar high-performance ratings. We might also assign the same or similar merit increases in order to further conceal our discomfort with differentiating the performance of one staff member over the other; hence, signaling that in your eyes, everyone's performance is equal.

Failing to take action can quickly spiral out of control and be detrimental to us. By not addressing the performance immediately and forthrightly, it can signal to the employee in question that their performance is acceptable. Other staff who see that there are no consequences resulting from the behavior translate this to mean that standards are not held to accountability, and they may let their own performance slip. This can snowball into serious disruptions to your unit's performance and productivity. You now face an even more difficult task of reining in the behavior of many staff who are not performing to standard, instead of just one.

To minimize this from happening, intervene early. At the first sign that there is a performance issue underfoot, it's time to step in. This is your opportunity to initiate a *coaching conversation* in which you use a facilitative approach to guide the employee in getting their performance back on track. In this role, you are encouraged to do the following:

> ➤ Stay positive that the situation can be remedied and communicate this to the employee.

> ➤ Reframe this as "a challenge to face" instead of a "problem for me to deal with".

> ➤ Discourage finger pointing and blaming each other or others for the performance issue. This only enflames the situation, and it isn't productive to the problem-solving nature of the conversation.

> ➤ Investigate with an open mind (and heart) and a willingness to listen to the other side of the story. This might be a misunderstanding or a misperception that could be resolved expediently.

> ➤ Provide a clear and candid explanation of the following:

>> ➤ Problem behavior with specific examples of the behavior that is not acceptable

>> ➤ Why the behavior is a problem, with reference to implications at the individual, unit, and organizational levels

>> ➤ How to reinforce the expected job performance and conduct

> ➤ Provide the employee with ownership of the problem and the outcomes:

>> ➤ Work with the employee to accept the rules

>> ➤ Take responsibility for their actions

>> ➤ Exercise self-discipline in determining how to resolve the problematic behavior

Added to this, here are a few questions that you might want to keep in your pocket as you are coaching employees through the problem-solving exercise:

> ➤ What happened?

> ➤ Why did it happen?

> ➤ Is there anything you'd like to tell me that will help me better understand why you are unable to meet the performance standards?

> ➤ What will you do to minimize the probability that we will have a similar conversation about performance in the future?

> ➤ What are the timelines to achieve these changes?

> ➤ What obstacles do you anticipate and how will you overcome them?

> ➤ What support do you need from me?

> ➤ What is your understanding of our conversation today, and what do you commit to do differently to reach the performance standards?

Wrap up the conversation by documenting the highlights of the conversation and the steps that the employee plans to take to remedy the situation. Provide a copy to the employee for their reference. The paper trail is important if the behavior recurs.

# Deja vu – when the behavior recurs

We can accept mistakes that arise occasionally, but we expect that once we've had a conversation about the job performance or workplace conduct, the employee will remedy the situation and get back on the expected performance track. If the behavior recurs, then we have more of a problem on our hands!

We return to a coaching conversation; yet, it requires us to be more direct in the performance-management conversation:

> ➤ Review with the employee the conversation from your last meeting, including remedial steps they committed to take and support you committed to provide
> ➤ Confirm the accuracy of the action plan as written
> ➤ Discourage finger pointing and blaming, which have a greater propensity to show up in this second conversation
> ➤ Remind the employee of the rationale behind performance standards and their responsibility to meet performance standards.
> ➤ Invite the employee to explain what didn't work for them in the action plan and what changes are needed
> ➤ Recommit mutually to a revised action plan
> ➤ Inform them that they will receive a formal written reminder of this
> ➤ Express confidence in the employee's ability to make the changes in the behavior that they've committed to

Provide a revised copy of the agreement to the employee, and issue them a formal written reminder.

But what happens when the behavior resurfaces....again?

# When it's time to say goodbye

I'd like to share a personal story with you. I've condensed it considerably so that it doesn't drag needlessly through the chapter, but there are enough details for you to get the gist of a conversation with one of my staff.

> *Geoff, this is our third conversation in less than 6 weeks about why you keep losing your temper with colleagues and customers. We discussed what ignites your self-described "short fuse", you committed to making changes, including seeing a counsellor and working 1 day per week from home where you have solitude, and I offered my office as a safe haven whenever you need time to decompress. This is the last conversation I'm prepared to have with you about this. Over the weekend, I have an important question for you to consider: Is this still the place where you want to work? On Monday morning, I want to know the answer.*

You thought I was going to fire him on the spot, didn't you! Tempting, especially when we are at our wits' end, and we don't know what other options are available to us after several failed attempts to get performance back on track. I suggest we have one more option available.

Invite the employee to make time for reflection on the same question that I asked Geoff: *Is this still the place where you want to work?* If they haven't demonstrated a willingness or ability to change up to this point, then it's time to invite them to take a few days to think about whether the job is right for them and whether or not they want to abide by the company's standards and expectations. It is an expression of the company's hope that the employee can and will turn the situation around. Ask them to consider the following points:

> Their long-term personal and professional goals

> Does this organization still appear to be the place where their goals can be met

> Based on the feedback they've received, are they willing and able to make changes:

>> If yes, what does the change look like and how will they make it stick

>> If not, perhaps it is time to consider leaving the organization

When the employee returns with a decision, you're going to be on the receiving end of either of the following:

> **I've decided to stay**: Work out a brief action plan for change. Make it crystal clear that this is a probationary period, and if the behavior reoccurs, it is grounds for dismissal. There are no chances left.

> **I've decided to leave**: Follow through with your organization's standard procedures when someone announces a resignation.

I continue to be amazed at how many employees choose to self-select out of organizations after they've given thought to whether they really want to be there. Many employees who I've seen leave companies after taking time for reflection told me that it had been too exhausting trying to work in an organization that clashes with their values and expectations. They knew all along in their hearts that there was a disconnection between their personal aspirations and the goals and expectations of the organization; they just needed time to think this through. According to them, the best gift they gave themselves and their families was to leave the organization and find a better fit elsewhere.

Even when performance is no longer what it should be and we are all hanging by the threads of our frayed nerves, I think we can still manage these final difficult conversations in ways that preserve the dignity and respect of everyone involved.

Are you wondering what happened to Geoff? First thing Monday morning, he came into my office with his resignation letter. Today, he is a well-respected and successful Vice-President of Operations for a leading fiber-optics company.

# Reframing challenges as opportunities

*I think we are logrolling.*

Logrolling is the practice of praising others with the expectation that they will reciprocate with the same gestures of high praise. As it relates to this chapter, logrolling shows up when we invoke peer feedback into performance appraisals, such as the 360-degree feedback focus groups that we discussed earlier. Peers simply rate each other highly or offer vacuous and noncommittal feedback which has limited value to the professional development of others. It could be caused by many factors. Some of them are as follows:

> ➤ Climate of apprehension that feedback will be used for summative and not formative purposes as communicated

> ➤ Not prepared to risk the backlash that could arise from giving honest feedback, such as spiteful and destructive feedback in return

> ➤ Not seeing the value of extending themselves to give the depth and breadth of feedback that we are asking for

> ➤ Uncomfortable giving constructive feedback publicly to colleagues who are also friends

Let's reframe this as an opportunity for our staff. In order to minimize logrolling, start by inviting the staff into a climate-setting exercise where they are asked to provide input into the characteristics of effective feedback sessions. Ask them to give you insight into the approach to facilitation that would encourage them to freely give and receive input about performance. Also, ask them to articulate the specific type of feedback they would like to receive that would be meaningful to their personal and professional development. In doing so, you and your team begin to better understand each other's needs and begin to co-create a climate that is conducive to rich and collegial dialogue.

Added to this, encourage your staff to reframe the feedback as learning moments in which they help colleagues and friends view a situation from a perspective that they have not yet considered. In doing so, they might be helping others shift their thinking and actions considerably. This could make a significant contribution to their professional development. In turn, you might establish a climate where the staff who are on the receiving end of these learning moments extend the same care and consideration to help their colleagues and friends experience the same.

# Leaning in to change

What about YOU?

Throughout this chapter, we've focused on the approaches, tools, and practices that you can use to manage daily performance, develop performance appraisals, and manage less-than-satisfactory performance along the way. Equally important is taking time to reflect on your personal approach to engage with your Gen Y staff during the performance-management process.

Here are a few questions to guide your reflection (and perhaps, your journal writing) about the changes you could make. Consider selecting one of the following questions and thinking deeply about your course of action:

> What are you doing *too much of* or *too little of* in your approach to guiding and supporting your Gen Y staff?

> What do you want to start doing that will be *just right* for balancing your busy day and giving Gen Y the attention they need?

> What is working, and not working in your current approach to formally evaluate your Gen Y staff?

> Play a video in your mind of the last round of appraisal interviews you conducted. What did you do well before, during, and after the meetings? What would you like to change in your approach to facilitate these meetings and what might that entail?

> Is there an employee in your midst who is not performing to standard? Plan your approach to have a performance-management conversation with this person. Be mindful of answering the question: what do I want to achieve by having this meeting?

Please join me online (www.eyeofthetigerconsulting.ca) to share your insights and experiences with managing performance.

# Google it

Here are a few additional resources for those of you who would like to continue to explore performance management:

> M., Armstrong and A., Baron, *Managing Performance: Performance Management in Action*, Chartered Institute of Personnel and Development, 2005

> R., Lepsinger and A., Lucia, *The Art and Science of 360 Degree Feedback*, Jossey-Bass, 2009

> K., Patterson, J., Grenny, D., Maxfield, R., McMillan, and Switzler, *Crucial Accountability: Tools for Resolving Violated Expectations, Broken Commitments, and Bad Behavior.* New York: McGraw Hill Education, 2013

> B., Sember and T., Sember, T, *Bad Apples: How to Manage Difficult Employees, Encourage Good Ones to Stay, and Boost Productivity*, Avon, MA: F+W Media, 2009

> D., Van Tiem, J., Moseley, and J., Dessinger, *Fundamentals of Performance Improvement*, John Wiley and Sons, 2012

# Meeting the Gen Y community – introducing…Abdulmohsen Almuhanna!

*What can supervisors do on a daily basis to manage and support your daily performance?*

Abdulmohsen has worked for supervisors who have been exemplary and those who failed miserably at managing and supporting daily performance. The disappointing experiences were earmarked by excessive top-down decision making, telling the staff what to do without providing a rationale, and heavy-handed criticism rather than praise of staff efforts. Abdulmohsen shared one of the more memorable responses he received from a supervisor, *"Why should I praise you for your work; it's your job. You're not doing us a favor by doing the work as expected."* For Abdulmohsen, an environment like this is fear inducing and demeaning. It didn't take long before this became too stressful and he resigned from the company.

At the core of a positive experience is working with supervisors who do the following:

> ➤ Value respect and show it in simple gestures such as a pat on the back or a kind word

> ➤ Distribute work equally among their staff so that everyone is held equally accountable and feels like an equally contributing and empowered member of the team

> ➤ Show they care about their staff by patiently guiding them with an equal balance of praise and constructive feedback that is delivered respectfully and focused on precise instructions for corrective action

Also, Abdulmohsen stressed the importance of supervisors genuinely listening to Gen Y's suggestions that he describes as, *"not a better way, but another way"* to get work done. Gen Y's ideas are worth listening to because they work at the ground level more so than their supervisors; hence, Gen Y is more attuned to the needs of guests, clients, and customers. According to Abdulmohsen, believing that Gen Y has something to contribute instils tremendous confidence in them, from which they are willing to go to great lengths to be fully engaged and contributing members of the team.

Abdulmohsen realizes that not every suggestion will have merit, and if this is the case, he encourages supervisors to spend time explaining why a suggestion isn't doable. In doing so, Gen Y learns how to become critical thinkers about the implications of their proposals, and the lessons learned will be valuable when Gen Y is promoted and expected to exercise their own leadership in making decisions. As Abdulmohsen said, *"I want to know in my heart that my supervisor wants me to learn".*

Added to this, Abdulmohsen reinforced the importance of never surprising Gen Y, for example, not informing them of changes to daily protocol that cause them to make mistakes in delivering the service that guests, clients, and customers expect.

Abdulmohsen leaves us with this final message, "The small gestures of kindness and the daily helpful hints that you give randomly through the day to help us get better at our jobs are more important than those big gestures that you think are important."

> *Abdulmohsen was born in Saudi Arabia. He is completing his Bachelor of Arts in Hospitality Management at Royal Roads University in Victoria, British Columbia, Canada, and he aspires to be a manager in the service industry. Abdulmohsen says he is "a changed person" since coming to Canada. He's maintained his values and strong cultural roots and has embraced all the newness of living and studying in Canada. Abdulmohsen describes himself as a highly curious person always wanting to know about the world around him. Never being one to rely on what the media tells him, you'll find Abdulmohsen combing the Internet in search of answers to his questions about world events, trends, and cultures. Abdulmohsen's mother is a strong and constant influence in his life, helping him appreciate the beauty of diversity. She reminds him that, "None of your fingers are exactly the same; and people are not the same either. Even though people may come from a specific country, no two people are alike."*

# Summary

In this chapter, we were hyper-intentional about the sustainability of our workplace initiatives for Gen Y by exploring the tools and practices for performance management. We began by discovering the secret sauce for managing daily performance, moving from what's too much to what's too little and then to what's just right. We then unveiled a new GPS for Gen Y and got you thinking about your own GPS. This required us to do some blue sky dreaming so that we could set our three coordinates. We finished with a discussion about what to do when performance gets a flat tire. This took us into the domains of managing the unexpected, responding to déjà vu, and saying goodbye.

Being hyper-intentional can pay off in spades when we develop a signature approach to performance management, which is the talk of the Gen Y town!

We now move into the next chapter to make sense of recognition and rewards for our Gen Y performers. Who gets a gold star?

# >7

# Rewarding Peak Performers – Goodbye Plaques, Trophies, and Recognition Pins

*A plaque on the wall acknowledges the Employee of the Month?*

*You can't be serious!*

Those legendary plaques, trophies, and recognition pins aren't exactly what Gen Y envisions as rewards for exemplary performance in the workplace. Overall, our reward and recognition systems are perceived by our Gen Y workforce as bland, disappointing, and tiresome. Most frequently cited are concerns that our practices:

➤ Aren't reflective of Gen Y's values and expectations

➤ Fall short of inspiring performance that meets and exceeds work standards

➤ Create an unflattering impression of how we celebrate star performers

The reward and recognition systems that currently exist in our organizations were the ones that many of us were introduced to years ago when we were studying to be managers. These practices, once touted as leading edge, are now outdated and destined for the rewards and recognition graveyard. Given the significant change in our workplace demographics, it's time to breathe new life into how we celebrate the achievements of our top-ranking performers.

The need for reform in how we will incentivize our staff is more pressing than ever before. In recent years, our reward practices have become one of the top reasons for Gen Y's exodus from our organizations. When our star performers, who are flagged as our future organizational leaders, march out the door, the ensuing damage penetrates deep into the crevasses of our organization and weakens the key performance indicators that are the drivers of our organization's prosperity. These losses can be punishing and difficult to recover from.

The keystone to design a highly acclaimed reward and recognition system rests in our ability to leverage the expectations of our Gen Y workforce and strategically tie rewards to our business goals, objectives, and values in a cost-efficient and effective way. In this chapter, we'll discuss how we can achieve this. We'll examine approaches we can use to create a system that:

> ➤ Aligns more closely with Gen Y's vision of performance rewards and recognition
> ➤ Gives your organization a competitive boost in attracting and retaining Gen Y
> ➤ Motivates Gen Y to soar beyond predetermined job standards and expectations
> ➤ Is cost conscious so that it weathers the most difficult recessionary climate and it won't empty your organization's wallet
> ➤ Can serve as the new benchmark standard in your industry and, in doing so, position you as a leader in honoring the achievements of Gen Y stars

In order to reach these outcomes, we tap into the following topics:

➤ Incentivizing peak performance with financial rewards

➤ Recognizing staff—possibilities beyond cash

➤ Incorporating a few tantalizing workplace perks

➤ Sometimes, it's about doing nothing at all

The overall intent of this chapter is to offer you a starter kit of approaches you can use to rejuvenate your organization's reward and recognition system. As you read through this chapter, reflect on how you can tweak the approaches offered in order to design a system that speaks to the uniqueness of your organization's culture. Also, consider how the approaches can be adapted to meet the demographic composition of your entire workforce so that the staff who are not in the Gen Y circle are also recognized for their achievements. Be willing to explore new terrain beyond what is proposed and to keep searching for ways to lead the charge.

# So, what's burning?

*Can't I just give them a paycheck and be done with it? Isn't that recognition enough? Whenever I put guidelines in place for rewards, there is always someone griping that the system doesn't work. They complain that the criteria to earn rewards are impossible to fulfil, the rewards are lackluster and not worth the extra effort, and the differentiation in rewards between star and superstar employees is wretchedly small. It's a futile battle. I can't please anyone.*

Getting the policies and practices for our reward and *recognition system just right* is a tricky business. It is fraught with unforeseen landmines that can cause us to question what we were thinking when we decided to venture down this path. We could be plagued by staff concerns that rewards are not fairly distributed, require more effort than the reward is worth, or don't suit the values and expectations of the recipients.

Yes, we could choose the easier route of simply paying our staff their wages and avoiding the hassles associated with exerting the extra muscle to design an incentive program. On the surface, this might be appealing, but in reality, it can cause massive problems for us in attracting, motivating, and retaining Gen Y superstars who are intentional in their search for companies with impressive reward and recognition systems. By not putting energy into creating a first-rate incentive system, there is a higher probability that our Gen Y stars might leave us prematurely or bypass us completely during their job search. Hence, we risk losing the most gifted of the bunch to our competition. Specifically, we lose out on the following:

➤ A rich source of innovative and strategic thinking that is the hallmark of an organization

➤ Talent we want to groom to become the next generation of leaders who shape our organization's legacy

In order to minimize these risks and put in place a reward and recognition system that works for you and your organization, it is important that we stay grounded in one fundamental reality:

*Success is achieved when we accept that it is impossible to please everyone.*

Success can only be achieved when we let go of the quest to please everyone. The complexity of human nature means that some people will never be wholeheartedly supportive of and committed to the decisions we make and the directions we take. In the case of incentives, it is best to set our sights on a more realizable goal of designing a system that aims to fulfil the needs of the majority. Yet, how do we get there?

Incentive systems that have the greatest chance of success are the ones that are designed in consultation with all parties that have a stake in the process. By drawing all stakeholders into the decision-making process, we are more likely to identify and invest in incentives that are aligned with Gen Y's values and with our organization's goals and objectives.

As you proceed through the design phase, be mindful that there are scores of incentives from which you can choose. What you want to avoid is jumping on the *flavor of the month* bandwagon, that is, copying the trending incentives simply because they are being used in other organizations. Some of these popular incentives might be worthwhile additions to your incentive program, but before you arbitrarily implement them, do a little detective work to ascertain whether they are right for your organization. The litmus test to determine which rewards are best suited for your organization consists of asking if the rewards:

> ➤ Fit your organization's culture and philosophy
>
> ➤ Link to your organization's values, goals, and objectives
>
> ➤ Contribute to the goals you want to achieve through your reward system
>
> ➤ Align with the needs and expectations of your Gen Y staff
>
> ➤ Can be sustained given the realities of your organization's budget

Envision your initial blueprint for a reward and recognition system as a work-in-progress. Launch it from a place of good intentions, whereby you attempt to balance the scale of employees' needs and organizational expectations, yet are willing to revise your plan often until you close in on a best-fit system that is grounded in integrity, equity, and fairness. This is a tall order, so let's start putting some ideas on the table.

# Incentivizing peak performance with financial rewards

A few years ago, I facilitated a retreat for aspiring Gen Y leaders, and one of our activities was to create a storyboard that represented their vision of the future. Specifically, the guiding question was, "What does your life look like when you are living into your full potential?" Envisioned were grand-scale entrepreneurial ventures with common threads of philanthropy and sustainability, winding through the stories and connections with influential people that could advance their careers. Also, most stories told the tale of the riches Gen Y hoped to have as a result of their efforts. They reveled in the promise of paychecks that could give them the purchasing power for the latest electronic toys, vacations, cars, and nice places to live.

This envisioned lifestyle has become the generational moniker for Gen Y. Although Gen Y has been criticized as having unrealistic expectations of what is required of them in order to acquire this lifestyle, they persist in voicing their expectations. Of all the generations in our workplace, Gen Y is considered the most vocal in expressing frustration if rewards aren't in place to acknowledge their performance. Yet, what satisfies their needs and expectations? What does incentivizing for Gen Y entail?

Before we answer this question, there is an issue that we need to address:

*As important as money is to Gen Y, it is by no means the singular motivator for them.*

Money is important, but our reward and recognition system needs to be more sophisticated than simply doling out cash payments. In order to create a reward and recognition system that is considered truly motivational by Gen Y, we need to find the right balance of financial and nonfinancial incentives. In this chapter, we'll offer a variety of monetary and nonmonetary approaches that you can use to acknowledge Gen Y performance. We begin with a discussion about incentivizing Gen Y using money and then move into nonmonetary ways to recognize performance.

# Performance-based reward system – rewarding superstars

In *Chapter 5, Inspiring Star Performance– Reaching Seriously for Sirius*, we spent time on job restructuring, specifically, encouraging Gen Y to explore innovative ways to enhance their jobs through projects within and beyond their job descriptions. Now, it's reward day! We are searching for an incentive system that does the following:

> ➤ Best suits the diverse project-based nature of the work that Gen Y does

> ➤ Links rewards to performance and our organization's values, goals, and objectives

> ➤ Meets Gen Y's preference for rewards that can be customized to recognize the breadth of contributions they make to the organization

> ➤ Motivates Gen Y to reach for, and beyond, their potential

The answer lies in performance-based reward systems, that is, incentive plans that explicitly link pay with productivity, profitability, or some other measure of organizational performance. A performance-based reward system salutes our highest performers who have the most noteworthy and forward-propelling impact on our organization's bottom line.

Before we drill into the details of performance-based reward systems, we want to be crystal clear with our staff that rewards are given for performance that *exceeds* the predetermined expectations of the job description and the outcomes of projects that were articulated on their GPS-tracking reports. Rewards are not given for performance that *meets* the standards. Completion of work according to standards is acknowledged through paychecks as well as through the praise that we give them as part of our commitment to manage daily performance.

The success of a performance-based reward system lies in the frontend conversations we have with our staff during the conceptualization of a new project. Not only is it important to discuss with our staff their action plan for completing a project, but it is integral to communicate the criteria for reward eligibility. As Gen Y is known to have a more skewed perception of the amount of work and effort that constitutes eligibility for rewards, it is important that we are explicit about when rewards kick in. In doing so:

➤ Staff can track their own performance and gauge for themselves when they qualify for performance-based rewards

➤ We minimize misunderstandings about the types of performance that are and aren't rewarded

If we choose not to have this discussion, a host of responses ranging from withdrawal to anger could surface afterwards, when Gen Y accuses us of not honoring our agreement to reward their performance. If Gen Y concludes that our reward system does not have the integrity and fairness that they were led to believe, we risk losing their trust in us, which is difficult, if not impossible, to regain. From there, you are in the express lane toward the following:

➤ Declining future performance because they realize that exerting extra effort has a disappointing payoff.

➤ Serious questions being asked by Gen Y about whether they want to continue working with you.

➤ Reputational damage when Gen Y starts text messaging about their experiences.

To avoid these calamities for you and for your organization, invest the extra time to make the connection between performance and rewards. Here are a few items to include on your agenda for this discussion:

➤ Clear, concise, and realistic metrics to meet and exceed performance standards and expectations

➤ Process to track metrics during the course of the project to ascertain progress and to flag trouble spots that could impede success

➤ Resources to be made available to support Gen Y in being successful

➤ Similar projects completed by other staff and how they were rewarded, which can be precedence setting in terms of financial compensation

➤ Explain whether rewards are to be distributed based on individual or team merit, and provide a rationale for the decision

➤ Articulation of who will make the final decisions pertaining to allocation of rewards

The criteria have been communicated, and now, we are left to consider who gets the distinguished honor of being called a *superstar* in our organization.

# Identifying the superstars

The integrity of our reward system hinges on procedural justice, that is, having the right set of tools in place to identify the *superstar performers* in our workplace. A structurally sound and accurate process to ascertain whose performance exceeds standards and is worthy of honorary recognition has many benefits for our organization. Some of them are as follows:

➤ Minimizes the number of complaints and grievances about unfair and discriminatory practices when our superstars are publically announced

➤ Allows our organization to showcase the right superstars as role models who inspire the performance of others

➤ Inspires staff to continue striving for and exceeding performance standards that are beneficial to our organization's bottom line

➤ Garners far-reaching staff support and commitment for the reward system, which is important when job candidates and new recruits ask the staff about their perceptions and experiences

➤ More likely to rally staff cooperation in revising the reward system when it is already standing on a foundation of fairness and equity

➤ Reduces the strain on you when you are no longer required to field endless questions from disgruntled staff about an incentive system that is flawed

Our best bet to accurately identify peak performers rests in developing and sustaining a valid and reliable performance-appraisal process. Our work in *Chapter 6, Performance Management– Becoming Hyper-Intentional About Sustainability,* on performance management was geared purposefully toward developing an appraisal system that provides the evidence we require to make informed decisions about which employees are in the upper quartile of performance in our organization. Performance-appraisal processes that best support our decision-making process in a performance-based reward system will:

➤ Position the GPS document as the centerpiece in the evaluation process, as it contains the following key decision-making data:

➢ Identifies specific goals that employees will work toward over the course of the year

➢ Describes the anticipated outcomes with focus on how the achievement of goals aligns with vision, mission, and strategic goals at the individual, team, and organizational levels

➢ Includes details about how outputs will be measured and documented

> ➤ Capitalize on an internal 360-degree feedback process which:
>
>> ➢ Captures Gen Y's many roles, contributions, and achievements as witnessed by the staff who have worked closely with them over the course of the year and that can't be captured in the feedback from one person
>>
>> ➢ Has a high degree of reliability, especially when similar feedback is given by several staff
>
> ➤ Conduct comprehensive appraisal interviews that cover:
>
>> ➢ Gen Y's self-assessment of their performance over the year
>>
>> ➢ Your feedback on Gen Y's achievements, contributions, and overall success based on last year's GPS report
>>
>> ➢ Gen Y's impressions of the 360-degree feedback they received

To complement the performance-appraisal system, consider putting in place a system to track, evaluate, and compare the performance of your employees. With this mechanism in place, you and your Gen Y staff can:

> ➤ Have reliable information at your fingertips to ascertain whether project outcomes were reached and to determine who is and isn't eligible for rewards
>
> ➤ Monitor the progress on projects and celebrate milestones along the way and at the end
>
> ➤ Detect early signs of obstacles that threaten the achievement of stated outcomes
>
> ➤ Strategize approaches to minimize or eliminate obstacles
>
> ➤ Revise action strategies to achieve goals if original plans are on wobbly footing and stagnating achievement of projected outcomes
>
> ➤ Have access to data that justifies decisions made around the allocation of rewards

Tracking progress can take many forms and can be adapted based on the resources available to you. The exact data to be collected depends on the nature of the projects Gen Y is involved in and the corresponding metrics that have been circled as the pinnacles of success. Quantitative and qualitative data can be gleaned from your organization's databank, which houses records on key performance indicators, interviews with the staff most closely affiliated with the projects, and surveys administered to clients, customers and external partners.

As we close this section, it is important to mention that the identification of *superstar performers* in our organization carries the risk of creating a competitive culture that can foster resentment and divisiveness. In order to minimize this from happening, look for ways to recognize the achievements of all of your staff. This could take the form of recognizing staff achievements informally at team meetings and during more formal organizational celebrations. In the section on *Reframing challenges as opportunities*, there are suggestions on how you can acknowledge your staff for achievements other than overall superstar performance, such as risk taking and exemplary leadership on a project.

# Fine-tuning our process – differentiating between low-end, middle, and top performers

Should we be cognizant of *how many* of our staff are given superstar status? Yes, indeed. Assigning too many staff to the top quartile can do considerable damage to a program that began with good intentions. Adverse consequences could include the following:

> ➤ Diluting the impact and distinction of performance-based pay that originated as a coveted reward for the most highly acclaimed performance in our organization

> ➤ Quickly depleting the funds that were set aside for reward payouts

In order to avoid these outcomes, consider putting additional parameters in place around reward eligibility. For example, you may want to implement a forced distribution protocol whereby you distinguish between your low-end, middle, and top performers. This could take the form of a 10-75-15 distribution where:

> ➤ 10 percent of staff are assigned to the low-end category, where performance, for the most part, is below par

> ➤ 75 percent of staff are put in the middle category, where performance meets or slightly exceeds standards

> ➤ 15 percent of staff are named in the top performance category, that is, the red carpet of honorary contributions and achievements to the organization

You are now positioned to decide on the size of the reward differential that should exist between each of these three levels of performance. For example, you might elect to have a 35 percent differential between the middle and top performers on your team. You can then translate the percentage into a cash amount based on your annual budget for the performance-based reward system. As you decide on the percentages and cash values for each performance level, be mindful to have payout differentials that will be perceived as fair and equitable by your staff. This would be an ideal place to consult with your staff to get their input on what would be appropriate.

Now that we have the structure to reward performance in place, where does the money come from on payday?

# Determining fund size – how fat is your wallet?

Our next order of business is to determine the fund size, that is, the amount of money from our organization's treasury that will be reserved to reward performance. Ideally, we'd like to implement a process that:

> ➤ Is perceived by the staff as a fair financial return for their achievements

> ➤ Does not require exhausting and complex accounting gymnastics to reconfigure our current system

> ➤ Is cost responsible and won't burn a hole in our organization's already lean wallet

➤ Can be maintained and adjusted with ease to meet our organization's changing financial status

➤ Can be easily comprehended by our staff; this increases their perception of procedural justice in the system

One of the options available to us involves making changes in the fund that is currently reserved for merit increases. This is a logical and financially astute place to start, as there is growing concern that merit increases no longer serve us well. Merit increases have lost their appeal in the lineup of performance rewards for three key reasons. They are as follows:

➤ They lost their clout as motivators when they became awarded almost automatically, that is, some managers feel compelled to give even their weakest employees a merit increase in order to avoid confrontations with the staff about why they received no merit increase. This signals to all employees that the link between performance and merit increases is broken, hence devaluing the once highly lauded annual accolade.

➤ Merit increases are permanent calculations on an employee's base pay. This means that even though an employee's performance may be substandard in subsequent years, they still reap the annual financial benefits from the previous year of performance glory.

➤ As merit increases have been dished out to everyone, the amount of money available to reward shining superstars on our team has significantly depleted, hence losing their luster as a motivational force in our reward system.

As merit increases are losing their motivational punch, consider transferring a portion of the money set aside for merit increases into a performance-based reward fund. Instead of allocating across-the-board annual merit increases to your employees based on how well they performed their work within the parameters of their job description, save a portion of the money to reward performance that exceeds standards. The actual amount allocated is at your discretion. However, if you are looking for a guideline, consider setting aside 25-30 percent in a given accounting cycle for rewarding high performers. This way, you'll have money in the coffers to recognize employees through the merit system as well as to reward star performers.

Another option is to allocate a straight percentage from your company's net income to establish a performance-based reward fund. Again, the exact percentage is at your discretion. Our earlier discussion about identifying and tracking the metrics for projects will be critical in determining what specific percentage should be held in reserve for employee payouts. As a general rule, the projects that have the greatest impact on your key performance indicators are the ones that should be compensated at higher percentages.

In some cases, the amount of the reward is determined on a discretionary basis, but typically, a target bonus is set for each eligible position, and adjustments are then made for greater or less than targeted performance. Performance ratings are obtained for each employee, and preliminary incentives are computed. Estimates for the total amount of money to be spent on incentives are thereby made and compared with the bonus fund available. If necessary, individual estimates are then adjusted.

Whatever approach you choose, remember to do the following:

> ➤ Communicate frequently with your staff from the original discussion about reward eligibility to the final allocation of rewards

> ➤ Be transparent and open in addressing questions that the staff have about the process and the differentiated rewards they receive

> ➤ Train new managers who join your organization so that they are equipped to join you in making fair and equitable decisions pertaining to rewards

> ➤ Orient new recruits so that they know how to become eligible for rewards

# Rewarding team performance

In some cases, there is such strong team collaboration on a project that it is difficult to separate the contributions of each team member and then assign the right rewards without arousing concerns about inequity and unfairness. To avoid this, we might want to explore other reward options in order to do the following:

> ➤ Preserve team bonds

> ➤ Encourage future team collaborations

> ➤ Sustain fairness and equity in our reward system

> ➤ Avoid the endless parade of employees complaining about injustice

You may want to consider rewarding teams using one of the following approaches:

> ➤ All team members receive the reward earned by the highest achiever

> ➤ All members receive the reward earned by the lowest achiever

> ➤ All members receive the reward equal to the average achievement by the team

Much like performance-based rewards for individuals, there needs to be a measurable definition of team performance or productivity that is communicated to the team before they embark on their project. There also needs to be an accurate tracking system to ascertain if, and when, these predetermined standards and expectations are exceeded and eligible for a reward.

Even though cash incentives are tantalizing for team-based achievements, Gen Y is even more attracted to noncash incentives. A growing trend in team incentives is the use of outdoor adventures such as skiing, white-water rafting, kayaking, and hiking to reward teams. These outdoor adventures have a host of benefits. They are as follows:

> ➤ Celebrate team achievements

> ➤ Foster team spirit and fun, which are valued in a Gen Y work world

> ➤ Reduce stress accumulated during the course of busy work days

> ➤ Provide opportunities for personal growth and development

> ➤ More cost effective than cash payouts

A cash incentive is quickly forgotten and is sometimes perceived as insufficient, whereas experiential rewards are team-bonding experiences that resonate with Gen Y long after the events.

# Recognizing staff – possibilities beyond cash

Even though money is important to Gen Y and appreciated at the time it is received, it is *here today and gone tomorrow,* that is, it is quickly spent and forgotten. Hence, it can weaken the intended purpose of rewards and recognition. To limit this from happening, there is another category of incentives that is equally salient for us to adapt alongside financial rewards. The added bonus is that it can be far less cost draining on our organization than monetary incentivizing. If we are committed to design a reward and recognition system that is earmarked as a drawing card for Gen Y, then let's cast our gaze beyond money and into a domain that is often overlooked. It falls by the wayside due to the busyness of our day or because we don't appreciate the magnitude of its impact on morale, performance, and retention. Incentives that have even greater allure for Gen Y are those that are nonmonetary.

What follows are a few ways in which we can recognize employee achievements without digging deep into our pockets.

## E-recognition – congratulatory messages go viral!

As we've discussed throughout the book, technology is a sixth sense for Gen Y. It permeates every fiber of their existence. It is the source of their knowledge, the vehicle for sharing information with others, and the platform for building and sustaining their networks. The airwaves are constantly buzzing with conversations and news flashes, and Gen Y is at the hub connecting feverishly and continuously in all directions.

On this digital highway awaits an opportunity for us. Consider how we can capitalize on the flurry of online activity with *e-recognition*, that is, a digital platform that showcases the best of our staff. E-recognition could take the form of a Twitter feed or a link on your website that serves as a venue for broadcasting news about your staff's achievements. Whatever option you choose, it is about using technology as a way to:

> ➤ Convey stories about your employees' achievements and contributions
>
> ➤ Serve as a means for other staff to chime in with their congratulatory messages
>
> ➤ Build momentum for other staff to keep reaching for their own successes

So that the full weight of populating the site with messages does not fall exclusively on your shoulders, encourage everyone in your organization to participate. Anyone who has a story to share about a colleague or a team's achievement is invited to post on the site and to invite others to join in with congratulatory messages. Watch the excitement and pride that spreads like wildfire when employees receive one congratulatory message after another splashed across their computer screen in recognition of their work. It is the ultimate adrenaline rush for our Gen Y staff. Also, it contributes significantly to the creation of a culture of inclusivity and appreciation that Gen Y wants to be associated with. Guidelines to make it work include the following:

> ➤ Encouraging real-time announcements so that the site doesn't get dragged down with ancient history postings from weeks or months ago

> ➤ Showcasing contributions to the organization and to the community at large

> ➤ Contributing stories that comment on specific behaviors associated with the achievement or contribution

> ➤ Explaining how the achievement aligns with one or a combination of your organization's values

> ➤ Commenting on the impact that the achievement will have on the organization

> ➤ Inviting others to offer their congratulatory remarks

In order to sustain the momentum for e-recognition, consider leaving space on the agenda of your staff meetings to recognize employee contributions. This regular placeholder, preferably at the beginning of meetings where it can establish a positive tone for engagement, can be used for anyone, including you, to acknowledge someone on the team who is worthy of recognition. Then, you or a staff member can post the accolades for a wider audience to see.

# Personalized recognitions – beyond another gold-plated watch

*A fancy silver candy dish*

*A fleece-lined company jacket*

*A gold-plated watch*

*Along with your gift, you receive a certificate and a company pin*

Our organizations spend an exorbitant amount of money on rewards and recognitions. Added to this, we spend a considerable amount of time thumbing through catalogs that feature trinkets, gadgets, and knick-knacks. Someone far away in corporate recognition land decided that these were trending status symbols that we must adorn our staff with when they do something extraordinary. We ruminate endlessly over which items we should crown our star performers with until our brains ache, and we can't bear the thought of looking at one more silver candy dish. Then, there is the added bonus round of agony that comes from making sure that the monetary value of the gifts equates with the level of achievement. Finally, we make a decision as to which mementos we will bestow upon our employees that will serve as eternal keepsakes which remind them of our undying gratitude for their service and contributions.

Right?

Go see where you'll find those symbols of undying gratitude. That fancy silver candy dish you gave to Jasmine is being used to hold paper clips, the company jacket you gave Jordan has been relegated to the back of his closet and neglected, and the gold-plated watch you gave Greg? Who needs a watch when we all have smart phones?

Gen Y shakes its heads in disbelief at the tokens of appreciation that we come up with. These gestures are perceived by Gen Y as:

➤ Antiquated practices that may have appealed to other generations but haven't been adapted to the value system of the latest generation in the workplace

➤ Lacking in flexibility and choice, which are the mainstay of their generation

➤ Missing the mark on the fun and excitement that they expect from our organization, even in the rewards that are given

For these reasons, let's scrap the plaques, mugs, and pen sets traditionally given. Instead of being the key decision makers in the recognition department, let's permit our employees to decide how they'd like to spend the money assigned to their achievements. The choice is theirs as to whether they want to spend their reward money on that which is fun, career-enhancing, or philanthropic. Also, let's give them the option to either spend the money as awarded or accumulate reward money and use it for a larger purchase. Whatever they choose, they are spending reward money in ways that are deeply personal and meaningful to them; hence, we avoid wasteful expenditure on paraphernalia that have little or no value to them.

To guide our staff in the decision-making process and to ensure the choices made align with the overall purpose of our reward system, let's put a few parameters in place. For example, the money can be allocated toward:

➤ Professional development tied to their career aspirations

➤ Launching a new project that is aligned with our organization's vision, mission, or strategic direction

➤ A community initiative or charity that aligns with their values and that of the organization

➤ Their personal wellness, which extends in many directions such as fitness, art classes, theatre, yoga, travel, or a hobby

Also, consider creating a digital storyboard on your company's website where reward recipients can voluntarily post photos and stories about how they spent their reward money. The benefits of this include the following:

➤ Showcase the contributions of your staff

➤ Serve as a memory board of your organization's culture and showcase how your organization is living its values

➤ Inspire recognition pathways for other staff

➤ Showcase the launch of new projects within your company and in the community

➤ Serve as a recruitment tool that gives job applicants a glimpse into your reward system and, in doing so, reveals your organization's culture

➤ Market your organization to new clients and customers, especially if you are in a competitive industry that would benefit from differentiation from your competitors

# Spontaneous bursts of caring – just because

One of my Gen Y staff members once told me:

> *Sometimes, motivation has nothing to do with formal reward and recognition systems. It's about recognizing the power of spontaneous bursts of caring.*

When Gen Y goes job hunting, they look for jobs that meet their salary and reward expectations, but equally important is finding a company that values and appreciates them. A family-like atmosphere in which there is care, compassion, and interest in getting to know them as people is a top contender for first place on their decision-making checklist when they are considering whether or not to join our organization.

*Spontaneous bursts of caring* are equally as important to Gen Y as the incentives you have in place to reward their performance. These *bursts* are random and unexpected gestures of appreciation, which show your Gen Y staff that you care about them as individuals. These actions can have a similarly powerful impact on inspiring Gen Y to stretch toward peak performance and beyond and convincing them to stay with our organization.

What *spontaneous bursts of caring* have you shown recently to your staff?

If this isn't something you've been doing, now's the perfect time to begin. However, only venture into this area if you are prepared to be sincere and genuine in your actions. If you are doing this to be strategically appropriate, then don't bother. Gen Y can quickly figure out whether you are sincere or disingenuous. If your actions appear to be fake, Gen Y soon becomes indifferent to your gestures; hence, the purpose of showing appreciation is defeated.

If you are prepared to offer *sincere* appreciation, then take time to honor and appreciate your staff. Showing your appreciation can happen after you've seen extraordinary effort and collaboration by your team and, at times, when you simply want to celebrate. The point to stress here is the importance of showing appreciation occasionally. If repeated too often, the *spontaneous bursts of caring* can become devalued as rewards.

Signs of appreciation can take the form of the following:

> ➤ Lunch or dinner at a local Gen Y hangout.

> ➤ A catered buffet lunch at the office.

> ➤ Gift cards for the movies, their favorite store, or online purchases.

> ➤ A more lavish splurge such as hiking, renting a boat for the day, skiing for the afternoon, bumper car racing, or leading the pack in bungee jumping (okay, maybe not).

> ➤ Workday flexibility, that is, coming in a few hours late or leaving a few hours early one day. This needs to be coordinated so that it does not disrupt project deadlines.

> ➤ A day off, which is not taken out of their vacation allowance. Time off is visible to the team as a reward, and it is greatly valued by a generation that places high priority on work-life balance.

By celebrating your team through *spontaneous bursts of caring*, you also make the workplace a fun place to be, which is one of the high-priority attributes of an organization that Gen Y wants to stay with. We can be a fun place to work and, at the same time, be committed to achieve the high standards that are mandated by our organization's goals and objectives. You can actually leverage both!

# Incorporating a few tantalizing workplace perks

Even though the ideas presented in this section are not traditionally found under the umbrella of recognition for star performance, they do warrant an honorable mention. They can make the difference between a mediocre and a thriving rewards-based culture. Offered are a few suggestions about the type of workplace that inspires Gen Y to do their best work and, in doing so, increases the probability that their performance meets and exceeds workplace standards and expectations. These suggestions are a drawing card for our Gen Y workforce, because they are specifically targeted at fulfilling Gen Y's lifestyle needs, especially the needs for flexible work options, autonomy, and work-life balance.

# Work space – here, there, and everywhere

Gen Y has a preference for mobility through their day. They tend not to do well in sedentary situations and prefer to have choices in regards to the physical space in which they work and when they work. The atmosphere is important to Gen Y; the right space for working can inspire their most creative and innovative thinking. We'll likely find them getting more done and to a higher standard when they have the autonomy to make their own decisions about where they want to work, what hours they prefer, and how they would like to complete their work. Yes, we need to hold them accountable to you and to their team for being available for meetings and for tasks that require them to be in a certain place at a certain time. Yet, beyond these expectations, let's give them the freedom to chart their own direction.

This autonomy and flexibility can take the form of working from home, at the local coffee shop, or at the park. Also, let's give them some workspace options within the four walls of our organization. As informality and open spaces are preferred by Gen Ys, consider how space in your company can be converted accordingly. This will unquestionably depend on your budget and the physical space you have in your organization, but here are a few examples to get you thinking about space allocation:

> ➤ Breakout rooms with a leisurely vibe, that is, couches and a coffee bar or cafe
> ➤ Outdoor patio converted into a workspace
> ➤ Games room, which is the incubator for innovative new collaborations
> ➤ Art room with whiteboards and e-boards for brainstorming sessions
> ➤ Meditation room for personal reflection

Sweeten the pot even more with a few additional workplace perks. These include the following:

> ➤ Paid overtime, which is especially important to a generation that is not keen on working extra hours that infringe on their work-life balance
> ➤ Subsidize their travel during the day so that they can go to places that inspire them to do their best work
> ➤ Fitness membership that allow them to look after their wellness needs and be creatively inspired

# Expatriate opportunities – pack your bags!

Of all the generations in our workplace, Gen Y has the strongest desire for short-term assignments and collaborations that involve travel, especially internationally. After graduating from secondary or post-secondary education, many Gen Ys choose to travel before entering the workforce. The allure of exploring unfamiliar cultures, having life-changing experiences, and cultivating new friendships is gripping and becomes that which they want to continue doing in their careers.

Consider opportunities for Gen Y to do the following:

> Lead or work with teams on international projects already in progress

> Join teams that are heading on international expeditions to pitch new partnership ideas

> Collaborate with other Gen Ys who work for international branches of your company in launching initiatives to attract, engage, and retain more Gen Ys to your organization

> Train members of your staff who will be on expatriate assignments in countries that they have traveled to

> Explore with you opportunities for collaboration in other countries based on their experiences and the networks they have cultivated

Gen Y is ideally suited to be our ambassadors internationally given their:

> Curiosity about the world

> Adaptability to different cultures

> Flexible approach to living

# A philanthropic generation

Take a peek at Gen Y's resumes, and you'll see an interesting trend. Gen Y has a deeply entrenched commitment to philanthropy, which appears to be more prevalent in this generation than others. Gen Y's desire to make a difference in the community is embedded in their value system, and it is evident in the personal leadership they have exercised early in their lives. For the most part, their philanthropic roots date back to their secondary and post-secondary schooling and take the form of volunteer work, internships, placements, and cooperatives in local, national, and international communities. Many of them went on to pursue diplomas and degrees that equipped them with the skills, knowledge, and abilities to be able to contribute more significantly to the causes that are important to them. In some cases, they deferred entry into paid positions in order to pursue humanitarian interests. Many who have returned from these projects remain committed to spreading their philanthropic wings throughout their careers.

Encouraging and supporting our Gen Y staff in their community pursuits can create a favorable impression of our company as a place where Gen Y wants to work. This could take the form of the following:

> Link Gen Y's work assignments to community initiatives

> Encourage them to explore partnerships between your organization and the community

> Carve out time once a week, for example, for them to engage in community initiatives that also serve as a powerful way for your organization to establish its community presence

> Involve Gen Y in leading workplace initiatives that support community fundraising initiatives

By allowing Gen Y to engage with the community, we may be on the receiving end of new community partnerships that we never thought possible until Gen Y exercised their leadership to make the connections. You may find new ways to establish your presence in the community which leads to creative and innovative new projects that benefit your organization and the community at large.

# Sometimes, it's about doing nothing at all

*Great! Fantastic!*

*You are doing a super job!*

*Wonderful! That's amazing!*

*That's the best work I've seen you do! I wish I could clone you!*

Can there be *too much of a good thing*? Yes, and this is a classic example.

Although praise and recognition are power-house motivators, they can also have an adverse impact. In our overzealousness to be more diligent in recognizing staff's accomplishments, we run the risk of showering Gen Y with so much praise that it is perceived as disingenuous; hence, it loses its punch as a motivator. When Gen Y comes to realize that recognition is given indiscriminately, it then becomes no more than vacuous noise bestowed upon them. Consequently, we lose our credibility in giving sincere and meaningful praise.

Some of the work that our Gen Y staff engages in is so intrinsically rewarding that there is no need for us to intervene. That is, their work is so personally gratifying that they don't need the financial and nonfinancial rewards that we might be inclined to heap upon them. They are so consumed with the work they are doing and fuelled wholly by the satisfaction that comes from doing that which speaks deeply and passionately to their values that they don't need or expect anything in return. They know their work is important, and no one needs to affirm, confirm, or reinforce this.

Our challenge and opportunity is to find the right balance between recognizing work and letting staff relish in the intrinsic satisfaction derived from the work they are doing. The performance-appraisal interview is the perfect place to have these discussions. As this is the time when you discuss Gen Y's goals, action plans, and outputs, it might be a natural next step to discuss how they would like to be acknowledged for their work. Engage Gen Y in conversation about the following:

> ➤ Activities for which they expect to be financially and non-financially recognized
> ➤ Work that is intrinsically satisfying and does not require financial or nonfinancial recognition
> ➤ Rewards and recognition they would value as they carry out their job accountabilities

In doing so, we leverage the complexities of financially and non-financially rewarding our staff and *sometimes doing nothing at all.*

# Reframing challenges as opportunities

The downside of reward and recognition systems is that some of our staff might lean toward *playing it safe*. They might be somewhat risk adverse and decide to stay within their comfort zone, that is, commit to projects and set goals that are easy victories. This will more likely secure them the coveted awards that we have to offer.

Let's reframe this for our staff. Consider a way to acknowledge members of your team who have been courageous enough to step outside their comfort zone and engage in riskier initiatives. They may have fallen short of reaching the anticipated target or missed the goal completely because of a glitch in their action plan, but our focus is on acknowledging their *willingness to take risks*. In doing so, we communicate to staff that our workplace is a safe climate for them to take risks. As well, we signal to staff that we support their willingness to go in new directions, even though the end result may be a disappointing miss.

How can you acknowledge the staff in your team who are willing to take this courageous leap? Be creative and have some fun with this. Remember, Gen Y values a playful work atmosphere, and this would be right up their alley. Consider a new batch of awards in your organization such as the following:

> ➤ Extraordinary effort award
> ➤ Courageous experimentation award
> ➤ Dogged determination award
> ➤ Awesomely persistent employee award
> ➤ Flying-without-wings award

Perhaps the recognition comes in the form of a gift certificate or monetary value that can be used for professional development to support the work they are experimenting with.

In doing so, we create a culture that recognizes staff who have the courage to step into the unknown and experiment. Eventually, one of those wild experimentations that failed a few times might one day propel our organization in a new direction, which hits the mark in setting us apart from the competition.

# Leaning in to change

Is there a financial or nonfinancial reward that grabs your attention? Throughout this chapter, we've focused on a variety of ways you can reward and recognize your staff. Consider selecting one approach that you read about that might work in your organization. Take the idea to your staff and seek their input on whether this would make good sense as a new addition to your current reward and recognition system.
A few questions to guide your investigation are as follows:

> ➤ What is the value of adding this approach to our current complement of rewards and recognition?
> ➤ How can we adapt it for use in our company?

➤ What policies and procedures do we need to put in place to enhance the probability that its implementation is perceived as fair and equitable?

➤ How can we sustain it as a value-added reward?

➤ What changes might be required in other aspects of our reward and recognition system in order to accommodate this new addition?

Please join me online (www.eyeofthetigerconsulting.ca) to share your insights and experiences in adding this new approach to your current reward and recognition system.

# Google it

Here are a few additional resources for those of you who would like to continue exploring reward and recognition systems:

➤ D., Deeprose, D, *How to Recognize and Reward Employees: 150 Ways to Inspire Peak Performance*, American Management Association, 2006

➤ A., Gostick and C., Elton, *The Carrot Principle: How the Best Managers Use Recognition to Engage their People, Retain Staff, and Accelerate Performance*, O.C. Tanner Company, 2009

➤ B., Nelson, *1501 Ways to Reward Employees*, Workman Publishing Company, 2012

➤ D., Pink, *Drive: The Surprising Truth About What Motivates Us*, Riverhead Books (also available on Ted Talks), 2009

➤ Pink, D, *Ted Talks: The Puzzle of Motivation*, 2009

# Meeting the Gen Y community – introducing…Victoria Kovalenko!

*What are the rewards and incentives that attract you to an organization and motivate your high performance?*

Victoria started our conversation with a lovely story about her days working as a hostess in a restaurant where she was questioning whether she should really give her heart to the job. The answer and her ultimate decision to stay with the company became crystal clear when her supervisor said, *"We love you here, and we love your energy."* That's all Victoria needed to hear in order to commit wholeheartedly to her job.

For Victoria, the greatest rewards we can give our staff are genuine appreciation of who they are and the work they do and our willingness to really get to know them as people. Gen Y will perform up to the work standards and beyond when we communicate that we sincerely like them and value their contributions to our company, especially when they go freely out of their way to accommodate a customer, support their team members, or make suggestions that add value to our operations. Also, the timing of our feedback is critical. Aim to give feedback as soon as you witness or hear that your Gen Y staff have done something worthy of applause. Showing our appreciation can also extend beyond verbal recognition, that is, consider taking the staff out for a coffee or for lunch or offering tickets to an upcoming concert or sporting event based on what you know they like.

Added to this, Victoria mentioned that offering Gen Y new challenges and opportunities to develop their skills and abilities is also an important component of rewarding staff. She advises us to check in often with the staff to offer praise and constructive feedback and to assist them as needed. However, refrain from micromanagement; it's a motivation killer for Gen Y.

Victoria noted that money motivates Gen Y to apply to our organization, but retaining Gen Y is dependent on creating a climate of recognition.

> *Victoria was born in Russia and immigrated on her own to Canada when she was 15 years old. She was raised by her mom and grandmother who taught her the importance of earning rewards in life based on having a strong work ethic. Victoria envisions building her career in the restaurant industry where she can be an exemplary manager and extend family values into her work with staff. Yet, don't be surprised if you someday see Victoria on the cover of a fashion magazine. Victoria would love to be a model!*

# Summary

This chapter was our foray into the world of rewarding peak Gen Y performers. We shed the plaques, trophies, and recognition pins and embraced a new package of financial and nonfinancial rewards. We started our voyage with an exploration of financial incentives and then moved into ways to reward performance by not digging so deep into your wallet. We went viral with e-recognition and learned that there are ways to recognize our staff beyond another gold-plated watch. We then discussed those spontaneous bursts of caring and came to realize that sometimes, it's about doing nothing at all. Our final inquiry was into how we can reward and recognize those bold and courageous bouts of experimentation that our staff are willing to engage in.

We now turn our attention to *Chapter 8, Mentoring the Next Generation of Leaders – Legacy Building, One Gen Y at a Time*, where we discuss the leadership role you play in mentoring Gen Y on their career development journey and in developing the talent you need for the future of your organization.

# Mentoring the Next Generation of Leaders – Legacy Building, One Gen Y at a Time

*You're leaving? Wait! You can't leave! What about your future here?*

How often have you come across this situation? Gen Y walks out the door to begin employment elsewhere, and you are left wondering what you could have done to keep them from leaving.

Since we started working together in this book, we've been on a journey, exploring how to transfer new learning from each chapter into practice in order to create *the right* workplace culture for Gen Y. Our work has spanned across the organizational horizon. We have:

> Revamped our training programs to accommodate a techno-savvy generation

> Reconfigured work assignments to meet Gen Y's needs for variety, challenge, and fun

> Remodeled our rewards and recognition system to hit the target in how we honor best performance

> Learned a new language to communicate effectively with Gen Y so that conversations with them are awesome

What else could Gen Y possibly want from us?

There's one more element in the equation for us to consider: *have we paid attention to Gen Y's career and lifestyle aspirations?*

Gen Y, like all generations, is interested in career-development opportunities. However, the crowning difference is the *pace* with which they envision themselves progressing within our organization to reach the promised land. They want to progress quickly, starting now. The quest for opportunities to grow and develop personally and professionally is a top priority for Gen Y. Even in their early days with us, they seek to know the programs we have that can put them on the fast track to their career destination.

Knowing this about Gen Y, let's not delay in getting the career conversation rolling. As soon as you are confident that you'd like to keep someone on your team for the long haul, initiate the career-development process. Even though we may not be able to accommodate Gen Y's need for speed and immediacy in their professional advancement *exactly* as requested, we can cocreate a new career reality that is attractive to them and to us. By doing so, we:

> ➤ Plant a strong and compelling vision for our Gen Y staff of their future with our organization, so they'll want to make a long term commitment to us

> ➤ Secure our organization's legacy by having a team of qualified Gen Ys to take the leadership reins in our organization

The roadmap to reach these goals is revealed in this chapter. Specifically, our focus is on the leadership role you can play in mentoring Gen Y on their career-development journey and—equally important—in developing the talent needed so that you have the *right staff,* with the *right skills,* in the *right roles* for your organization's future. To get us there, we'll cover the following topics:

> ➤ Getting YOU primed for the mentoring journey ahead

> ➤ Parachuting Gen Y into their future—their wish list and your map

> ➤ Hey! Can I get a little support here?

Mentoring has the potential to become the quintessential ingredient in professional development for our Gen Y workforce, enabling them to reach their career goals and enabling us to fulfill our mandate of building organizational prosperity through the management of human capital. In doing so, we seal our organization's competitive advantage.

I smell smoke. A concern has been ignited for many of us.

# So, what's burning?

*Why would I waste time mentoring Gen Y when they have no intention of staying in my company? I'll invest all this time and money in professional development, and then, they will leave. My investment literally walks out the door and into another organization!*

We are angered to know that our employees, who choose to leave our organization, might march through the competition's front door, fully trained and prepared to assume new work accountabilities *at our expense.* Our competition won't need to shell out money for Gen Y's professional development, because we've already footed the bill! This is a sobering reality that causes many of us to rethink whether we want to invest our limited resources into mentoring initiatives for Gen Y.

Yet, before we completely go to the dark side and dismiss mentorship completely, consider the benefits to be reaped from this unique one-on-one coaching opportunity. Investing in mentorship carries many benefits, including the following:

> ➤ Accelerates career progression, meaning we can get our Gen Ys ready for leadership roles sooner rather than later

> ➤ Stands as an unrivalled approach to transfer organizational wisdom, skills, and abilities from seasoned to younger workers

> ➤ Reduces job ambiguity, which decreases work-related stress and enhances job performance, productivity, and efficiency

> ➤ Enhances job and career satisfaction

> ➤ Advances development of leadership skills attributed to the one-on-one coaching between you and your Gen Y staff member

> ➤ Serves as our strategic advantage, especially in regards to recruitment and retention

If we go down the rabbit hole thinking that Gen Y will irrefutably leave us, we increase the probability of a self-fulfilling prophecy. This means that we might consciously or unconsciously act or react in ways that push Gen Y out of our organization and into the welcoming arms of our competition. We may be causing Gen Y to leave at a faster rate because of how we connect or don't connect with them about their career prospects. We may not even realize that we are doing this!

Is it possible to break free from this? Definitely! However, as we proceed through this chapter, let's be mindful that no pathway proposed guarantees that Gen Y will stay with us. As we've come to realize, there are few certainties when it comes to working with others. Nevertheless, we can develop new ways of supporting Gen Y in their career journey that weakens their desire to flee for greener pastures where they anticipate their careers will be better served.

In order to enhance the attractiveness of our organization to Gen Y, we'll explore the fundamentals of mentoring that equip us to engage with them in career building and nurturing conversations. We'll focus specifically on how to:

➤ Maintain open and transparent channels of communication

➤ Detect early signs of complications

➤ Increase our confidence in order to step into tough conversations, if needed

➤ Monitor frequently whether Gen Y's career progression is on track

➤ Check periodically whether the process is working effectively for us as well

Let's now turn our attention to the mechanics of mentoring Gen Y in ways that inspire their professional development within our organization and communicate that we are committed to working with them to become the leaders they aspire to be.

The journey begins with *you*.

# Getting YOU primed for the mentoring journey ahead

Career-development conversations with our staff usually kick off with heavy-duty mental gymnastics, that is, meticulously formulating a career-advancement strategy. This usually takes the form of establishing career goals that align with the organization's strategic compass, charting an exact set of action strategies to achieve the said goals and forecasting outcomes to be realized when the goals are achieved.

As important as these considerations are to career mapping and execution, there is another ingredient in the formula that is equally important. On the surface, the ingredient may seem trivial, but—if negated—it puts the entire career-advancement process in peril. It is an ingredient of **good conversations** that often remains in the shadows but one that should be on our radar screen. It has the power to differentiate us from other leaders in how we mentor Gen Y.

Our home game advantage in mentoring begins with mastering the art and science of *setting the right tone for dialog.* The challenge and opportunity are to set the climate for collaborative and meaningful mentorship that compels Gen Y to:

➤ Make our organization their professional home

➤ Flourish to new heights in their career, beyond what they thought possible

➤ Hone the competencies required to be future leaders in our organization

How do we achieve this? It starts with *you* accepting a special invitation.

# An invitation to get over ourselves

One Friday morning, a Gen Y staff member walked into my office, parked herself in a chair across from me, and blurted out, *"Will you take over the role of mentoring me? It's just not working with Dr. "X". He just doesn't get it."*

I sat for the longest time trying to figure out what exactly *"it"* was. My young office visitor also tussled with this. She wasn't sure what prompted her to walk out of his office and waltz into mine. However, in the end, *"it"* came down to *sandbox basics*, that is, lessons we learned in childhood about how to be in the presence of others. Yet, for some of us, these life lessons drifted from consciousness and practice. These sandbox basics reveal themselves in the words we use, our tone of voice, and subtleties in our gestures.

Regrettably, some of us are oblivious to how we present ourselves to others in these three areas. Is our presence received by others as a welcoming embrace or a knockout punch?

The core of our success in connecting deeply and meaningfully with Gen Y hinges on the *sandbox basics*. In order to create a climate characterized as collaborative, authentic, and supportive, here are a few guidelines to consider:

> ➤ Canvass feedback from others about how your choice of words, tone of voice, and nonverbal messages are perceived

> ➤ Act on this feedback so that you move closer to setting the right tone for dialog

> ➤ Let go of preconceived notions of what career laddering should entail

> ➤ Refrain from projecting your values and expectations onto others

> ➤ Withhold judgment on the rightness or wrongness of what Gen Ys want to do with their lives

> ➤ Avoid jumping in with unsolicited advice

> ➤ Let go of assumptions that your way is the best way and the only way

> ➤ Stay grounded in unconditional positive regard, even though Gen Y's career aspirations are different from what you envision for them

> ➤ Enter into the mentoring relationship with the right attitudes and beliefs about supporting Gen Y

> ➤ Be courageous enough to admit that you cannot mentor someone if you don't have all of these qualities

Furthermore, as you know, Gen Y has a voracious appetite for career advancement that is aimed at seizing the leadership reins sooner than later. In response, we often push back reminding Gen Y that there is a prescribed developmental pathway in our organization that unequivocally *must* be respected and followed in order to earn a coveted leadership seat. This exasperates Gen Y. In response, they push back with a litany of reasons why our rules don't make sense. What ensues is a battle of wills.

Why do we keep re-engaging our Gen Ys in the same weary debate? Who says Gen Y *absolutely must follow the prescribed pathway to leadership?* Here's our opportunity to break free from the vicious cycle. When faced with this unrelenting tug of war, we have an opportunity to exercise our leadership to find a solution. It begins with our willingness to suspend our entrenched views on what Gen Y's career trajectory *should* be and enter into an exploratory playground with them. I'm not suggesting we scrap the carefully laid out plans that are the backbone of our organization's talent management and development. I'm simply inviting us to be open and receptive to other options offered by Gen Y. They might actually have refreshingly new ideas that result in giving our talent development programs a much needed dusting off. In doing so, our programs become a better fit for the newest generation in our workplace.

If Gen Y hasn't completed all the steps in our organization's career laddering program, but they have foundational leadership skills coupled with willingness to do the job, then consider letting them fly. Their passion and ambition are exactly what we need in leadership roles if we want to differentiate ourselves in the marketplace.

However, if you aren't quite ready to take the leap with me on this, then let's start incrementally. Perhaps there is a way to meet in the middle by creating an assistant leadership role where Gen Y can be mentored and groomed before they step into a full-fledged leadership position. Yet, underscored here is the importance of keeping Gen Y in the assistant role only long enough to build their capacity and to assure you that they are ready to fly forward. Hopefully, the end result is something everyone can live with.

Now that we are in the right mindset for the journey, what tools do we need?

# Blueprint for your training – yes, training for YOU too!

Mentoring is often viewed as a one-way street, where our attention is focused entirely on the training and development needs of our staff. Yet, equally critical to the long-term viability and success of mentorship is the training given to those of us who have agreed to serve as mentors. Even though you might be tempted to skip this step (I realize how incredibly busy you are, and you may doubt whether training is value added to the overall objectives in play here), I implore you to rethink this. Investing in training to prepare you for mentoring has the following paybacks:

➤ Requisite competencies to coach your staff skilfully toward their goals and those of your organization.

➤ Consistency in how mentoring is conducted across your organization so that Gen Y has equally positive and enriching experiences; hence, we minimize the number of grumblings about inequalities in practice.

➤ Increased likelihood that you choose to remain a mentor in the future because you now have tools to manage the complexities and dynamics of mentoring.

➤ Gen Y has a positive and enriching experience, which increases the likelihood that they set their sights on fulfilling their career aspirations in your organization

> ➤ Gen Y's commitment to stay means you are on track with your legacy-building work to have the right staff, with the right skills ready to assume leadership roles

> ➤ Communicates commit to your own professional development, which earns Gen Y's respect and admiration, and in turn, they have another reason to continue working with and for you

Developing a standardized training program for mentors can be done in consultation with your Human Resources staff or a team of your colleagues who have an interest in jumpstarting the process. If the training expertise does not exist in your organization, consider working with an external consultant who can design and facilitate the training for you. This way, you have a program in place that equips mentors with the tools to coach efficiently and effectively. To get you started, here are a few topics to include in the train-the-mentor architecture:

> ➤ Adult-learning principles and practices to create climates conducive to learning

> ➤ Tools for goal setting and charting action strategies

> ➤ Art and science of cocreating learning experiences with Gen Y

> ➤ Coaching Gen Y to *learn how to learn*, that is, to become critical thinkers, fact finders, and networkers

> ➤ Giving timely and constructive feedback that shapes thinking and actions

> ➤ Proactive problem solving and decision making for you and for Gen Y

> ➤ Conflict management and resolution for those tough coaching conversations

> ➤ Facilitating rather than leading career development discussions

> ➤ Empowering others rather than micromanaging them

> ➤ Linking Gen Y with internal and external networks and resources

> ➤ Moving Gen Y from dependence on mentors to leveraging independence and interdependence on organizational networks

Fully armed with our mentoring skill set, we are ready to coach Gen Y into their future.

# Parachuting Gen Y into their future – their wish list and your map

A three-year study took me into profit and nonprofit organizations across North America where I met Gen Ys who were in the early stages of their careers. With each conversation, I became increasingly aware of the importance that mentorship plays in Gen Y's professional lives and the imperativeness of committing organizational resources to their career advancement. Eighty-five percent of the Gen Ys that I spoke with identified mentoring as the cornerstone of their career development and a key determinant in their decision to join an organization. However, Gen Y's perceptions and experiences with mentoring have been disappointing and discouraging.

Most disturbing was my discovery that only 32 percent of them were satisfied with the mentoring they have received so far in their careers, 38 percent would have preferred better support systems, and 21 percent received no mentoring.

Mentorship, with its capacity to parachute Gen Y into their careers and to be at the forefront of talent development in our organizations, doesn't need to teeter precariously on the edge of disappointment for our Gen Y workforce. We have an opportunity to turn this situation around not only for the benefit of Gen Y but also for our organization. Our future generation of leaders is standing right in front of us with a wealth of insights and personal experiences that can shape our thinking and approach to mentorship. Let's unpack their words of advice and discuss the implications for practice.

# The great revelation – what's on Gen Y's wish list?

Life gets noticeably easier for us after the *great reveal*, that is, when we finally discover Gen Y's wish list of needs and expectations as they pertain to mentoring. When Gen Y's mentoring needs and expectations are unearthed, we are better able to deliver the *right* professional development, pitched at the *right* intensity, in order to achieve the *right* outcomes for them and for us.

So what is Gen Y looking for?

Gen Y expects that we will first set the stage for mentoring by helping them make connections between their career ambitions and the organization's mandate and accountabilities. Specifically, mentoring needs to crystallize their understanding of the following:

> ➤ Role and accountabilities of their current job

> ➤ How current accountabilities ladder into the strategic mandate of the organization

> ➤ Competencies they are expected to develop in order to be promoted into higher level positions

> ➤ Pathways available to develop these competencies

> ➤ Expectations, challenges, and opportunities that come with higher level positions

Drilling down further, Gen Y is looking for a rewarding learning experience that will sharpen their professional presence and catapult them into their desired careers. Specifically, they are looking for mentoring that can:

> ➤ Enhance their professional visibility and credibility in the eyes of their colleagues and senior members of the organization, the industry, and the community in general

> ➤ Open doors to prominent networks that enable their career aspirations to be realized

> ➤ Bring clarity to performance expectations, standards, and behavior that position them to become star performers in the organization

➤ Coach them on the following:

- ➤ Effective and expedient ways to develop the competencies required to reach their career goals
- ➤ Unspoken ways to thrive in the organization and industry
- ➤ Maneuvering the intricacies of office politics in order to preserve their professional reputation
- ➤ Resolving conflicts in ways that minimize the likelihood of stinging and damaging implications
- ➤ Knowing when to lead and when to follow
- ➤ Knowing when to speak and when to remain silent

➤ Managing disillusionment when faced with unchallenging work

➤ Be a platform for their values to flourish, especially their desire for personal flexibility, professional satisfaction, immediacy, and continuous learning as a way of life

➤ Provide ongoing feedback that is developmental, invites self-assessment, and is delivered informally and formally

➤ Encourage active and free experimentation in their work and throughout their involvement in the organization

➤ Allow them to capitalize on their own problem-solving abilities when they stumble rather than micro-managing them every step of the way

➤ Facilitate their development by asking probing questions rather than providing all the answers

➤ Introduce them to unconventional approaches to career management so that they can bypass traditional pathways heavily travelled by others

➤ Fulfill their need for daily contact with you in order to build close working bonds

So, what does Gen Y want from you?

Gen Y also weighed in on the profile of personal attributes and competencies that they expect from their mentors. A burgeoning list of qualities were identified, so for ease of communication (and not to completely overwhelm you with the wish list), the top themes have been presented. According to Gen Y, a mentor's credibility hinges on the following:

➤ A track record of leadership contributions to the organization's strategic vision, mission, and mandate

➤ Coaching skills with signature strength in the ability to give and receive honest feedback and promote self-confidence in rising Gen Y leaders

➤ Openness and transparency in collaborating with others

➤ Ability to juggle multiple responsibilities during tight deadlines

➤ Knowing when to be a leader and when to be a follower

➤ Resilience and ability to find life lessons in emergencies and crises

> ➤ Leveraging life-work commitments and inspiring others to do the same

> ➤ Being task focused, yet making time to maintain workplace relationships

> ➤ Fostering genuine working relationships with staff at all levels in the organization

> ➤ Ability to break free from organizational hierarchies and promote equality across the organization

Now that Gen Y's wish list has been revealed, we need a map to help them navigate into their future.

# Your map – guiding Gen Y to their career destination

Career discussions can be pressure cookers, especially if Gen Y's expectations collide with organizational realities. This is not what we want! We don't want to be embroiled in a discussion that spirals downward into a contest of wills and ends badly by deflating Gen Y's spirit and yours. In order to avoid this, let's map out our route for how we can launch the conversation on a positive note, create a climate of engagement, explore the possibility curve of career laddering for our Gen Y staff, and remain grounded in what is doable within our organization.

The road to achieve these outcomes is paved with good questions. As we discussed in *Chapter 4, Unlocking the Secrets to Awesome Conversations with Gen Y*, the soul of awesome conversations with Gen Y is our willingness to be perpetually and authentically curious rather than evaluative in how we connect with others. This is especially true in career discussions where we need our Gen Y staff to be forthright about their intentions so that we can make prudent decisions about how to fulfil those needs. Here are a few questions to get us into the mindset of curiosity:

> ➤ What is your blue-sky vision for your professional and personal future?

> ➤ What are you currently doing to reach your blue-sky vision?

> ➤ What would you like to continue doing, stop doing, and start doing in order to reach your blue-sky vision?

> ➤ How can I work with you to help you realize your envisioned career?

After setting the right climate, we enter into the next phase of discussion, which is more strategic in nature. The following points are included in this discussion:

> ➤ Establishing goals and learning outcomes for the partnership that align Gen Y's blue-sky vision with our organization's vision and mandate

> ➤ Clarifying job and organizational accountabilities, opportunities, and expectations

> ➤ Strategizing the specific pathway to reach the said goals and outcomes

> ➤ Agreeing on the right metrification to measure and evaluate success

> ➤ Ironing out the logistics of working together

However, let's pause for a moment.

Even though setting goals and charting action strategies are fundamental terms and conditions of our partnership with Gen Y, doing so upfront could be highly problematic. Asking Gen Y early in the mentoring relationship to produce detailed goals, action strategies, and metrics that are aligned with the strategic imperative of the organization leaves Gen Y bewildered. Their minds just aren't in the game yet! Also, at this point, they likely have limited professional and organizational knowledge and experience to draw on for an undertaking of this magnitude. In my conversations with Gen Y, some of them admitted that they have resorted to identifying a few random goals and action strategies in order to be done with this and to avoid any questions that their supervisors might have about their competency. Knowing this, it is more judicious of us to temporarily shelve these potentially taxing and unproductive discussions about goals, strategies, and metrification, and to give Gen Y time to explore possibilities before we nail down the specifics.

So, where do we go from here?

As you recall, Gen Y has an unquenchable thirst for experimentation, which is perfect for us to capitalize on. Imagine transforming your organization into an experimental playground for Gen Y where they explore possibilities as intuition guides them and use insights gleaned from their wanderings to set their career goals and action strategies.

In *Chapter 5, Inspiring Star Performance– Reaching Seriously for Sirius*, we encouraged Gen Y to experiment freely as part of formulating their work plans. Now, we revisit this familiar practice, but this time, experimentation is for the purpose of advancing careers. As it relates to career development, experimentation can take the form of the following:

➤ Observing executive meetings to plant the vision of what it will be like for them to be at the boardroom table, participating in and chairing high-level discussions

➤ Job shadowing you or other leaders held in high regard to learn the finer skills associated with the career they envision

➤ Participating in committees that will help them develop the requisite competencies for the roles they aspire to have

➤ Encouraging them to take a facilitative role on a committee or to be a champion of change on a workplace initiative so that they can test drive new skills

➤ Attending networking functions that allow them to canvass career advice from practitioners in the industry that inspire them

In this exploratory lab, Gen Y comes to better understand their passions, talents, untapped potential, and gaps in their skill set. With these new insights, they are able to express their professional development needs and expectations with greater conviction, from which they can set more precise and substantial goals and action strategies that support their careers.

To diffuse the probability of goal setting becoming merely an academic exercise, review goals and action strategies during your check-in meetings with Gen Y, link goal-setting initiatives to performance evaluations, and tie them to rewards and recognitions in your organization. This way, Gen Y's career goals are discussed often, which allows you and Gen Y to celebrate milestones and refine professional-development paths as needed.

# Can I get a little support here? – mentoring the mentors

*Ken, will you return to a mentoring role this year? - No*

*Mary, a new recruit could really benefit from your mentorship. - No*

*Bev, can you mentor Ksenia? She's asked specifically for you. - No*

One rejection followed by another...

This was the unforeseen response I received after designing my first mentorship program, which was for a broadcasting company in Western Canada. Initially, the project was greeted with cheerleader enthusiasm from my team of mentors, but this soon waned. By the second year, I was pleading with them to stay on board.

What happened? What was overlooked? In the debriefing session that followed, the team acknowledged the structural integrity of the program and commented on the early indicators that the program was contributing to the achievement of the company's succession-planning objectives. However, the accolades stopped there, and they soon confessed their reservations about the program. Quite simply, mentoring grew to become an isolating experience for them. Over the course of the year, they found themselves:

➤ Struggling on their own to identify the best ways to engage Gen Y, often second guessing the professional development pathways they proposed

➤ Battling their own apprehensions and insecurities about coaching

➤ Commiserating over their own limitations and missed career opportunities that were resurrected when Gen Y asked them about their own career trails

What I came to realize is that a support network for mentors was missing. *My mentors needed mentors!*

This was my watershed moment. It was the realization that our best work is done only when we are with a community of travelers on a similar journey. Let's explore this further.

## Throwing a mentoring life raft to YOU

By establishing a support network for mentors, we have a forum whereby those who serve in a mentoring capacity can guide each other on the journey. This is especially important when we hit a crisis point in mentorship. For example, we might face a conflict with Gen Y that rattles our confidence and leaves us uncertain about how to rectify the situation. By having a circle of partners in mentorship, we have a designated place to discuss issues of concern and repairing conflicts before they cause irreparable damage. Some of our colleagues may have experienced the same or similar conflict from which we benefit by hearing about their solution strategy, implications of the approach that was followed, reflections on what went well and what they would have done differently, and words of wisdom on how to lead the coaching conversation.

Alongside guiding us through sticky situations, the circle provides a forum for you and your colleagues to:

> ➤ Report progress on career goals and how they ladder into organizational initiatives

> ➤ Swap best practices to work with Gen Y

> ➤ Celebrate mentoring successes with each other

> ➤ Boost morale during rough patches in the mentoring partnership

> ➤ Contribute to each other's professional development as coaches

> ➤ Bring forth recommendations to enhance rewards/recognitions and training programs for mentors

> ➤ Advise on policy and procedure changes that are applicable to mentoring or any area of your organization

After these discussions, we return to our mentoring assignments, having experienced a much-needed opportunity to vent our concerns. Also, we are now armed with a new set of possibilities to manage complex situations and a rejuvenated outlook about our role and accountabilities.

Long-term support networks can serve our organizations well. Specifically, they sustain the momentum of leaders like ourselves who have committed to mentor Gen Y. They increase the likelihood of attracting other organizational leaders to the mentoring role, because it is evident that strong supports for mentors are in place, and they communicate the importance of a community of mentors guiding Gen Y in their professional lives.

Given the benefits associated with a circle of partners for *mentors*, might a support network for *Gen Y protégés* be equally advantageous?

# Throwing a life raft to Gen Y too!

By establishing a parallel support network, Gen Y has personal space to host conversations about their mentoring experiences. These forums enable Gen Y to benefit from each other's unique perspectives and words of wisdom, which are signature strengths of peer support groups. By pooling their collective wisdom and resources to solve problems and chart directions, Gen Ys empower each other with new ideas and approaches that they can take back to the workplace and apply.

Especially noteworthy is the synergy that emerges when Gen Ys from across organizational units, representing a mix of professional disciplines and orientations, come together. In these exchanges, Gen Y begins to grasp the universality of their cohort's experiences, which, in turn, mobilizes them to work together to support each other's professional growth and development. Also, this collective rallying around causes of mutual interest can reduce the likelihood of professional silos taking root. Emergent is a community that stays together to fulfill personal, professional, and organizational directives long after the mentoring support network disbands.

Dialoguing monthly, either face-to-face or electronically, with each other in these self-managed teams provides a channel for Gen Y to do the following:

> ➤ Share their experiences and significant learning

> ➤ Offer each other input on refining career goals and priorities

> ➤ Brainstorm pathways for goal achievement

> ➤ Offer peer support and resources

> ➤ Seek input on how to manage difficult situations that they may not be comfortable addressing with their mentors until they've consulted with their peer group

> ➤ Build professional networks with their Gen Y colleagues across the hall in other departments

> ➤ Awaken refreshingly new insights regarding their assumptions, business philosophy, and approaches to leadership

Each month, they reunite to report on outcomes, which will either be the cause for celebration or lead to putting issues back under the microscope for a second look.

With each passing month, it is anticipated that Gen Ys will become increasingly more confident in their personal wealth of talents and abilities for problem solving and decision making and realize the power of networks for support and guidance. As a result, we likely will see the transformation of our Gen Y protégés from being dependent on us to becoming independent and interdependent on their colleagues—a collaboration that will hold them in good stead as they are promoted to leadership roles and eventually become the legacy builders in our organization.

# Reframing challenges as opportunities

*I start out with good intentions to mentor my staff. Then, the demands of the day take precedence and, before I realize it, the time that was once devoted to mentoring gets strangled out of my day.*

This is a common occurrence in the workplace. Far too often, mentoring programs quickly meet their untimely demise. Many leaders have confessed that mentoring can be an exhausting addition to an already overburdened and unpredictable work schedule. Given a business landscape of unprecedented and unpredictable change and a workplace culture characterized by chronic hours, fatiguing workloads, and shrinking deadlines, mentoring typically takes a backseat. It is treated as an initiative that is done from the side of our desks, instead of one of the centerpieces of our operations. Hence, good intentions to develop mentoring programs are trumped by other, more pressing, organizational demands. Consequently, mentoring programs eventually lose steam and get squeezed out of the system.

It's time to reframe this. If mentoring is truly a priority for our organization, then our journey begins with asking a tough question:

> *What changes must be made to accommodate mentoring; that is, what do we need to remove from our daily list of accountabilities so that we leave space in our schedule for mentoring?*

In order to sustain mentorship as a priority item, we need to look deep into our organization. Consider conducting an audit of your workplace to ascertain the *give and take*, that is, what can be eliminated, revised, or added to your operations in order to accommodate the addition of a mentoring program. A mentoring program can only be successful if we are prepared to make changes in current practices. Preferably, something has to be removed from our to-do list to accommodate the addition of a mentoring program. We cannot afford to simply add mentoring to an already over-burdened system and expect it to fly. The viability of a mentoring program is dependent on our willingness to dive deep into our operations in search of functionalities that are due for revision. This could include a review of the following:

➤ Policies, procedures, programs, and activities in each functionality

➤ Work design, practices, technology, and communication channels

➤ Mechanisms for employee engagement, decision making, and support

➤ Management-staff working relationship

Apply the same rigor to review the *give and take* in your own job. What can you remove, adjust, or add in order to embed mentoring more prominently into your work schedule?

By engaging in *give and take*, we uncover and minimize—perhaps even eliminate—stress points in our organization and in our jobs that make it difficult to implement and sustain mentoring programs. Good intentions to have a flourishing mentoring program can now become our organization's lived reality.

# Leaning in to change

The role you play as mentor to your Gen Y staff is instrumental to their professional development. It is an art and science and a challenge and an opportunity. Let's reserve space here to reflect on what you can start doing today in order to enhance your presence and effectiveness as a mentor to your young staff.

Take some time to reflect on the following questions:

➤ What is your vision of the exemplary mentor that you aspire to be for your Gen Y staff?

➤ What are you most proud of in your approach to mentoring Gen Y?

➤ How can your strengths be capitalized on in new ways when you mentor Gen Y?

> ➤ In what ways would you like to enhance your approach to mentoring so that you can be the best possible career Sherpa for your Gen Y staff?

> ➤ What are your personal *gives and takes* in order to enhance your mentoring partnership with Gen Y?

Also, is there someone in your life who has mentoring skills that you admire? Consider having a *conversation* with that person to hear more about the story of their mentorship. Perhaps, this person can mentor *you* in discovering your own storyline for success as a mentor.

Please join me online (`www.eyeofthetigerconsulting.ca`) to share your insights and experiences with mentoring. I'm looking forward to reading about how you are challenging yourself in new ways to enhance your presence and skill in mentoring.

# Google it

Here are a few additional resources for those of you who would like to continue exploring ways to groom the next generation of leaders in our organizations:

> ➤ T., Allen, L., Finkelstein. and M,. Poteet, *Designing Workplace Mentoring Programs: An Evidence-Base Approach*, Wiley-Blackwell, 2011

> ➤ M., Benko, *Ted Talks: Mentoring the Next Generation*, 2013

> ➤ K., Russell, *Ted Talks: Modern Mentoring: The Good, The Bad and The Better*, 2011

> ➤ D., Stoddard, *The Heart of Mentoring: Ten Proven Principles for Developing People to Their Fullest Potential*, NavPress, 2009

> ➤ L., Zachary, *The Mentor's Guide: Facilitating Effective Learning Relationships*, Jossey-Bass, 2011

# Meeting the Gen Y community – introducing...Hande Gulsen!

*What are your long term career goals? What workplace initiatives would you like to see in place to support your career aspirations?*

I had the pleasure of meeting Hande when she emailed me about the exciting work she is doing in her Masters thesis on Gen Y and mentoring. I couldn't wait to invite her to contribute to this book!

In relation to her own mentoring needs and expectations, Hande welcomes the opportunity to be mentored by someone who is willing to commit at least a year to her professional development, and someone who is interested in guiding her in the development of her skills and knowledge. She has rich theoretical knowledge from her university studies and now wants to build her confidence in real work-life situations. Hande describes her ideal mentor as someone who, "*helps, guides, teaches and allows her to feel comfortable and self-confident*" and someone who will open the doors to new career possibilities by providing continuous training and development.

Equally important to Hande is the opportunity to engage with colleagues. She believes organizations should provide time for staff to socialize in order to rejuvenate their thinking, build strong working relationships between all generations and departments in the workplace, and decrease organizational hierarchies between staff. Such activities could include meeting for coffee or playing billiards or strategy games.

She says, "mentoring, candid communication, and socialization are the most attractive features of the workplaces I would like to be involved in".

*In 2010, Hande graduated from Foreign Language Education at Ba kent University in Turkey. Currently, she is pursuing a Masters' degree in International Business and Management at Kozminski University in Poland. She also attended an exchange program at EM Lyon Business School in France.*

*Hande worked as an English teacher for two years. She also completed an internship with a mass marketing department in Turkey where she contributed to the development of marketing communications and assisted the Director of Communications with initiatives to present a positive corporate image. She attended My Challenge group as an intern in Poland where she evaluated target markets, proposed marketing strategies, and established client communication.*

*During her free time, Hande enjoys meeting with her international friends who help broaden her point of view and give her an opportunity to share her perspectives. Also, she is involved in sports, participates in the Toastmaster's Club to develop her leadership and speaking skills, and volunteers her time to nongovernmental organizations. Hande was recently involved in arranging a Mother's Day celebration for a nursing home.*

# Summary

This chapter took us into the world of mentorship, specifically, how we can support our Gen Y staff in their career pursuits and contribute to the talent-development and management initiatives in our organization. We began by getting ourselves primed for the mentoring journey ahead. This included a personal message to get over ourselves and what our own blueprint for training should entail. The chapter then took us into wish lists and maps, where we explored Gen Y's mentoring needs and expectations and the ways we can engage with Gen Y to make their dreams a reality. We finished the chapter with a look at life rafts for Gen Y and for you.

All the trails explored in this chapter converge to achieve one goal—guiding us toward mentoring the next generation of leaders to become the legacy builders of our organization. We are building capacity—one Gen Y at a time.

We now head into *Chapter 9, Retaining Gen Y – What Else Does it Take to Keep Them?*, which introduces us to the approaches we can take to retain Gen Y in our workplace.

# 9

# Retaining Gen Y – What Else Does it Take to Keep Them?

I'm going to let you in on a secret.

There isn't a recipe that, if followed scrupulously by mixing, sautéing, and blending the right ingredients, will—presto—ensure that the Gen Ys we actively recruited and handpicked for our team will actually commit to making our organization their professional home. No matter what airtight retention practices we put in place, there is no guarantee that Gen Y will stay in our organization for the long haul.

Why then do we need a chapter on how to retain Gen Y?

This is because we at least want a fighting chance at keeping them longer than they currently stay in our organizations.

Our business world is inundated with advice on how to improve employee retention rates, and we need to become shrewd consumers of this knowledge. Tips, models, and frameworks that claim to be *best retention practices*, *secrets of the trade*, and *never before revealed techniques* are in abundance in business literature. Yes, there are some brilliant pearls of wisdom that rightly deserve to be considered, but we should also be cognizant that not all of the practices in the mix are a good fit for us. When we find ourselves staring down the barrel of tumbling retention rates that threaten the viability of our organization, we are vulnerable and more susceptible to any lifeline that promises to rescue us. At times like this, it is tempting to latch on to new practices that catch our eye, especially if they come in neat, user-friendly packages such as *five easy steps to enhancing employee retention*. That's alluring!

In reality, retaining Gen Y is far more intricate than simply plugging in a set of guidelines. This is our challenge and opportunity heading into the final chapter of the book.

In this chapter, we'll bypass discussing steps, models, and frameworks in favor of more grassroot approaches to improve employee retention. The goal is to provide you with a different twist on how to do the following:

> ➤ Keep a finger on the pulse of Gen Y's needs and expectations throughout their employment with you so that you can be more *proactive* rather than *reactive* in managing employee retention

> ➤ Minimize the probability that Gen Y will be snooping through *help wanted ads* posted by the competition

This chapter focuses on proactive measures that position you to get a crystal clear read on what is happening in your organization so that you can make smart decisions about what needs to change in order to improve employee retention. To get us there, we'll cover the following topics:

> ➤ Putting your organization's culture on your radar screen

> ➤ Developing your sixth sense to the noise around you

> ➤ Oh no! They're leaving!... Let them

As we go through this chapter, note that your leadership, more than ever, is instrumental to the success of retention efforts in your organization.

# So, what's burning?

In Silicon Valley, California, known as the epicenter of the world's most sophisticated high-tech innovations, I was privileged to meet a thriving venture capitalist who shared his views on employee retention. He said:

> *I'm not sure why we start hyperventilating whenever we talk about retention of our Gen Y staff. If they want to leave, let them. What's the big deal? We just hire replacements and resume doing business. Everyone's replaceable. Let's not be so obsessed about keeping everyone.*

He's right. There is no need to keep *everyone*, we just want to make sure the *best ones* don't walk out the front door permanently.

Some of you might be in an industry, occupation, or geographic region where you have few, if any, worries about staffing, that is, the supply of qualified talent surpasses your demand. No sooner does someone resign than you are able to find a replacement without much effort, angst, or lag time between the resignation and replacement. Hence, you probably don't feel the pinch to be mindful of employee retention.

You might be in nirvana right now where supply trumps demand, but this is unlikely to last forever. When the tide turns and the supply dwindles, are you ready to ride the surf in another direction, that is, do you have a plan in place to develop and sustain a stable workforce, which has direct implications for the productivity, effectiveness, and efficiency of your organization?

Whether you are fortunate to be in an enviable position right now, or the reverse is true for you and your company, employee retention should always be a high priority. It is an imperative regardless of how the pendulum swings on the supply-demand curve for your organization. If you don't keep employee retention on your radar screen, you risk getting swept up in a vicious cycle of resignations and replacements. You find yourselves on an unrelenting treadmill of the following:

➤ Recruiting, interviewing, and selecting staff to replace employees

➤ Training new staff to reach performance standards

➤ Coaching new staff through the learning curve until they become acclimatized to new accountabilities, which is often accompanied by increased reliance on you and your tenured staff to provide assistance as needed

➤ Correcting errors made by new staff to minimize adverse consequences on other organizational units, customers, clients, and suppliers

➤ Managing responsibilities associated with the announcement of a staff member's resignation, including the following:

    ➢ Restructuring of workload in your unit until replacement staff is hired

    ➢ Managing the consequences of workload reassignment for your remaining staff, which can include higher stress and fatigue levels that can lead to lower performance and productivity

    ➢ Scheduling overtime for deadline-specific work

    ➢ Managing the exit strategy for departing staff, including interviews, and termination of benefits and privileges

In this cycle, an inflated amount of time and money is devoted to managing the logistics of staffing. This detracts from the time you need to plan and execute initiatives that give your organization the strategic upper hand in the marketplace and to build industry partnerships that are integral to your organization's future. You also risk losing the competitive advantage because you don't have a stable and reliable workforce that is fully functional and meeting performance standards. As a result, customers or clients might be on the receiving end of substandard quality or service while new staff are getting up to speed in their new jobs and do not have the experience to make the right business decisions.

Do you really need these headaches?

By being more vigilant and proactive in our approach to managing employee retention, we minimize the aforementioned hassles that fall squarely at our leadership feet. In doing so, we take the initial and integral steps toward establishing a stable and reliable team that works with us to achieve our departmental and organizational goals and mandate, fulfill our organization's vision and mission, and contribute to the long-term viability and success of our operations.

So, how do we get to this headache-free zone? We start by paying attention to the signals that are being transmitted from Gen Y to you. Are you ready to receive incoming messages?

# Putting your organization's culture on your radar screen

Many of us wander in the business wilderness, hunting for an antidote for our organization's retention ailments. When we stumble upon an organization that has found the miracle cure—and has an impressive display of dashboard metrics to prove it—we pounce on the solution and claim it as our own. We hurriedly inject the remedy into the veins of our organization, and we wait eagerly for it to breathe new life into us. However, much to our chagrin and more often than we'd care to acknowledge, we are faced with the unwelcomed and raw truth that the wonder drug that held such promise just doesn't work. It doesn't fit the culture, infrastructure, or strategic direction of our organization.

Practices that are a reverberating success in one organization can fall flat in another. Why is that? For the most part, the perfectly marvelous idiosyncrasies in the community of employees that we manage make it nearly impossible for us to simply parachute a practice from one organization into another and to expect the same or similar results.

In reality and on a more optimistic note, we need not look further than our own doorstep to find solutions to our retention problems. The answers to the majority of our concerns can be found *within* our own organization. We have the capacity within to heal what ails us and restore our organization to retention health.

How do we do this?

It's about being more deliberate and strategic in how we manage the web of relationships, systems, practices, and procedures within our organization. It requires us to look through a new lens and ask a different set of questions. In doing so, we are propelled into richer and more conscious awareness of what is actually happening in our organization. If we listen intently and thoughtfully, we become privy to new insights that put us on track to fostering a workplace culture where Gen Y feels highly valued and engaged and chooses to make our organization their professional home.

# The view under the microscope – one step back and two steps forward

Remember that treadmill we talked about—the one that keeps us on a dizzying cycle of managing resignations and replacements and leaves us in a cold sweat just thinking about it? We want to get off that treadmill as fast as possible.

In order to do so, we need to change one of our workplace behaviors that, for many of us, has been a customary way of doing business since we began our careers. This behavior is engrained so deeply in our psyche that, at first, we might be reluctant to let go of it. However, improving employee retention is incumbent upon embracing change in this area.

What am I referring to? I'm referring to our collective *need for speed*, that is, the frenzied and constant push forward in hot pursuit of *the next best thing* on the horizon. The pattern is unremarkably predictable—we plan, we launch, and then straightaway, we chase another initiative in anticipation of further advancing our organization's position in the marketplace. Unarguably, the business world expects and demands a sense of urgency. We are expected to be in the spin of scanning the market with lightning speed, constantly being in the throws of conceptualizing new products and services, pushing lucrative proposals forward, and launching new products and services ahead of anyone else.

That's survival in the business world. I get it.

In what I'm about to propose, I'm not asking you to do anything that puts your organization in peril. I'm simply appealing to your good business sense to think about the strategic importance of leaving space for a *different set of behaviors* that can have a profound effect on employee retention, especially keeping the Gen Y staff. It is an approach to doing business, whereby you make changes before employee retention rates become sluggish and sabotage your organization's ability to maintain a stable workforce.

In order to *go forward* successfully in business and become an industry leader that is ahead of the curve in getting new products and services to market, you are invited to *take one step back*. Make time to reflect on how well the practices, systems, and protocols you have in place to manage Human Resources have served you in attracting and engaging Gen Y. For the most part, this entails assessing the degree to which all the initiatives that you've been introduced to in this book are contributing to creating a workplace culture that Gen Y is attracted to, inspired to work in, and plans to stay in. *Taking one step back* involves putting the following practices under an evaluative microscope:

> ➤ Recruitment initiatives that consist of paying attention to content and tone and are in line with the actual job

> ➤ Use of social media to establish and sustain your professional network

> ➤ Onboarding and training that are "sticky, stickier, and stickiest"

> ➤ Your mastery of the language to have awesome conversations with Gen Y, including conversation connectors and checking assumptions

> ➤ Conflict management and resolution strategies, including shifting gears, signaling new directions, and seeing what's in the rear-view mirror

> ➤ Practices that inspire star performance by encouraging Gen Y to explore new horizons within and beyond their jobs, and by teaching them how to fall

> ➤ Approaches to manage performance, including knowing what's too much, too little, and just right

> ➤ Rewards and recognition for peak performers, which go beyond plaques, trophies, and recognition pins

> ➤ Mentoring programs that prepare Gen Y to take the reins of leadership when it's time for us to leave

> ➤ Initiatives to encourage multigenerational unity and enforce zero tolerance for behaviors that are counterproductive to establishing a culture of inclusivity

To help you manage this daunting task that I've just laid at your feet, consider framing the assessment around three core questions. These questions were introduced earlier in the book, but, with a slight revision, they serve us well here. Consider drilling down into what we are called to:

> ➤ Continue doing because there is evidence that supports success

> ➤ Stop doing because it doesn't serve Gen Y or us well

> ➤ Start doing because we received feedback that there is still more we can do

It is in this roadmap that we find the answers to our questions about employee retention. At the end of the day, employee retention is about being mindful—at all times—that we, as organizational leaders, are expected to be responsible for and responsive to our employees. It's about using all of our available resources to enhance the probability that the ways in which we structure work, treat our staff, and engage them in the workplace community are perceived and experienced by staff as efficient, effective, fair, and gratifying. Quite simply, when employee retention is managed well, all of our practices are taken care of and endorsed by staff. Their stamp of approval signifies that we are on track to fostering a workplace where they can stretch into their potential, be the very best they can be, and contemplate staying with us a little longer than we expected.

Yet, before we do the victory dance down the halls of our organization, are we able to *park our ego for incoming messages?*

# Parking one's ego for incoming messages

Six years ago at a town hall meeting for staff in a publishing company, I witnessed their president self-destruct. During the question and answer period, the newest Gen Y recruit approached the microphone to give feedback to the president. Right before our eyes, feedback that was offered innocently and respectfully was taken out of context, mangled, and left for dead on the carpet. It was an historic awakening for the staff. Years later, the staff still recount vividly the day that the president went armed into a feedback session as if it was guerilla warfare and displayed the most unbecoming array of defensiveness, denial, and disrespect. He did a masterful job of completely missing the point of the feedback and, in turn, doing irreparable damage to his professional reputation.

It was the day that *the president's ego got in his way.*

Although this story highlights an extreme example, most of us likely can recall a time when our own egos got the better of us. This usually happens when feedback is offered, especially feedback that hits a vein because deep down—in those dark places where we don't want to go—someone has uncovered an unflattering truth about us or confronts us with one of our weaknesses. Feedback of this nature can be gut-wrenchingly raw and painful for us to hear, especially when it comes from a younger person. We might also experience similar discomfort even when the feedback isn't about us. That is, the feedback might be about an organizational issue, but we take it personally because we assume it is an attack on our competency.

Either way, when our ego takes its position as an army-of-one defending our raw underbelly against perceived attacks, we become unhinged, and a torrent of ugly outcomes surface. First of all, we lose our ability to actively listen and hear what is, and isn't, being said by the speaker, and this can result in inappropriate responses, which erode our credibility in the eyes of the speaker and staff who witness the exchange. When this happens, the staff might be reluctant in the future to come forward with feedback, knowing how we respond. When feedback is no longer forthcoming, we could experience personal and professional isolation from the realities of what is happening in our organization. This could lead to detachment from our staff because communication is less open, honest, and comfortable. If this awkwardness persists, the staff likely will seek employment elsewhere.

These outcomes are especially problematic when we are in need of staff's feedback on their lived experiences in our organization, in order to make smart decisions about ways to improve employee retention. If we want to position ourselves to receive constructive feedback that will allow us to exercise good judgment, then it's time to *park our ego for incoming messages*.

Receiving authentic feedback from staff is dependent on our ability to establish a climate in which it is psychologically safe for them to speak openly without fear of retribution. As we've already covered the give-and-take of effective feedback in *Chapter 4, Unlocking the Secrets to Awesome Conversations with Gen Y*, let's reserve this space to lay out guidelines that are helpful in advancing our work on employee retention.

*Parking our ego* entails adapting the following new behaviors:

➤ Be aware of your ego, that is, know under what circumstances it shows up, with what intensity, and the role you allow it to play

➤ Acknowledge the presence of your ego when it surfaces, and then, wilfully move it to the back of your mind so that you can focus on the conversation at hand

➤ Reframe all feedback as learning opportunities

➤ Seek out a trusted colleague who can provide you with honest and supportive insights about your approach to giving and receiving feedback

➤ Reframe your organization's quest to improve employee retention from a responsibility that rests exclusively on your shoulders to an opportunity for all staff to contribute to community building

➤ Stop thinking that you have to be the *perfect leader* and aim for being *perfectly yourself*

It is with this mindset that we are best able to listen intently to what is communicated through words, tone of voice, and nonverbal behavior; remain curious about the messages communicated; and receive feedback generously and graciously. Also, we can be gentle with ourselves and others if feedback comes *at* us rather than *to* us, that is, feedback is given by others in ways that are not as tactful, diplomatic, and respectful as we would like.

Now that your ego is in check, are you ready to develop your *sixth* sense?

# Developing your sixth sense to the noise around you

*Sensing what is beyond the ordinary*

*Reading between the lines*

*Intuitive knowing*

The preceding descriptors capture the common ways we understand the *sixth sense*. Yes, it also conjures up images of extra-sensory perception, clairvoyance, and ghost stories about the deceased coming out of the bushes. As fun as it would be to take an extra-terrestrial journey with you, we might be better served if we stay clear of goblins and keep our focus on the sixth sense as the development of our *intuitive selves* for workplace purposes.

At the heart of developing our intuitive selves is honing our *subtle perceptual ability*, which can be a powerful tool in our approach to leadership, especially as it applies to our work on improving employee retention. It can give us an advantage, far ahead of others, in reading people and situations in the workplace, and it can position us to be proactive in solving problems before they disrupt performance and productivity. In turn, this might enrich our working relationships at all levels in the organization, because we are attuned in new ways to clues in conversations and in the workplace environment.

Developing our sixth sense involves becoming cognizant of the *noise around you*, that is, being vigilant in a different way to the signals that we get from Gen Y about how they perceive and experience the workplace. In this section, we'll discuss how to connect with polar opposite participation styles in the workplace—Gen Ys who choose to be vocal and those who choose to be silent. This is about paying attention to what is and isn't being said by Gen Ys.

## Embracing the celestial sounds of whining

*Again? He's always complaining about something!*

*Here it comes! Another toxic comment!*

*Doesn't she ever stop whining?*

Sometimes, you can be taken to the edge of sanity with the incessant buzz of complaints from your employees about workplace happenings that don't meet their expectations. As maddening as it can be to have complaints hurled randomly at you with laser precision, they can be the best gifts you ever receive from your staff. Here is an opportunity to explore a different perspective of what's really at play in your organization.

If you are willing to look through a different lens, you will come to discover that those Gen Y staff who remind you constantly about the organization's shortcomings and point their finger at you with advice on what you *should* and *need* to do, in reality, care deeply about the organization. Beneath what you perceive as *whining,* you will likely uncover their *hope* and *faith* that you, in your leadership capacity, can mobilize organizational resources to change the situation that is the source of their distress. Underlying all the bravado of their complaints, they believe strongly enough in your leadership to exert the energy to tell you—and sometimes, return to tell you a second and third time—that there is something wrong and that they are confident you are the person to make change happen. They are banking on your intervention.

When Gen Y comes to us with their concerns, we are faced with choices. We can either respond in a way that leads to a resolution that serves the needs and expectations of all parties involved or fuels Gen Y's decision to resign, leaving us with another casualty and another reason to be concerned about employee retention in our organization.

In order to increase the probability of finding a harmonious resolution to the issue at hand, it's time for us to *embrace the celestial sounds of whining.* This entails adapting a new approach for how we engage with Gen Y when they appear at our doorstep with a complaint. In *Chapter 4, Unlocking the Secrets to Awesome Conversations with Gen Y,* we learned the foundational skills for managing these conversations; in this chapter, we further build our skill capacity. When faced with this situation:

> ➤ Be patient with Gen Ys who might be brimming with emotions when they bring their complaint forward

> ➤ Keep your own evaluative voice in check and come from a place of curiosity and empathy

> ➤ Look beyond what you might perceive as *whining* to get at the heart of the issue and how Gen Y experiences it

> ➤ Listen and watch unconditionally to understand what is being communicated through words, tone, and nonverbal behavior

> ➤ Refrain from interrupting Gen Y regardless of how far from the main issue they meander

> ➤ Ask guiding questions to get an accurate understanding of the issue

> ➤ Invite Gen Y to discuss possible alternate solutions and the implications of each

Having said this, there might be cases where we choose *not* to accommodate staff members. Their requests might be unrealistic, that is, they are not aligned with the organization's values or strategic mandate, are outside your jurisdiction as a leader, or are not feasible under the current budget. We might also choose not to accommodate staff members because their complaints are unfounded.

When Gen Y is told that their request is denied or their complaint will not be investigated further, they may feel so strongly about the response that they decide to terminate their employment with us. For some of you, this might be a welcomed relief. We are reminded that employee retention is not about saving *everyone;* it's about saving *our best.*

Alongside *developing your sixth sense to the noise around you*, it is important to respond to the *white noise*, which can be equally as deafening.

# Silence ain't golden

*No news is good news, right?*

Not really. No news is your signal that trouble is underfoot.

It's the silence, not the ongoing whining, that we should be worried about.

As you recall from our earlier discussions, for the most part, Gen Y has a tendency to avoid engaging in *uncomfortable* conversations with those of us in authority—not always, but often. If Gen Y is discontent, disgruntled, or experiencing any niggling upset about what is or isn't right in the workplace, they are more likely to vent their aggravations to their peer group rather than to us. Depending on what the issue is, the venting could be to a small group of friends, or it could be splattered far and wide across Twitter and Facebook. I'm sure you will agree that neither option is attractive or desired.

Another important point to consider is that the silence could be the source of a more deep-seated problem lurking in our organization. Silence could signal that Gen Y has given up on us. Perhaps, after several attempts to plead their case for change, we ignored them, trivialized their concern, or responded in a way that failed them.

They may have lost their confidence in us to exercise our leadership capacity to remedy the situation that was the source of their distress. They were hoping we'd pull through for them, and this didn't happen. Over time, apathy settled in and they:

> ➤ Stopped caring enough to voice their concerns

> ➤ Chose to confine themselves to working within the parameters of their job description and to not get immersed in discussions about organizational issues

> ➤ Started asking themselves about what's in store for them if they stay with us

> ➤ Began envisioning a more promising future elsewhere

If these issues fester long enough, Gen Y might be compelled to leave our organization. How absolutely distressing this would be, since most of the issues that are rattling around in their minds and causing them anguish likely can be resolved or at least minimized. If we were privy to what was behind Gen Y's oath of silence, we would have a fighting chance to work with Gen Y to find a resolution.

Knowing that silence can be a signal of a soon-to-erupt volcano of problems from an employee retention perspective, there are courses of action that we can take. Your leadership is required to take initiative in the following ways:

➤ Watch for changes in your staff's participation, for example, staff who were once highly communicative are now reticent.

➤ Approach these staff members to convey your perception of the change in their behavior that you have witnessed and to communicate your concern, especially the losses to the workplace community when they choose to be less participative.

➤ Communicate clearly and precisely why you are approaching the staff member, that is, are you genuinely concerned about them or are their performance and productivity issues associated with their change in demeanor? It is imperative to differentiate accordingly so that you can frame the discussion as an informal conversation or a performance-management discussion.

➤ Invite the staff member to validate your observations and to share with you the reasons behind the shift in their participation. Be extra careful here. If there are no performance problems associated with the change, your line of inquiry could be perceived as a violation of their privacy.

➤ Ask the staff member what you can do to bring them gradually back into full participation in the workplace.

This conversation with your Gen Y staff member can be the first step in taking the situation from *white noise* to *lots of noise*.

However, we also need to be cognizant that despite our best intentions and efforts to improve employee retention, some Gen Ys may still choose to leave.

# Oh no! They're leaving!... Let them

*More money? More vacation time? Better benefits? A new job?*

*What can I offer that will stop you from walking out that door?*

A hailstorm of questions pelted my star Gen Y performer the day he submitted his resignation. Totally blind sighted by the announcement, I fired one corporate perk after another in his direction in a desperate attempt to convince him to stay. Despite my finest effort to persuade him to rescind his resignation, his decision was final.

As I replay the scenario in my mind, I'm grateful he declined the offer for more cash in his pocket, more time in the sun or on the ski slopes, or a job that elevated him to a higher position within our organization. Any of these outcomes would have had damaging and far-reaching implications. No matter what agreements I would have put in place to safeguard the confidentiality of the negotiated terms, news of the arrangement would have undoubtedly leaked out. As you are aware, deals done under the veil of confidentiality have a mysterious way of spreading far and wide through the corporate grapevine. Once news would have broken that a staff member was getting a host of corporate goodies to stay with the organization, other staff would expect and demand the same. The relentless pressure to restore fair and equal treatment of staff would have been palpable. If not taken care of, it wouldn't have taken long before other employees, en masse, would be stampeding toward the exit door with resignation flags waving and with bullish determination to find other organizations that treat them better.

Letting my star performer go was the best gift for him and for our organization. Let's explore how it can be the same for you.

# Putting the stick down – don't beat yourself up

Imagine yourself in a position where you've conscientiously and exhaustively deliberated over a situation, announced your decision, and then, someone tries to coax you to reconsider. Likely, a range of reactions float to the surface, one being dismay that someone is actually trying to persuade you to retract a carefully considered decision.

Gen Ys have a similar response to our eleventh-hour attempts to get them to reconsider their resignation from our organization. According to Gen Y, it baffles them that such attempts are made when they have psychologically disconnected from our organization and are ready to move on. For Gen Y, enticements to stay with the organization, which are common offerings to Gen Ys with sought-after expertise in the industry, would have been received more favorably if they had been negotiated into their employment contract when they were thinking about joining our organization. Persuading them to stay once their sights are set elsewhere is perceived as *too little and too late*.

If you notice a trend in which Gen Y staff are leaving in droves from your organization then, as we've been discussing in this chapter, it's your green flag signaling you to forge ahead with a plan to minimize turnover before it disrupts the core of your operations. However, if such a trend does not exist, that is, the occasional resignation letter comes across your desk and turnover is not a burning issue that keeps you awake at night, then please *put the stick down*. Don't beat yourself up over what you *should have* or *could have* done to prevent a few of your staff from leaving. In such cases, let's face some realities about resignations:

> There is an infinite number of reasons why Gen Y might no longer be satisfied with the organization, and we are setting ourselves up for failure by trying to accommodate every single person who decides to leave.

> In some cases, Gen Ys struggle to pinpoint the exact reason for wanting to leave. They simply have a feeling that the culture is not right for them.

> The resignation could be coming from a Gen Y staff member who:

> ➢ Entered the organization with an explicit personal commitment to stay for only a set period of time

> ➢ Is someone you don't want to keep long term, which means the resignation creates a vacancy to be filled by someone better suited to the organization

➤ Despite our best efforts to offer more meaningful work or incentives, it is not meant to be, that is, Gen Y is ready to move on and to explore opportunities elsewhere.

Instead of trying to lock the front door so that Gen Ys don't escape, let's *hold the door open for them as they leave.*

# Holding the door open for Gen Ys as they leave

Do you realize that supporting Gen Y's departure from your organization can be one of the best strategic moves you'll ever make? Gen Y might serve you better *outside* of the organization than working for you!

In cases where you wish the Gen Y staff members would have stayed in your organization and built their careers with you, there are many new opportunities awaiting you. As we've discussed, Gen Y is the most entrepreneurial of the generations, and if they leave your organization to establish their own business, be the first in line to invite them into a discussion with you about partnership opportunities. Collaboration of this nature is mutually beneficial for you and Gen Y as it provides an opportunity to join forces on initiatives that can strength both your positions in the industry. Also, you can capitalize on Gen Y's competencies, including their technological prowess and their entrepreneurial skills, and they benefit from your strategic business intelligence gleaned from years of being in the trenches of the industry.

Partnerships could take the form of:

➤ Being an angel investor for a fledgling operation

➤ Special projects, such as a new product line or service, that bring the distinctive competency portfolios of your company and theirs together

➤ Your participation on Gen Y's advisory board to offer advice on how to shape the direction of their business based on your years of experience doing so

➤ Gen Y serving on your advisory board to provide their insights on how you can attract Gen Y clientele to your organization and how you can revamp your organization's practices to better accommodate a Gen Y workforce

➤ Shared services and resources such as staff exchanges during peak periods or for special projects that require a specific skill set

➤ Involvement in community events that showcase the collaboration of both parties

> ➤ Company merger which can:
>
>> ➤ Position you and Gen Y as a united and strong front that can compete even more aggressively in the current marketplace
>>
>> ➤ Expose both businesses to a potentially wider client base
>>
>> ➤ Capitalize on the skills of both to more strategically and aggressively respond to change in a volatile business climate

Even if Gen Y doesn't leave to start up their own business, but they choose to join a rival, still consider how you can stay connected with them. Your ex-employees remain part of your professional network, and occasionally getting together to share ideas, coach and support each other, and swap professional references could be tremendously valuable to you and Gen Y.

Hence, instead of being apprehensive when resignation letters arrive from Gen Y, we should reframe this as a welcomed opportunity for collaborations that benefit both parties and position us to shape new directions in our industry.

# Reframing challenges as opportunities

*They're leaving us?*

*What did we do wrong?*

*After all we've done for them!*

*You just can't please Gen Y no matter what you do!*

All too often, these are our initial responses when we get word that Gen Y is leaving. We become consumed with questions about what went off track and, before we realize it, we've entered that dark dungeon of negativity. We get caught in a downward spiral of negative talk that is exhausting, defeating, unproductive and destructive, and leads to feelings of professional helplessness and hopelessness.

These thoughts can then affect how we act and react to Gen Y, leading up to their official departure date. When we know that they won't be around much longer, we might:

> ➤ Become increasingly more brief in our conversations with them
>
> ➤ Exclude them from upcoming meetings
>
> ➤ Refrain from seeking their input on job-related issues
>
> ➤ Be disinclined to answer their questions about the exit protocol, especially those questions that are important to them but not on our agenda of importance
>
> ➤ Initiate the recruitment and selection process to hire their replacement without their input
>
> ➤ Remove workplace privileges ahead of their departure

> ➤ Reassign their job duties and accountabilities without consulting them and while they are trying to bring closure to their commitments

The aforementioned can happen without our conscious awareness.

Is this the last impression of your leadership that you want Gen Y to take with them? Do you want to risk the possible implications to your professional reputation if Gen Y chooses to share with others their end-of-work experiences in your organization?

Here's our opportunity to reframe the situation.

In those days leading up to Gen Y's resignation, let's create a positive last impression that will reflect well on you and your organization. Consider the following ideas as starting points for creating this impression:

> ➤ Engage genuinely with Gen Y to know more about their new job opportunity

> ➤ Ask them to share with you their needs and expectations during the last few days to ensure a smooth transition from endings to new beginnings

> ➤ Invite them to contribute to the recruitment and selection of their replacement, if they wish to be involved

> ➤ Canvass their feedback on what you and your organization are doing and are advised to do in order to become a first-rate employer

> ➤ Honor and celebrate their accomplishments in your organization before they leave

> ➤ Commit to staying professionally connected

In doing so, Gen Y is more likely to leave your organization with a favorable last impression that will serve you well in the long run.

# Leaning in to change

Developing your sixth sense to detect what *is* and *isn't* being said by your Gen Y staff is vital to your success in managing employee retention. Your adeptness at reading spoken and unspoken messages from your Gen Y staff positions you to respond to employee concerns before turnover rears its ugliness and weakens your organization's ability to sustain a stable workforce.

Take some time to reflect on how you plan to develop your sixth sense in order to uncover that which is hidden from view in your organization's culture.

Consider using the following questions to guide your approach to engage with Gen Ys who are vocal about workplace happenings:

> ➤ What will you do to keep your emotions in abeyance when someone approaches you full throttle to raise a workplace complaint?

> ➤ What questions will you ask to get to the heart of their concern?

> ➤ What will you start doing differently to get a better read on what is being communicated by Gen Y through words, tone, and nonverbal behavior?

> ➤ How will you engage Gen Y in new ways so that they feel like they are being heard and understood by you?

> ➤ How will you encourage them to be part of the solution to the problem that they've presented?

The following questions might be helpful in shaping your approach for engaging with Gen Ys who have chosen to be silent on issues:

> ➤ What signals to you that it's an appropriate time to engage Gen Y in a discussion about the changes you've noticed in their workplace participation?

> ➤ What do you hope to achieve from the conversation?

> ➤ How will you prepare yourself to enter into this conversation?

> ➤ How will you set the climate for the conversation so that Gen Y experiences and perceives this as a positive and unthreatening exchange?

> ➤ How will you convey your concern about their declining workplace participation?

> ➤ What will you watch for during the conversation that signals a need to shift the way you lead and participate in the conversation?

> ➤ How will you encourage Gen Y to break their silence on workplace issues?

As always, I'm eager to know about your experiences leading to a change in your organizations. Please join me online (www.eyeofthetigerconsulting.ca) to share your insights and experiences as you develop your sixth sense. Also, please feel free to share any of your experiences by applying new insights about employee retention from this chapter into practice.

# Google it

Here are a few additional resources for those of you who would like to continue exploring ways to enhance employee retention:

> ➤ S. Byrd, *Employee Retention: 31 Most Asked Questions on Employee Retention*, Emereo Publishing, 2014

> ➤ B. Kaye and S., -Evans, Jordan, *Love 'Em or Lose 'Em: Getting Good People to Stay*, Berrett-Koehler Publishers, Inc., 2014

> ➤ P., Marciano, *Carrots and Sticks Won't Work: Build a Culture of Employee Engagement with the Principles of Respect*, McGraw-Hill Books, 2010

> ➤ A., Meyer, *Ted Talks: What do Employees Want the Most?*, 2011

> ➤ J. Phillips and A., Connell, Managing Employee Retention (Improving Human Performance), Elsevier Butterworth Heinemann, 2011

# Meeting the Gen Y community – introducing...Dr. Ganesh Ramachandran!

*What advice would you give to business leaders who are wondering what they can do to keep Gen Y from seeking employment elsewhere?*

If we want to keep Ganesh from seeking employment elsewhere, we are advised to pay close attention to the type of work we offer. For Ganesh, the most important quality that he seeks in a position is meaningfulness. He wants assignments that are personally fulfilling and worthwhile, and he wants to know that his input is valued in achieving the organization's goals. He does not want to stay with an employer who does not give him free rein or one who is apathetic to his contributions.

Ganesh has witnessed many friends changing jobs or taking time off work precisely because their roles do not give them a sense of purpose. Ganesh says, "*I feel that people of my generation do not like to blindly follow orders. They like to be empowered to complete their tasks and to be recognized for their contributions.*" Ganesh also wants us to know that strict hierarchies in our organizations are passé in today's workplace.

Ganesh's ideal workplace would provide ample opportunity for socializing. He especially enjoys when *"professional activities can be done in a relaxed and informal setting."* Of crucial importance to Ganesh is the quality of interactions with colleagues. He wants to be in the company of others that he respects and enjoys working with. According to Ganesh, "*Many of my peers would like to interact socially with their colleagues. It helps a great deal to be part of a team with a sense of camaraderie.*" Having said this, Ganesh encourages us to be proactive in our efforts to build teams in our workplace.

It is a pleasure to introduce you to Ganesh. He completed his undergraduate degree with a major in Physics from India and his PhD in Physics from a leading university in Canada. Ganesh worked for two and a half years as a post doctoral researcher in a reputable academic institution in Germany, and he has also been actively involved in advising international students on campus.

Ganesh envisions his career in an academic setting where he can work closely with a team to find solutions to leading-edge problems, be free of administrative constraints, cultivate international collaborations, and exercise his autonomy in deciding who he will collaborate with and be mentored by. According to Ganesh, "*I find the greatest fulfilment when surrounded by motivated people who enjoy doing what they do.*"

During his free time, Ganesh enjoys traveling. He especially enjoys those travel opportunities that allow him to attend conferences and meetings and then schedule time to explore the surrounding sites. Ganesh enjoys musical performances and exhibitions that are offered in bigger cities and the opportunity to attend social events where he can make new friends.

# Summary

This chapter had one final message for us about retaining Gen Y. We began with *putting your organization's culture on your radar screen* by *taking one step back and two steps forward* and exploring how to *park one's ego for incoming messages*. We then voyaged into the world of the *sixth sense* where we *embraced the celestial sounds of whining* and came to realize the inherent dangers associated with silence from our staff. We finished with the realization that some Gen Ys are bound to leave our organizations regardless of the initiatives we put in place. To this, we responded...*let them.* We explored how Gen Y's departure can actually be the best thing that ever happened to us.

We now head into our final chapter. Are you ready to lead like a conductor so that your organization can sing in semi-perfect harmony?

# >10

# Multigenerational Unity – Singing in Semiperfect Harmony

*Maestro steps onto the podium at center stage, raises his baton, and the orchestra begins to play. The percussions break the silence of the night and beckon the other instruments to join in, the strings hear the call and begin to play, the brass answer with their unmistakable voice, and finally, the woodwinds chime in. If you close your eyes, you can hear the most enchanting four-part harmony filling the room.*

This is the harmony of the orchestra that we hope to replicate in our organizations.

Throughout the book, we've had our eyes riveted on Gen Y. We've put the spotlight exclusively on how to attract, engage, and retain them. As we come to the end of the book, I'd like to offer a few thoughts about how we can integrate Gen Y into our organization alongside the other three generations. In doing so, we create a rich and vibrant harmony in the interactions of the four generations that are in our workplace—Gen Y coupled with Gen X, Baby Boomers, and Traditionalists, also known as the Silent Generation. With this extraordinary synergy, we can reach the height of collaboration that leads to landmark innovations, which set us apart from our competition and position us for success in our industry.

In order for us to have a common language for our discussion, here is a brief description of each of the other three generations in the workplace, courtesy of the research done by Zemke (2000). The intent is not to label each generation but to provide a few attributes that differentiate each generation so that we understand their similarities and differences.

➤ **Generation X (1965-1980)**:

   ➢ Core values—independence and informality

   ➢ Work ethic and values—self-reliant, want structure and direction, skeptical, unimpressed by authority

   ➢ Communication—direct and immediate

   ➢ Work is a difficult challenge, a contract

➤ **Baby Boomers (1946 – 1964)**:

   ➢ Core values—loyalty, optimism, and involvement

   ➢ Work ethic and values—driven to work and succeed, efficiency, champion causes, question authority, bottom-line oriented

   ➢ Communication—prefer in-person communication

   ➢ Work is an exciting adventure

➤ **Traditionalists or Silent Generation (1922-1945)**:

   ➢ Core values—conformity, honor, and discipline

   ➢ Work ethic and values—hard work, respect authority, sacrifice, duty before fun, follow the rules

   ➢ Communication—formal, such as memos and letters

   ➢ Work is an obligation

Disappointingly, few organizations are collaborating in four-part harmony. One of the top challenges that organizations grapple with today is bridging generational differences in the workplace. Differences in attitudes, priorities, expectations, and work styles have contributed to misunderstandings and disagreements that are pervasive, persistent, and polarizing. While conducting my research, I had the pleasure of meeting many organizational leaders who noted that conflicts arising from generational differences are major contributors to the lowest levels of employee engagement experienced in the workplace over the past few decades.

The discord permeates all aspects of organizational life, from informal exchanges in the hallway to formal discourse in the boardroom. It chips away at relationships with others, affecting how we listen to, respond to, and collaborate with each other, and even whether we choose to join a conversation or volunteer for a project when we find out who will be there. The unresolved riffs that accumulate over time can lead to low morale and withdrawal, followed by low performance and employee turnover. If left unattended, they contaminate the sacred organizational ground of productivity and threaten the viability of our organizations that we've been trying desperately to sustain in a volatile economy.

So, what do we do? How can we exercise our leadership to bridge differences and foster generational unity that contributes to sustainable organizational effectiveness?

This chapter provides tools we can use to unite the multigenerational cohorts in order to capitalize on their contributions and maintain high levels of employee satisfaction and engagement while reaching organizational goals. To this end, we'll cover the following topics:

➤ Setting the right tempo for working together—Maestro, please set the stage

➤ Multigenerational collaborations—singing an octave higher

➤ Establishing community circles that keep us singing in semiperfect harmony

You might be curious as to why the title of this chapter refers to semiperfect harmony. As you may recall from previous chapters, we discussed the quest for perfection that many of us pursue. In reality, it is impossible to define perfection, let alone achieve it, especially as it pertains to human relationships. By seeking *semi*perfect harmony, we set our sights more realistically on being *the best we can be*. We'll aim for our best, realizing that we won't always be in perfect sync with each other. Occasionally, we'll strike the wrong cord and cause conversations to go off key. That's okay. We'll learn from this and keep building our capacity for stronger workplace relationships.

# So, what's burning?

Do you recognize these exchanges between an older and younger employee?

> ➤ Why do you come in to work so late every morning?

*Why do you work so late every night?*

> ➤ Why aren't you in the office today?

*I'm working from home.*

> ➤ Let's meet in my office tomorrow.

*Can we Skype instead?*

> ➤ Do you have any work ethics at all?

*Yes, but I don't live to work like you do.*

> ➤ I would appreciate some respect!

*So would I!*

The friction can be palpable. Some of you might be asking, "*Will we ever be able to create workplace harmony given the enormity of the chasm that exists between the four generations? Are we being too idealistic in our pursuits?*"

At first glance, I agree that the task before us seems daunting, thorny, and a trip into fantasy land. I appreciate the reservations you have, and for years, I've wrestled with the same concerns. Work expectations, attitudes, and styles are entrenched so deeply in the psyche of each generation that it is difficult to fathom workplace unity on such a grand scale. To further complicate the situation, we are inundated with literature on generational differences, which may cause inadvertently more harm than good. Even though authors have good intentions to educate us, they may be widening the generational gap by putting the spotlight squarely on how we differ from each other instead of focusing on the universals that unite us. As a result, many stereotypes abound in the workplace about the generations, and for the most part, these perceptions have been formed about each generation regardless of individual performance. Inarguably, particulars about what distinguishes one generation from the other are important, but they are the *starting point* on a much longer journey.

When we consider this more deeply, we have never faced a human resources challenge of this nature. This is the first time in history that four generations are working alongside each other in the workplace. Unfortunately, there isn't a play-by-play manual for how to manage the complexities of this, so evidently, we will face a few hiccups along the way.

Even though we have an arduous mission ahead of us, it is doable. As organizational leaders, we are in a pivotal role to champion change. It won't be easy, and it promises to get messy before we find our footing. However, it's possible. Success in closing the generational divide is incumbent on us doing the following:

> ➤ Equipping ourselves with new tools to chisel a way forward
>
> ➤ Taking risks (and risking a few mistakes) until something sticks
>
> ➤ Listening deeply to sage advice from others along the way
>
> ➤ Persevering like never before

I ask you to look beyond "*what*" makes each generation different and reflect on a pertinent question—"*so, what now?*"

Along the way, you might experience some pressure from others who expect you to plug in some practices and be done with it. In a world that expects and demands quick fixes, this nudge to expedite implementation of new initiatives is nothing new to us. However, in the domain of human interactions, change happens incrementally over time. Change of this magnitude is not a sudden burst of 180-degree transformation in how we value, respect, and appreciate others. It takes time to shift attitudes, assumptions, and views about each other and build trusting relationships.

*We need to build change slowly.*

This is an important message for us to carry in our pocket as we proceed deeper into the chapter and a message you may want to share with others when they give you a gentle (or not so gentle) poke in the arm to hurry change along.

Having said this, maestro, please set the stage.

# Setting the right tempo for working together – maestro, please set the stage

Have you ever thought about the role of the conductor in an orchestra? The conductor is the only one during the performance who doesn't make a sound. Maestro doesn't play an instrument or utter a word, yet he or she plays a critical role in the following:

> ➤ Unifying the musicians
>
> ➤ Setting the tempo
>
> ➤ Executing clear instructions through the wave of a baton
>
> ➤ Listening intently
>
> ➤ Shaping the sound accordingly

The conductor is there to frame the musical score. However, the magic of what we see, hear, and ultimately experience during the performance comes not from the conductor, but from the ensemble itself—four voices in unison.

Here lies a message about the role we are invited to play in creating four-part harmony in our own organizations. Like the conductor, we have an integral role to play, but once our job is done, we get out of the way and let others create the magic. As organizational leaders, we *frame the musical score*, that is, we put in place parameters and set the tone for multigenerational collaborations to take place. Once the framework is established, we step back and allow the synergies of four generations coming together to bubble and to take shape. If at any time our leadership is needed to resolve an issue or to advise on a situation, we indeed step in. However, for the most part, we set the stage and let working relationships evolve and mature.

What specifically is the role that we play as organizational leaders in setting the stage for multigenerational collaborations?

We begin by establishing a *culture of inclusion*—a workplace that is guided by a fundamental norm that welcomes, encourages, and nurtures differences. Everyone in the organization—without exception-—has a voice and is invited to contribute their unique gifts, talents, experiences, and viewpoints. Respect and appreciation of others are internalized and explicit in actions and reactions to each other. We move away from viewing the world dichotomously, that is, "*us*" vs. "*them*", "*older*" vs. "*younger*", and "*better*" vs. "*worse*" and shed the generational labels that often stand in the way of our ability to dialog fully and meaningfully. From this, we emerge not as Boomers, Gen Y, Gen X, or Traditionalists, but as valued members of a multigenerational community coming together with distinct voices to work toward a common goal.

How do we create a culture of inclusion? We start by selecting a new song sheet to sing from.

# Singing from a value-based song sheet

Wherever you are in the organization, the room is buzzing with facts, opinions, and recommendations. You'd be hard pressed to find anyone bringing their personal values into discussions. Values—those deeply coveted principles that serve as the compass for one's actions in life—rarely get aired in discussions. For the most part, values are not recognized as appropriate inclusions because they speak to matters of the heart, which are perceived by many people as insignificant babble in a predominantly left-brain work world. Hence, they remain hidden.

Yet, values are the most powerful unifying force available to us. If we unmask the values buried beneath each other's language of facts, opinions, and recommendations, we begin to see the real people in front of us—their hearts and minds are revealed. In doing so, we come to realize that we have more in common with those around us than we initially thought. We've been focusing for so long on how we are different that few of us have thought to ask *how are we alike?* If we can get past explicit differences associated with each generation, we discover the universal values that bind us. It is from this place that we begin to see ourselves traveling in the same direction toward organizational goals.

Making values explicit in our organization means establishing a new norm that widespread sharing of values is welcomed and encouraged. Invite staff to bring their values into discussions to help everyone better understand each other. This could include sharing values in the following areas:

> ➤ Views, opinions, and insights on a topic

> ➤ Critique of a workplace situation or proposed course of action

> ➤ Recommendations for change

> ➤ Rationale for the decisions they make and stand behind

As an organizational leader, consider how you can model the way by making values explicit in the messages that you communicate to your staff. *Articulate the values behind your views, your decisions, and your recommendations*, and also include values in your rationale for organizational change, whether it is to embark on a new project, expand into new markets, or shift strategic direction. I recall the president of a telecommunications company sharing initial thoughts with his staff about partnering with a nonprofit company in Africa in order to provide educational resources to schools in the villages. He spent most of the time articulating how this project spoke to his personal values of *making a difference in the world* and *leaving a legacy of goodness*. Staff of all generations rallied around the idea and behind the president because the values he espoused were also important to them. The values were a unifying force for good in the world. Throughout the project, these values served as the compass for making decisions and solving problems.

When conflict surfaces in discussions, encourage staff to discuss the espoused values that ground them in their positions. Take this one step further. Even though we make values explicit in our discussions, this might not go far enough. We can sometimes draw erroneous conclusions about the meaning that others attach to values. For example, disagreements and misunderstandings can ensue over values such as respect, trust, accountability, and making a difference. All four generations cite these values as important, but each generation differs in their description of the workplace behaviors associated with each value. When tension mounts, invite staff to describe specific workplace behaviors that signal to them the presence and absence of the values they espouse. This way, a clear picture of values and associated behaviors are conveyed. In doing so, we are better able to leverage a *meet in the middle* outcome, as discussed in *Chapter 4, Unlocking the Secrets to Awesome Conversations with Gen Y.*

When we can be open and transparent about our values, we come to appreciate the power of our interconnectedness. With values in hand, we can now pay attention to our tempo.

# Establishing contractual agreements for our working relationships

Have you ever entered into a contractual agreement with someone? Perhaps it was a contract for a car loan, mortgage, or job offer. We negotiate the deal, reach an agreement, and then memorialize the terms and conditions of our agreement in writing. Any agreement that is important to us is put in writing. In doing so, our agreement becomes binding and serves as our point of reference to define the relationship, describing the expectations of both parties and describing the terms and conditions of the relationship. Also, the written agreement prevents us from forgetting what we verbally agreed to, and it prevents confusion about what is expected from both parties. If anything goes astray, we can refer back to the agreement to resolve the discrepancy.

If it's important to put agreements in writing, then let's consider the applicability of contractual agreements to our workplace relationships. If we are serious about our commitment to establishing and sustaining multigenerational unity in our workplace, then let's put our commitment to each other in writing! Let's seal the deal!

In a modified version of the aforementioned contract, this written document serves as a blueprint for how multigenerations in our workplace will work together. It is not a legally binding agreement, but it carries the spirit of a contract. It binds staff to their commitment, and it serves as a point of reference if any questions arise about the nature of their working relationship.

## Welcome to your team charter!

Our contractual agreement takes the form of a team charter that delineates how we commit to working in four-part harmony. It is our way of *setting the tempo*, that is, it reminds us of our commitment to workplace unity, and it serves as our compass for how to act and react to each other. The team charter helps us keep a steady pace toward our goal, even if a few disagreements threaten to take us off track.

For every team that you bring together in your organization, whether it serves an ad hoc mandate or is a permanent fixture in your organization, lead staff in creating their team charter. Carve out time at the first meeting for the team to review their mandate and discuss how they'd like to work together. Encourage them to disclose preferences, needs, expectations, likes and dislikes, and work styles. Guide them to drill down into specific behaviors they would like to see demonstrated that will contribute to a positive, enriching, and gratifying team experience for them. Please don't aim for a perfect team charter at the end of the first meeting. It may take several iterations of the document before it captures what the team wants it to say.

A team charter can take any form based on what the team values and what they want to make explicit about their interactions. Here are a few topics your team may want to include in the charter:

> ➤ Team's vision, mission, and values (what the team stands for)
> ➤ Composition of team and membership roles
> ➤ Decision-making process
> ➤ Guidelines for giving and receiving feedback
> ➤ Means by which conflict will be managed and resolved
> ➤ Approaches to honor differences
> ➤ Guidelines for fair and equal treatment of everyone
> ➤ Consequences of not honoring the team charter
> ➤ Definition and measurement of success (what are the milestones along the way and how will success be celebrated?)

Hammering out a team charter that everyone can agree on isn't easy. We are making the divergent needs, expectations, attitudes, and work styles of four generations in our workplace explicit. There likely will be some stray sniping and grumbling along the way; that is the reality of this task. Please remind your staff and yourself that the team charter is a *living document*. It is a *work-in-progress* that will always remain open to modification as the team is working together.

## Checking in and checking out

As you've likely experienced, some workplace initiatives never fully materialize. For example, some organizations spend a considerable amount of time crafting eloquently empowering and transformational vision and mission statements only to see them mounted on office walls and rarely, if ever, referred to again. They hang ceremoniously on the walls as a reminder of a distant commitment to do things differently, yet somewhere along the way, something went astray.

In order to avert a similar fate for our team charter, we are called to be more proactive. In order to sustain the team charter as a living document in our team's daily functioning, establish *check-in* and *check-out* processes, whereby time is reserved at the beginning and end of meetings to review the team charter. Check-ins and check-outs keep our commitments on our radar screen and provide us with a built-in opportunity to modify the team charter as needed. Added to this, they serve as early detection of conflicts that could potentially become explosive, derail working relationships, and spiral downward to affect performance and productivity.

I can hear you now, *"These check-ins and check-outs are going to swallow up too much of our meeting time!"* If we've made the commitment to bridging the multigenerational divide in our organization, we can't afford not to do this. The goal on the horizon is just too important for us not to be this assertive about our process. As we know, process has a direct impact on the key performance indicators upon which we build our organization's viability. The commitment of time to checking in and checking out doesn't need to be onerous or intrusive; 5-10 minutes at the beginning and end of each meeting will suffice. Here are a few guiding questions for check-ins and check-outs:

**Check-in:**

> ➤ What were your thoughts and reactions to the previous day's meeting?
> ➤ What do you invite us to continue doing, stop doing, and start doing as a result of your reflections on the previous day's meeting?
> ➤ What do we need to reinforce or add to our team charter to better support working together?
> ➤ What do you need from the team today?
> ➤ What do you bring to the team today?

**Check-out:**

> ➤ What are we doing well? (keep doing it and celebrate it!)
> ➤ What do we need to add to our team charter? (ask for examples of behavior that support new inclusions)
> ➤ What needs to be tweaked on the charter because it doesn't describe exactly who we are or who we want to be as a team?

The check-ins and check-outs help us *keep the beat*. The beat goes on....but along the way, watch for staff who are *B'ing flat!*

# Zero tolerance for B'ing flat!

If we've exerted all this effort to foster a culture of inclusion by making values explicit, composing a team charter, and pledging allegiance to regular check-ins and check-outs, then it would be judicious of us to safeguard our investment. For the most part, staff will welcome and applaud our initiatives to improve working relationships because the efforts ultimately make for more civil and pleasurable working experiences. Yet, there are bound to be a few staff who behave in ways that are counterproductive to the culture of inclusion that we are trying to establish. There are a myriad of reasons for their behavior, ranging from lack of awareness of the impact their actions have to extreme cases of malicious intent to sabotage others. It is imperative that we address these behaviors. If we don't take action, we risk the following consequences:

> ➤ We appear to pay lip service to creating a climate of inclusion and over time, few, if any of our staff, feel compelled to continue following the pathways for change

> We make a mockery of our collective commitment to creating a climate of inclusion, which doesn't set the right tone for future workplace initiatives around generational unity

> Bad behavior can become a precedent setting, that is, others may follow suit when they observe that there are no consequences of inappropriate behavior

By addressing unacceptable behavior, we turn the situation around. We underscore the importance of our commitment to a climate of inclusion, and we hold everyone accountable to the principles, standards, and practices that we collectively agreed to. This speaks volumes about your leadership and your commitment to building multigenerational unity.

*So, what do we do?*

# Striking the right chord

We communicate a widespread message of zero tolerance for behaviors that violate the integrity of the practices around inclusivity that we worked diligently to establish, and we remain steadfastly grounded in our resolve. If behaviors that detract from a culture of inclusion emerge, then it is incumbent upon us to step in and address this with the staff member in question. The exact conversation varies depending on the situation, but here are a few general guidelines:

> Describe the behavior you have witnessed or that has come to your attention.

> Ask for an explanation. Get all sides of the story before rendering a decision.

> Invite the staff member to propose a plan to rectify the situation and decrease the probability that this will happen again. Focus on specific behavioral changes.

> Inquire as to what you can do to support the person in making changes.

> If an apology is warranted, discuss the process for doing so.

> Check in with the person a few days later regarding progress.

How do you communicate back to other staff that witnessed the inappropriate behavior or got wind of it? This depends on the situation, so I am cautious about being overly prescriptive here. There is a fine line between communicating all the details about a situation and preserving the dignity of the parties involved. Think about the message you want to communicate to others. This message should convey that you are aware of the situation, you have discussed the situation with both parties, and what is being done about it. Also, reinforce your commitment to preserving the integrity of working relationships. If anyone has any questions or concerns, invite them to meet with you to discuss this further.

As we know, there are always exceptions to the rule, and here is one that many of you might be familiar with…

# Striking a different chord

I'm reminded of my days in unionized work environments where putting into effect zero tolerance for behaviors that violate the integrity of workplace unity were mind-crushingly treacherous. Implementing changes beyond the scope of the collective agreement was the ultimate test of my endurance, patience, and sanity (I failed the last test!). I can recall times when employees were in my office, accompanied by their union representatives, demanding that I show them the specific article in the collective agreement that they violated and threatening to file a grievance against me for overstepping management rights. For them, if it wasn't in the collective agreement "*they ain't doing it!*"

In the midst of this polarizing experience, there is a common ground upon which both parties stand. Encouragingly, most unions share our concern for fair and equitable workplace practices that is central to a climate of inclusion. Knowing this, it would be mutually advantageous to get this commitment reflected in the collective agreement. When you find yourself back at the bargaining table negotiating your next collective agreement, negotiate the inclusion of an article that outlines the principles and protocol that support fostering a climate of inclusion. Table language that makes "*respect for diversity*" and "*equal and fair treatment of everyone*" explicit in your agreement. This new language justifies your future plans for initiatives directed toward creating a climate of inclusion.

Until that time when your collective agreement expires and you can open it for the inclusion of new language, appeal as best you can to your staff's good judgment, professionalism, and spirit of collegiality to join forces in establishing workplace unity. Present your best case for how changes benefit not only the entire organization, but their colleagues and them personally. Emphasize the favorable outcomes that workplace unity will have for them.

However, despite your most noble efforts, some staff might continue to oppose vehemently even the hint of engaging in behaviors that are outside of the collective agreement. If this happens, shift your focus. Disregard the resistors and devote your time and energy to the staff who are rallying behind you. After all of your previous efforts, moving away from resistors is the greatest gift you can give to yourself and others. In my experience, one of the following two things will happen as a result:

> ➤ **Peer power**: The passion and excitement of staff who are onboard with changes are a contagion. Resistors feel the electricity generated by the changes and witness the benefits that their co-workers experience as a result. They soon find themselves swept up in the excitement and want to be included.

> ➤ **Self-selecting out**: The same passion and excitement exuded by staff who are onboard with changes eventually becomes so unbearably annoying and intolerable for resistors that they withdraw from others. In some cases, they choose to leave the organization. Either way, resistors lose steam in defending their cause and retreat deeper into the background. You can move forward with staff who are committed to the workplace unity initiative.

Now that the stage is set for workplace unity, let's take it up an octave.

# Multigenerational collaborations – singing an octave higher

Our attention turns to *singing an octave higher*, that is, implementing practices in our organization that encourage and support multigenerational collaborations, which allow us to capitalize on the diversity of thought, experience, and knowledge that each generation brings.

The most ground-breaking and progressive advancements in our organization come from the collaborations of our staff, who bring their most thought-provoking and unconventional ideas to the table, coupled with a wealth of expertise and thought leadership. In a room where the energy is high and the ideas are endless, staff confidently tackle anything that comes in their direction. They solve niggling problems, propose revolutionary ideas for new product lines and expansions into new markets, and find the courage to initiate partnerships with unlikely allies half way around the world. The possibilities for bottom-line success in our organization are endless when strong multigenerational collaborations are in place.

# Leveraging the generational mix in unconventional ways

Reflect on the current composition of staff on teams and permanent and ad hoc committees in your organization. Is there equal representation of the four generations on each one? Where can you more effectively leverage the generational mix on workplace teams and committees? Some of you might be thinking that there is a fairly equal balance of generations across your organization. I'm going to gently push you further here. Let's rephrase the question—in what *unconventional* places in your organization can you leverage the generational mix?

A few years ago, I was on a consulting project with a hospital in Texas, and my first meeting was with the Finance Committee. As staff started trickling into the meeting, I was confused by who walked into the room and confidently took a seat. I thought either *I* was in the wrong meeting or *they* wandered into the wrong room. There were the expected senior administrative stakeholders coming in, but also joining us were custodians, reception and hospitality staff, triage staff, and radiologists. Here sat men and women of every age representing all hospital units, professions, and seniority—*in the finance meeting!* Don't they realize this is a *finance meeting* that doesn't pertain to them?

Soon after thinking this, I was pleased to be in a hospital because I was choking on my words. At this hospital, there were no sacred or restricted meetings, no taboo topics reserved for only a few who occupy coveted senior positions. I was in an organization that valued and *lived the values* of openness and transparency and extended this into the far reaches of their organization. The mantra in this hospital is that if all staff are considered equally important to the efficient and effective operation of the hospital, then everyone has the right and privilege to be a welcomed and contributing member of every committee.

Generation-wide participation, like that which is practiced at the hospital, gives everyone a voice on issues of organizational importance, which has a number of positive outcomes. Some of them are as follows:

> ➤ Enhances employees' perception of value in the organization
> ➤ Contributes to a sense of ownership in and accountability to each other and the organization
> ➤ Increases employees' active engagement in decision making and protecting organizational investments
> ➤ Capitalizes on diverse and divergent thinking that enriches the quality of decision making

Are you willing to follow suit? If we know that organizational success is built on the diversity of many minds contributing their ideas and recommendations, then are you willing to leverage the composition of your committees in a way that reflects the four generational cohorts in your organization? Look for ways to bring a multigenerational mix into all meetings, even into meetings that traditionally have been reserved for a select few in the upper echelon: finance, marketing, forecasting, performance management, recruitment and branding, work design, operations management, production, and even strategic planning. On my research trails, an overwhelming number of Gen Ys said they would like to participate in strategic planning and implementation discussions. Even though they realize that they are not familiar enough with the organization to offer recommendations that are transformational, they still think they can add value by contributing insights about ways to encourage Gen Y to rally behind the strategic mandate.

At all costs, avoid faux inclusion, that is, going through the motions of having multigenerational representation but not creating opportunities for fair and equal treatment. A facade of inclusion soon becomes evident to everyone in the room. When it is unveiled, it is perceived as disingenuous, insulting, and can do irreparable damage by eroding trust levels within your organization. Create genuine opportunities for multigenerational collaborations by:

> ➤ Demolishing deeply entrenched hierarchies that position senior members as dominant speakers at meetings
> ➤ Removing restrictions on access to information, participation, and decision-making capacity
> ➤ Ensuring equal opportunities for people to speak in meetings
> ➤ Encouraging spontaneous, transparent, and genuine dialogue
> ➤ Seeking continuity in discussions by connecting ideas
> ➤ Challenging each other's assumptions and voicing divergent views constructively and respectfully
> ➤ Encouraging curiosity instead of sitting in judgment
> ➤ Allowing all members to be influenced by each other

This puts us on the path to establishing meaningful and authentic connections with each other. From here, we are en route to some impressive organizational outcomes as well.

# Informal conversations – a cappuccino moment

*I can't stop for coffee, I'm too busy.*

*Lunch? Can't—I'll grab something later.*

*No, sorry. I don't have time to chat right now; I have this deadline.*

The busyness of our work day characterized by mounting and competing pressures and deadlines leaves little time to engage with people on a personal level for more than a few brief moments each day. Out of politeness, we may ask a few brief questions of a personal nature but nothing that commits us to a conversation that lasts longer than a split second or two. We need not look any further than our favorite question of the day to test drive this theory—when we greet someone and ask, "*How are you?*" do we *really* want to know? Our *deep* conversations during the day are typically about project updates, problems we are consumed with fixing, and information we need from someone for a report we are working on.

Yet, it is through informal conversations that occur anytime, anywhere, and have absolutely nothing to do with work that we really get to know others. They share their stories and, in doing so, reveal their values, priorities, passions, and visions for the future. It is in knowing others informally that the foundation of working relationships is built; our familiarity and comfort with others gets transferred into the formal workplace committee meetings and boardroom discussions that we find ourselves in. Through informal conversations, we come to understand each other better, appreciate each other more, and even accept each other's quirkiness that reveals itself in the throws of a heated debate in the boardroom. When we know each other personally, we likely feel more comfortable speaking candidly in meetings.

*But I can't afford time for idle chit chat!* You can't afford not to. This is the fundamental reality of workplace relationships. The core of your success, your team's success, and your organization's success is rooted in the quality of the working relationships that you build and sustain. This starts with getting to know people informally.

I encourage you—I implore you—to *go have a cappuccino with someone!* Encourage others on your staff to do the same. It is not meant to be disruptive to your daily routines, and it isn't meant to cut into workplace productivity. Just spend quality time forging bonds that will serve all of us well in an organization that has made a commitment to unifying the multigenerations in our workplace. So, walk down the hall to someone's office, knock on their door, and invite them for a cappuccino and a chat. If your staff are working from remote locations, schedule a cappuccino moment over Skype or FaceTime!

# Establishing community circles that keep us singing in semiperfect harmony

How disappointing and frustrating it would be if our efforts to establish multigenerational unity were not sustained. Imagine if all our plans met an unexpected demise and were thrown unceremoniously onto the rubble pile of defunct projects. I'm sure you have witnessed organizational initiatives that began like a bolt of electricity surging through the veins of your organization with lots of hype, masterfully ambitious plans, and throngs of staff rallying around the cause. Yet, somewhere along the way, a few obstacles reared their ugly heads, momentum dissipated, and the curtain fell on what was originally heralded as a brilliant stroke of genius.

Knowing how important multigenerational unity is to our organization, *let's compose new music.* Let's put in place a practice that augments the probability that multigenerational unity remains on our radar screen and is a prominent feature in our organization's culture. Proposed are *community circles*—hierarchy-free zones of unrestricted conversations that provide a forum to discuss our progress in bridging generational gaps and to propose new initiatives to enhance workplace unity.

Like we discussed at the beginning of the chapter, here lies the opportunity for you to put a general framework in place for interaction and then step aside to allow the staff to dialogue. You are still physically present, but instead of influencing the direction, you are there to listen deeply to the exchanges. In doing so, you foster a bottom-up approach to leading, whereby the staff carry the accountability for introducing topics of interest and speaking as deeply and broadly about issues of importance to them. It is an untamed and free-floating dialogue that goes where the staff need and want the conversation to go, and it results in recommendations that are based on what the staff thinks are the best courses of action for change. In doing so, you capitalize on your staff's leadership skills and empower them to work with you on the challenges and opportunities that we face in creating a unified workforce.

## Instruments of our success

In my own experience in facilitating community circles, they are best organized as annual or semiannual events that are scheduled for a half or full day. Anything less doesn't allow for in-depth discussions that are the trademark of these events. Aim to schedule these events at a time of year when most of your staff aren't feeling the crunch of year end deadlines. If this is not feasible, organize a time when as many people as possible can participate. In departments where full coverage of services is required at all times, you may want to rotate staff attendance at community circles.

The activity being proposed will accommodate any number of staff as long as you have the space to fit them all in the room. I've sometimes taken staff outdoors for this activity (as long as we aren't in the dead of winter!) or to a community center nearby. I've also rearranged lobbies, dining areas, boardrooms, and loading docks to accommodate this event. Be creative in terms of where you can host this event.

To set a positive tone for dialog, start the session by asking staff to join you in creating a code of conduct for how we will work together. Added to this, communicate what you will do to foster a safe environment for the staff to speak truthfully, take risks to challenge current thinking and practice in the organization, and offer refreshingly new ideas. After the code of conduct is created, spend time generating a list of topics that the staff want to discuss. Again, nothing is off limits as long as it relates to the over-arching theme of multigenerational unity.

As a suggestion, if you are running a half day session, which translates to about 3 hours, try to limit the number of topics generated to a maximum of 21 (which really does suffice). This way, you can have seven questions for three rounds of conversations that are 30-40 minutes in length. Once the list of topics are generated, organize them into three bunches of seven questions and post the first set of seven questions around the room or in breakout rooms throughout your organization. Let the staff know where the first round of questions is posted and allow them to free-float in and out of conversations as they please. There are no restrictions on where they spend their time or for how long. They can spend their entire time chatting about one topic or move through all seven. After the first round is over, post the next batch of questions and repeat the process. There should be someone permanently stationed in each area to transcribe notes either on flipchart paper or a laptop. This way, you have a written record of the feedback generated.

Consider reserving 15 minutes at the end of the event for debrief. Use the time to canvass the following:

> ➤ General reactions to the community circle
> ➤ Significant learning that emerged for staff
> ➤ What worked well so that we can keep doing it
> ➤ What we can do differently next time

# How does feedback resonate with you – a prelude to success

The success of community circles hinges on your response to the feedback generated from your staff.

Feedback, especially if is it less than favorable, is not easy for us to accept; it can be perceived as personal criticism. Yet, if we get defensive or ignore feedback, the damage is far more potent and widespread than a bruised ego. If your staff perceive that their feedback is unwelcomed or disregarded, they can become jaded about the feedback process. This decreases the probability that they'll participate in future community circles. Why should they exert the energy to give feedback when nothing is done with it? If they do continue to participate in community circles, they likely will be less diligent about offering feedback that is genuine and meaningful and reflects a deep seated interest in collaborating with you.

What we do with feedback generated from community circles will determine whether people shut down and stop giving feedback because it is going on deaf ears, or whether they remain actively enthused about giving feedback, because they know that you are thoughtfully considering and acting upon it.

If we've invested time to establish community circles, then let's invest equal amounts of time to establish a culture of gratitude for feedback. Let the staff know that you will consider all the feedback gathered during the day and get back to them with a response. Don't feel compelled to respond during the community circle; use that time to listen and take everything in. Once you've had time to reflect on staff input, report back to them on the following:

> ➤ Recommendations you plan to act on first and your rationale for starting here. Also include timelines and champions of each initiative.

> ➤ Recommendations that you are unable to act on at this time, but ones that warrant review in 6 months to see if circumstances have changed. Include rationale for decision.

> ➤ Recommendations that need to be shelved permanently and your rationale for this.

Then, stay true to your word. Invite staff to get involved in change initiatives arising from the feedback, especially in the case where ad hoc committees will be struck to move recommendations forward.

Feedback is a continuous process of asking for input, responding accordingly, and then asking again to ascertain if the changes made are on track. Keep listening, refining, checking in, and being willing to go back to the beginning to rework your courses of action until the right fit is found.

# Reframing challenges as opportunities

*This entire initiative is doomed to failure. I can think of a few members of my staff who won't go for this warm and fuzzy harmony stuff and could sabotage the entire process. What's the point of doing this if you can't get everyone on board?*

Not everyone will be on board with everything we do in our organizations. There will always be naysayers who:

> ➤ Sit in judgment of organizational change

> ➤ Recite countless reasons why an initiative is flawed, impractical, and likely to fail

> ➤ Threaten the viability of a new initiative during its delicate early days

When faced with staff who object to the directions we propose and turn discussions into a battle ground, consider reframing their criticism. Consider it as *feedback*. At least, they care enough about the organization to voice their dissent and to explain why it doesn't make good business sense. Consider reframing how we manage conversations with our more skeptical employees:

➤ Give them the courtesy of thoughtfully listening, without interrupting

➤ Ask questions that reflect your curiosity about learning more about their position and the reasons behind it

➤ Engage them in discussion on the problem we are trying collectively to fix, that is, if we know there is a generational divide in the organization, how would they suggest we go about unifying the cohorts

In doing so, we invite our staff to step away from critiquing our efforts to joining us as equal partners in solving the problem that we face. Coupling their ideas with ours might make for an interesting cocreation of a new initiative to bridge generational differences, one that surprises everyone by its ingenuity and fits the culture of our organization beautifully.

# Leaning in to change

Are you thinking about how to integrate the team charter into your team's process?

The team charter is a very concrete tool that you can build immediately into your team's process. It makes expectations explicit, and it serves as a roadmap to keep your team on target to reach their vision of working effectively together. Take time to chart the approach you can use to introduce the team charter to your staff. Here are a few questions to consider:

➤ What are your talking points to introduce the team charter to your staff, that is, the goals and benefits of the team charter?

➤ How will you explain the process to develop and sustain a team charter in a way that showcases its value and is not perceived as another onerous task?

➤ What resistance might surface and how will you manage it?

➤ How will you facilitate this discussion in a way that gets the staff excited about creating their own team charter?

When your plan is ready, schedule a meeting with your staff and put these plans into action. I look forward to seeing you online (www.eyeofthetigerconsulting.ca) to share your experiences with the team charter and other initiatives underway in your organization to create multigenerational unity.

# Google it

If you are interested in learning more, please consult the following resources:

> ➤ S., Bartley, P., Ladd, and M., Morris, *Managing the multi-generational workplace*, CUPA-HR Journal, 58(1), 28-34, 2007

> ➤ M., Macon and J., Artley, *Can't we just all get along? A review of the challenges and opportunities in a multi-generational workforce*, International Journal of Business Research, 9(6), 90-94, 2009

> ➤ M., Wesner and T., Miller, *Boomers and millennials have much in common*, Organization Development Journal, 26(3), 89-96, 2008

# Meeting the Gen Y community – introducing...Gwen Hill!

*What are organizations doing effectively to bridge generational gaps in the workplace? What could they be doing differently?*

In Gwen's experience, allowing flexibility to flourish in our organizations is a key practice that contributes to harmonious working relationships across the generations. As long as the work gets done, Gwen encourages us to promote staff flexibility in hours of work, decisions to work from home or the office, and charting one's own approach to complete projects. In her own work environment, Gwen has strong working relationships with colleagues that span three generations. She credits the success of their collaborations to transparency, ongoing support, open communication, and a willingness to have fun. Gwen also mentioned that in her department, they "play to each other's strengths", that is, work is delegated to team members based on the competencies they bring to the job. For example, Gwen is often called upon to lend her expertise in social media and develop processes to a project.

Gwen would like to see more organizations develop mentoring programs that provide opportunities for Gen Y employees to be coached by more senior members of the workplace community. The goal of the mentorship program would be to "provide a guiding hand to new employees" as they make their way through the maze of organizational expectations and accountabilities; manage life, career goals, and aspirations; and face unexpected roadblocks. According to Gwen, the success of a mentoring program hinges on the following:

> ➤ Honest communication of expectations for the relationship

> ➤ A good personality fit

> ➤ Deep active listening

> ➤ Keeping the focus on the developmental needs of their Gen Y protégé

Speaking about staff who have more seniority, Gwen said, "I don't think they realize just how much they have to offer us."

*Originally from Ontario, Gwen now lives on the other side of Canada in Victoria, British Columbia. She is a writer, pilot, and self-described "process nerd". When Gwen is not working, she loves hiking with her partner and their dog, scuba diving, cooking Indian food, and travelling to absolutely anywhere.*

# Summary

We devoted this chapter to exploring how we can unite multigenerational cohorts in our workplace in order to capitalize on their contributions and maintain high levels of employee satisfaction and engagement while reaching organizational goals. We asked Maestro to lead the way in helping us create a culture of inclusion by singing from a value-based song sheet and setting the tempo with a team charter. We were then asked to take it up an octave and explore unconventional ways to bring generational harmony to life. We finished with establishing community circles that keep us singing in semiperfect harmony.

# Our last few minutes together...

I'm reserving this space in our last chapter for a farewell message. Even though I don't know you personally, I've immensely enjoyed spending this time with you. Even though you weren't sitting here with me as I hammered away on the laptop, or sometimes sat in infuriating and mind-numbing silence, trying to figure out what to write to you, you were always right in front of me. I envisioned you at work, exercising your exemplary leadership and managing the many challenges and opportunities you face leading forward and leading by example. I'm in awe of the work that you do with Gen Ys in your workplace, and I hope that I've given you a few new tools, techniques, and frameworks that you can apply in your own practice so that you can choreograph a new workplace reality for the Gen Ys in your workplace.

The book was never intended to be a quick fix. Change of this magnitude requires the following:

➤ Time and unfaltering commitment to doing things differently and doing them right

➤ Willingness to be immensely courageous and curious

➤ The ability to whether the naysayers that claim, *it can't be done*

➤ Heaps of patience to shift the culture *slowly* in your organization

All is doable. I have every confidence that you will be successful in this venture. Please be patient with yourself and others as you establish new workplace protocols and norms and stretch into a new reality of what your organization can look like.

And the last word goes to you...

I sincerely hope you accept my invitation to meet online, where, as a community of business practitioners and learners, we can:

➤ Share stories about our adventures in the land of Gen Y

➤ Commiserate over things that didn't progress as expected, but be gentle with ourselves in the process

➤ Celebrate our successes with gusto

➤ Co-create new ways of engaging with our Gen Y community and all generations in our workplace

➤ Establish a strong community of practice that we can rely on as we move forward in our careers so that we can build on our reputation of leadership excellence

End of the book? No, we're just beginning!

Until then...

Best regards,

**Carolin**

carolin@eyeofthetigerconsulting.ca
www.eyeofthetigerconsulting.ca

www.ingramcontent.com/pod-product-compliance
Lightning Source LLC
LaVergne TN
LVHW081340050326
832903LV00024B/1238